Black-Native
Autobiographical Acts

Black-Native Autobiographical Acts

Navigating the Minefields of Authenticity

Sarita Cannon

LEXINGTON BOOKS
Lanham • Boulder • New York • London

Published by Lexington Books
An imprint of The Rowman & Littlefield Publishing Group, Inc.
4501 Forbes Boulevard, Suite 200, Lanham, Maryland 20706
www.rowman.com

6 Tinworth Street, London SE11 5AL, United Kingdom

British Library Cataloguing in Publication Information Available

Library of Congress Cataloging-in-Publication Data

Names: Cannon, Sarita, author.
Title: Black-native autobiographical acts : navigating the minefields of authenticity / Sarita Cannon.
Description: Lanham : Lexington Books, 2021. | Includes bibliographical references and index.
Identifiers: LCCN 2021014702 (print) | LCCN 2021014703 (ebook) | ISBN 9781793630575 (cloth) | ISBN 9781793630582 (ebook) | ISBN 9781793630599 (pbk)
Subjects: LCSH: Indians of North America—Mixed descent. | Racially mixed people—United States.
Classification: LCC E99.M693 C36 2021 (print) | LCC E99.M693 (ebook) | DDC 973.04/97—dc23
LC record available at https://lccn.loc.gov/2021014702
LC ebook record available at https://lccn.loc.gov/2021014703

For Arturo

Contents

List of Figures

Acknowledgments

This book stems from research on Black-Native literature, art, and history that formed the basis of my doctoral dissertation. I am forever grateful to Professor Hertha Dawn Sweet Wong at UC Berkeley for introducing me to *The Life of Okah Tubbee*, the gateway book for my plunge into Black-Native studies.

I am grateful to my editor at Lexington Books, Judith Lakamper, for believing in the value of my project and for providing guidance every step of the way.

Many thanks to Dr. Adrienne W. Hoard for granting permission to use her exquisite artwork. When I saw the piece, I knew it would be perfect for the cover of the book.

I am also grateful for Valena Dismukes for granting permission to use a photograph from her stunning collection *The Red-Black Connection*.

I would not have been able to finish this book without the generosity of my dear friend Naomi Goldner, who offered me a quiet space to work every week when I couldn't use my campus office because of COVID-19 restrictions. I am eternally thankful for her kindness and encouragement.

My friend and colleague, Loretta Stec, has continually encouraged me to keep working on this book even when teaching and family commitments made it challenging to do so. I am heartened by her unwavering belief in me.

My MA American Autobiography seminar at San Francisco State University in Fall 2020 provided much-needed inspiration while finishing this book. Our weekly conversations over Zoom reinforced my belief in the healing power of telling our stories and of bearing witness to the stories of others.

I am thankful to my mother, Helen Wiley, for introducing me to the music of Jimi Hendrix.

My friend and colleague, José Alfaro, lifted my spirits during low points in the writing process. Through his example, he showed me the ways in which stepping outside the conventions of academic writing can facilitate individual and collective healing.

Eric, Linda, Sue, and Marc cared for my son so that I could finish this book. I am so grateful for the love they show Arturo every day and for their support of my professional endeavors.

Introduction

Authenticating Narratives

In 2008, Margaret Jones published a memoir about growing up as a half-white half-American Indian child in foster care in the ganglands of South Central Los Angeles in the 1990s. Published by Riverhead Books, *Love and Consequences* focuses on the author, a young girl from Southern California who at the age of eight is taken from her biological mother's custody after teachers notice signs of sexual and physical abuse. This girl, who goes by Bree after leaving her mother's house, is put into a foster home headed by a Black matriarch named Big Momma in South Central Los Angeles. In the memoir, Jones details how she became a gang member, sold drugs, and watched family and friends fall prey to gang violence and the criminal justice system. She also, however, discusses the bonds she developed with her foster family and friends in the neighborhood. And the story, despite its bleakness, has a happy ending: she escapes South Central by winning a scholarship to University of Oregon where she eventually earns a degree in Ethnic Studies. As a story of a young woman succeeding against the odds, *Love and Consequences* is the kind of feel-good tale that reinforces our belief in a just, meritocratic America. The reviews of the book (before its authenticity was debunked) reflect this attitude. Motoko Rich, for example, praises the "amazing job" Jones has done of "conjuring up her old neighborhood," (Rich 2008) despite the fact that some of the "scenes she has recreated from her youth . . . can feel self-consciously novelistic at times." (Rich 2008) And Mimi Read, who interviewed Jones for a huge spread in *The New York Times* Home and Garden Section in late February 2008 noted that "unlike several other recent gang memoirs, all written by men, Ms. Jones' story is told from a nurturer's point of view." (Read 2008) Read's piece, which is based on interviews with Jones in Eugene, where she (among other activities) raises her eight-year-old daughter and enjoys "putting up" jam, highlights the contrast between her past life in South Central and her current life in suburban Oregon: "With its shootings, pimps beating prostitutes in the street, and drug deals plainly transacted in front of children the Los Angeles neighborhood where Mrs. Jones lived is light years from her tame life now." (Read 2008) We as readers are invited to read it as a rags-to-riches story by Jones, whom Read calls a "consummate storyteller," a compliment that proved to be all too true (Read 2008).

Just a week after this *New York Times* story appeared, Jones was outed by her sister, Cyndi Hoffmann, and the world learned that Margaret B. Jones was, in fact, Margaret (nicknamed Peggy) Seltzer, a white middle-class woman who grew up in Sherman Oaks and attended a "private school that counts Mary Kate and Ashley Olsen . . . among its graduates." (Banks 2008) The reaction to the revelation of her lie was vehement. Sandy Banks, writing for the *Los Angeles Times*, noted that: "What ticks me off is the notion that it takes a white author's gripping memoir to cast the problems of ghetto blacks in a sympathetic light." (Banks 2008) Another writer for *The Nation*, Amy Alexander, expressed dismay at the manipulative nature of Seltzer's ruse (she stops just short of calling her a sociopath) and at the publishing industry's failure to verify Jones's story (Alexander 2008). Despite the many falsified or exaggerated memoirs in the past few years, this story elicited an unusually fierce reaction. Perhaps it was the elaborate nature of Seltzer's performance that stunned and disturbed so many people. She had fooled book critics, veteran journalists, (including NPR's Michele Norris, who interviewed Jones right before the book was released), and her publisher at Riverhead Books, Sara McGrath, whom she had worked with for three years while writing the memoir. Even Seltzer's agent, Faye Bender, believed her story and told *NY Times* reporter Motoko Rich that the "author had been using a false persona for years." (Rich 2008) An undated ten-minute YouTube video of Jones talking about her childhood (in African-American vernacular) posted by Media Assassin in 2008 lends credence to this claim (Media Assassin 2008).

Peggy Seltzer's story of ethnic impersonation is not a new phenomenon.[1] In fact, the history of racial transvestism, particularly in autobiographical genres, extends to the antebellum period. In the first chapter of her 2000 book *Slippery Characters: Ethnic Impersonators and American Identities*, Laura Browder discusses faux slave narratives written by white abolitionists, including a famous one from 1856 by Mattie Griffith entitled *Autobiography of a Female Slave*. Born into a Kentucky slaveholding family, Mattie Griffith, née Martha Griffith Brown, wrote this slave narrative in order to affirm her conversion to the abolitionist cause (Browder 2000, 32). Interestingly (and in contrast to Seltzer's fate), even after her true identity was discovered, Brown was welcomed warmly into the fold of the abolitionist movement, a gesture that reflects the paternalism of white abolitionists who, in Browder's words, were "unwilling to trust the slaves, despite their protestations, to tell their own stories adequately" and thus "created slave personae who were disgusted by black bodies, revolted by slave characters, and unable to see the truth about slavery without the intercession of wise abolitionists." (Browder 2000, 41) For white abolitionists, a narrative's "emotional authenticity" mattered more than its literal authenticity (Browder 2000, 33). But it is noteworthy that Seltzer's hoax occurred in what Sidonie Smith and Julia Watson call "the age of confession." (Smith and Watson 2010, 174) As Jones's story demonstrates, the collective investment in authenticity, particularly in relation to texts that are labeled as memoirs or autobiographies, is powerful. When we read an autobiography, we want to believe that we have entered what Philippe Lejeune calls the "autobiographical pact": the acknowledgment that "the *author*, the *narrator,* and the *protagonist* are identical." (Lejeune 2016, 35) Although scholars of life writing have pointed out that the written self is always already mediated and never a direct, transparent delivery of the self, "the autobiographical relationship depends on the narrator's winning and keeping the reader's trust in the plausibility of the narrated experience and the credibility of the narrator." (Smith and Watson 2010, 34)

Along with the rise of tell-all narratives, the turn of the twenty-first century has also seen a rapid growth in the visibility of multiracial people. U.S. President Barack Obama is probably the most famous mixed-race person in the United States (and perhaps in the world), and his memoir *Dreams From My Father: A Story of Race and Inheritance*, written in 1995 long before he was elected president in 2008, grapples with some of the issues that people who claim multiple ancestries face. While avoiding the tragic mulatto/a trope of a person who is caught between two communities and fits in nowhere, Obama nevertheless details some of the struggles that he faced as a Black biracial young man coming of age in the 1970s. One of the struggles that emerges in many narratives by and about mixed-race people is the issue of belonging and authenticity. To which group(s) do I belong? Am I authentic enough to belong to the communities that reflect my heritage? And who determines and measures authenticity? People of all races and backgrounds also struggle with these questions, but in a country that collectively sees racial categories as discrete (and that historically has thought about race in terms of a Black-white binary opposition), mixed-race people may be more acutely aware of these issues.

Along with the emergence of a focus on mixed-race identities comes the question of terminology. In their introduction to the collection of essays entitled *Rethinking "Mixed Race,"* David Parker and Miri Song ask, "Can we conceive of 'mixed race' without reifying 'race'?" (Parker and Song 2001, 2) This is an important consideration. Parker and Song assert that a celebration of hybridity, such as Gloria Anzaldúa's 1987 *Borderlands/La*

Frontera, actually promotes the "inherent biological superiority of 'mixed race.'" (Parker and Song 2001, 9) A term such as "mixed race" or "multiracial" may inadvertently reinforce biologically rooted notions of race: "To identify someone as 'multiracial' is to enumerate a genealogy that combines a number of distinct 'races' which that person now embodies." (Parker and Song 2001, 10) Moreover, the term "mixed race" may flatten important differences between various iterations of mixed-race identities; in other words, it is dangerous to "assume[e] all mixes are on equal terms." (Parker and Song 2001, 9) And as Minelle Mahtani and April Moreno point out, there is also the danger of characterizing "mixed race" solely "in terms of a white-non-white dichotomy." (Mahtani and Moreno 2001, 71) Despite the challenges that terms such as "mixed race" and "multiracial" present, I use them to refer to a group of people from a variety of backgrounds who are invested in claiming multiple ancestries. I aim to be as specific as possible when referring to the racialized identities of the subjects in this book as well as respect their particular self-identifications.

The term "mixed-blood," used to describe someone who has both Indian and non-Indian ancestry, is another signifier of hybridity that is potentially problematic. Some Native writers such as Louis Owens (Choctaw/Cherokee) and Gerald Vizenor (Anishanaabe) embrace the term as a way to "challenge[s] the biologization of Native identity as well as static and essentialist notions of indigeneity." (Teves 2015, 206) That is, "mixed-blood" may function as a way to subvert binary and simplistic understandings of Indian-ness. William S. Penn, in his introduction to the 1997 collection of essays by multiracial American Indian writers *As We Are Now: Mixblood Essays on Race and Identity,* coins a new term to describe this hybrid identity: "'Mixbloods' not 'mixedbloods' because they express the unified and inseparable strands of their heritage and experience. Mixblood instead of crossblood, though in this instance mainly because crossblood has been so long confused with 'mixed-blood.'" (Penn 1998, 9) Yet some Indigenous scholars, such as Craig Womack (Creek/Cherokee), wonder if "identifying as mixedblood, rather than as part of a tribal nation, diminishes sovereignty"? (Womack 1998, 32) Moreover, for some, any invocation of "blood" in reference to human identity is racist and has no place in twenty-first-century discourse. As Claudio Saunt, Barbara Krauthamer, Tiya Miles, Celia E. Naylor, and Circe Sturm assert: "Who would defend the terms *mixed-blood* or *half-breed,* with their obvious invocations of pseudoscience and animal husbandry (702)?" (Saunt, Krauthamer, Miles, Naylor, and Sturm 2006, 400) Like the term "mixed-race," "mixed-blood" carries a great deal of historical and cultural baggage. The choice to use such terms is a personal one, and in my discussion of the subjects in this book, I use the labels that they opt for themselves. However, when speaking broadly about people with polycultural and polyracial ancestries, I will use "mixed-race" or "mixed-blood," as these are the most common and legible terms, however inadequate and problematic they may be.

In this book, I yoke considerations of authenticity in life writing with questions of authenticity around mixed-race subjectivity. I focus on people whose ancestries, traditions, affiliations, and/or chosen communities represent both African and American Indian identities. Through a variety of autobiographical modes, Black Natives navigate narratives of racial, ethnic, and cultural authenticity. The mixed identities that they inhabit, embody, and perform are reflected in the hybrid forms through which they express those subjectivities. I analyze how Black Natives have inscribed themselves in a variety of genres, including scrapbooks, oral histories, music, photography, and performance, and argue that people who straddle Black and Indigenous communities disrupt biological, political, and cultural metrics of racial authenticity. Examining Black-Native self-inscriptions across a wide range of autobiographical modes from the early twentieth century illuminates the empowering possibilities of broadening staid definitions of autobiography and demonstrates the importance of questioning monolithic definitions of Blackness and Indigeneity.

The growth of autobiography as a subgenre within literary studies informs and is informed by poststructuralist and postcolonial theories that populate the late twentieth- and early twenty-first-century scholarly landscape. No longer limited to a life (bio) written (graphy) by the self (auto), autobiography has become a capacious term that refers to different kinds of media that are not necessarily textual and not necessarily about a single person. In the second edition (2010) of their indispensable guide to life writing, *Reading Autobiography*, Sidonie Smith and Julia Watson posit a distinction between life writing, which includes memoir and autobiography, and life narrative, which is a "general term for acts of self-presentation of all kinds and in diverse media that take the producer's life as their subject, whether written, performative, visual, filmic, or digital." (Smith and Watson 2010, 4) This distinction is a useful one for this project, which explores both verbal and non-verbal forms of self-expression. As many theorists of life writing and life narrative have asserted, the self does not exist a priori but is instead an "effect of autobiographical storytelling." (Smith and Watson 2010, 33) That is, life writing and life narrative are not simply documentary forms through which fully formed selves express themselves. Rather, the act of expressing oneself (and the mode of expression) informs and shapes the narrative that emerges. I borrow the term "autobiographical act" from Elizabeth Bruss's 1976 text *Autobiographical Acts: The Changing Situation of a Literary Genre*, in which she theorizes that autobiography is an "illocutionary act." (Bruss 1976, 5) Such an act "is an association between a piece of language and certain contexts, conditions, and intentions." (Bruss 1976, 5) Bruss asserts that there is "no intrinsically autobiographical form," but also acknowledges that there are "limited generalizations to be made about the dimensions of action which are common to these autobiographies, and which seem to form the core of our notion of the functions an autobiographical text must perform." (Bruss 1976, 10) That is, autobiography is defined not by what it is but by what it does. Although the authors of her study—John Bunyan, Jame Boswell, Thomas De Quincey, and Vladimir Nabokov—are more canonical and firmly grounded in textual forms than my subjects here, Bruss's emphasis on the "roles played by an author and a reader, the uses to which a text is being put" resonates powerfully with my project (Bruss 1976, 5). The relationship between the autobiographical actor and the reading/viewing/listening audience in the texts constitutes a key part of my analysis. Moreover, these autobiographical acts by people who straddle Black and Indigenous identities must be understood in terms of how they function within their particular historical, political, and cultural contexts.

Life narrative is an especially salient form for members of historically marginalized and oppressed groups. While it is perhaps most accurate to locate the origins of both American Indian and African-American literatures within the oral traditions of these respective groups, autobiography has been a crucial genre in the development of both literary traditions.

If we limit the definition of *autobiography* to written life narratives, American Indians have only been producing autobiography for the past 250 years. But as H. David Brumble III reminds us, our understanding of autobiography should not be limited by "a Western aesthetic and Western literary conventions." (Brumble 1988, 14) In his 1998 text *American Indian Autobiography,* Brumble examines six kinds of preliterate autobiographies written by Natives, including "(1) the coup tales, (2) the less formal and usu-ally more detailed tales of warfare and hunting, (3) the self-examinations, (4) the self-vindications, (5) the educational narratives, and (6) the tales of the acquisition of powers." (Brumble 1998, 22–23) Building on Brumble's work in her 1992 book *Sending My Heart Back Across the Years,* Hertha Sweet Wong considers oral and pictograph narratives from the Pre-Columbian period, a gesture that "expand[s] current definitions of autobiography, which all too often have not recognized non-Western self-conceptions and their con-sequent expressions and representations." (Wong 1992, 6) Brumble and Wong also place "as-told-to" life narratives under the umbrella of American Indian Autobiography. These narratives are "bicultural documents," (Brumble 1988, 11) the result of collaboration between an Indigenous person who shares his or her life story and a (usually) non-Indigenous person who transcribes and/or edits that life story. Some examples include Crow *Plenty-Coups: Chief of the Crows* (1928) and *Pretty Shield: Medicine Woman of the Crows* (1930), both of which were transcribed by Frank Linderman (Wong 1992, 90). Wong notes that these kinds of texts "were similar to the nineteenth-century slave narratives produced collaboratively by a European American abolitionist and an African American escaped or freed slave." (Wong1992, 202) Then there are life narratives written by American Indians themselves without the aid of an amanuensis, including Samson Occom's 1762 *A Short Narrative of My Life*, William Apess's 1829 *A Son of the Forest*, and Sarah Winnemucca Hopkins's 1883 *Life Among the Piutes: Their Wrongs and Claims*. More contemporary iterations of Native American autobiography include *The Names* (1976) and *The Way to Rainy Mountain* (1969) by N. Scott Momaday and *Storyteller* (1981) by Leslie Marmon Silko. All three of these texts evoke older oral traditions and include "graphic as well as verbal images." (Brumble 1988, 179) The hybrid identities of many mixed-blood Indians writing life narratives in the twenty-first century reflect the "incorporat[ion of] Native American oral and artistic modes into Euro-American written autobiography." (Wong 1992, 199) The critical and popular acclaim of Terese Mailhot's *New York Times*' bestselling autobiography *Heart Berries: A Memoir* (2018) marks a new wave of Indigenous life narratives that are reaching broader audiences without pandering to a white gaze. In an article for *Mother Jones* written shortly after the publication of her memoir, Mailhot asserts, "I am not a hopeless illustration, something for non-Natives to witness. . . . I don't want a joyous future nearly as much as I want the freedom to present the tragedy in our lives and not be bound to it." (Mailhot 2018, 64, 66) Autobiography continues to provide a mode for Indigenous people to tell their stories in ways that reflect their multiple cultural and artistic influences.

Autobiography, in the form of the slave narrative, has also been central to the political and literary development of Black people (Andrews, n.d.). The slave narrative provided an opportunity for people of African descent to express themselves, support the abolitionist cause, and reach a broad audience. Some of the most well-known of these narratives include *The Interesting Narrative of the Life of Olaudah Equiano, or Gustavus Vassa, The African* (1789), *Narrative of the Life of Frederick Douglass* (1845), and *Incidents in the Life of a Slave Girl* by Harriet Jacobs (1861). M. Giulia Fabi notes that William Wells Brown, who first entered the publishing world as the author of his own slave narrative in 1847, was "the first African American author to move openly into the realm of prose fiction" with his novel *Clotel* in 1853 (Fabi 1993, 641). And James Weldon Johnson's understanding of the market for African-American life writing led him to anonymously publish a book entitled *The Autobiography of An Ex-Colored Man* in 1912, a text ostensibly written by a light-skinned man of mixed African and European descent who crossed the color line to escape the dangers of Jim Crow life in the early twentieth century. Johnson even signifies on one of the tropes of the slave narrative genre, the authenticating preface, by writing his own authenticating introduction to the novel but attributing it to the publishers (Stepto 1979, 98). Fifteen years later Johnson revealed that the text was, in fact, a fictionalized novel, though loosely based on the life of his friend Judson Douglass Wetmore (Goellnicht 1996, 17). The rich tradition of African-American life writing continued in the twentieth century with authors such as Richard Wright, Maya Angelou, James Baldwin, Audre Lorde, and Barack Obama. Despite the vast diversity within African American autobiography, two recurring themes in all of these texts is the notion of writing as a form of freedom and the idea that the individual is often expected to speak both for herself and for her community. Nellie McKay writes that "[i]n the eighteenth and nineteenth centuries, displaced Africans" in the Americas found the genre of autobiography "critical in gaining the language they needed to enter white debates on the humanity of Africans, and to challenge western European discourses on freedom and race." (McKay 1998, 96) The personal narrative was a vehicle for "[d]efining black selfhood in a racially oppressive world." (McKay 1998, 96)

The genre of autobiography has proven to be an important medium not just for putatively monoracial groups such as African Americans and American Indians, but also for multiracial Americans. Justin Ponder notes that "scholars in mixed race studies claimed that . . . no self-representation can undermine stereotypes better than autobiography." (Ponder 2012, 63) In particular, he cites SanSan Kwan and Kenneth Speirs who argue that self-inscriptions by multiracial individuals are more powerful than studies about their lives and experiences (Ponder 2012, 66). Yet Ponder deftly unpacks the ways in which self-representation is not a simple act of self-revelation. He cites four important aspects of self-representation, particularly as it manifests in autobiography: "1) self-representation communicates with others, 2) self-representation requires signs that do not belong to the self, 3) self-representation often relies on stereotypes, and 4) self-representation constructs a racial subject that identifies through stereotypes." (Ponder 2012, 67) As with any performative act, the performance depends on an audience; or, as Judith Butler puts it, the story is only possible with a "you." (cited in Ponder 2012, 68) Ponder uses Barack Obama's 1995 autobiography *Dreams of My Father* as an example of mixed-race autobiography that resists the telos of the discovered self (to which so many narratives of life writing by people of all racial and ethnic backgrounds conform) and asserts that Obama resists the urge to control his narrative (Ponder 2012, 75, 78). For Ponder, the strength of Obama's writing comes from his refusal to own his representation. That is, the "subject may best subvert stereotypes with indeterminate self-representation." (Ponder 2012, 75) Indeed, this is a powerful gesture on Obama's part. But he is also speaking from a relatively privileged position compared to some of the subjects of this book. For example, Sylvester Long Lance's control of his narrative was literally a matter of life and death in the early twentieth century when Black men (and women) were being lynched at alarming rates.[2] I do not intend to dismiss the racism that Obama faced as a Black biracial man in the White House or to minimize the structural and casual racism that exists to this day. But I do think that the stakes of Obama's self-representation are quite different from Long Lance's, which is why historical contextualization of the primary texts in this study is so vital.

Life writing by Black Indians falls under the umbrella of mixed-race auto-biography. This tradition reaches as far back as the nineteenth century and includes autobiographies by Paul Cuffe, William Apess, and Okah Tubbee.[3] As Jonathan Brennan suggests in the introduction to his 2003 collection of essays *When Brer Rabbit Meets Coyote: African-Native American Literature,* it is possible to establish a genealogy of Black-Native literature that links these eighteenth- and nineteenth-century texts with more recent iterations of Afro-Indian identity in the works of contemporary writers such as Alice Walker, Toni Morrison, Sherman Alexie, and Leslie Marmon Silko. In fact, Brennan asserts that "there have been five centuries of African-Native American literature" whose "oral and written expressions" encompass a wide range of genres (Brennan 2003, 35). While Brennan's naming of the field of Afro-Native literature is important work, in this project I am less interested in tracing a path and more interested in investigating the role that medium plays in self-presentations of Black Indians since the early twentieth century.

While it may be impossible to pinpoint the onset of African-Indigenous encounters in the Americas, Jonathan Brennan offers one possibility in 1526, when Spanish colonists brought African slaves to present-day South Carolina (Brennan 2003, 1). The colony, however, was short-lived, as the enslaved peoples collaborated with the Native populations and rebelled against the Spaniards (Brennan 2003, 1). Other scholars have suggested that interactions between Africans and Indians in the New World extend even further back, as Ivan Van Sertima asserted in his 1976 text *They Came Before Columbus.* What is clear is that interactions between the two groups have been frequent and various, often mediated by European and European American coloniz-ing forces. As historian Theda Perdue and others have noted, Indigenous peoples were enslaved alongside African peoples: "Until the 1720s, Indians comprised a significant proportion of the slave labor force on southern planta-tions." (Perdue 2009, 22) This experience of enslavement led many Blacks and Natives to establish maroon communities as early as the seventeenth century (Katz 1997, 37). These maroon colonies consisted of Africans and Indians who had escaped slavery in order to create their own free communi-ties (Katz 1997, 38). In many instances, runaway enslaved people gained assistance from Native tribes and relied on them for survival in inhospitable terrain. According to historian Herbert Aptheker, there were about fifty maroon communities between 1682 and 1864 in the swampy, forested, or mountainous regions of the South and Southeast (Aptheker 1996, 151).

One of the most famous maroon societies was that of Black Seminoles. In the eighteenth century, enslaved Africans and "refugees from the Creek Nation [also known as Seminoles]" met in Florida and developed a powerful alliance (Katz 1997, 50). In this particular instance, Black people, who were more accustomed to the tropical climate of the Southeast because they had lived longer in the region, helped the Seminoles, who had migrated more recently, to survive in this new territory. These two groups also stood together in solidarity against "British and then U.S. slaveholders [who] were horrified by the strong relationships among red and black Seminoles" and did their best to undermine this formidable coalition (Katz 1997, 52).

Collaborations between enslaved Indians and Africans were not limited to the Southeast, as the earliest slave rebellion in New York City was led by a Native man, known only as Sam, and an African American woman, whose name is unknown (Miles 2009, 145–146). In 1708, they "killed [their] master, pregnant mistress, and all of their children with an axe." (Miles 2009, 148) Both were publicly and brutally executed, their deaths meant to serve as a warning to others who might have similar notions of insurrection (Miles 2009, 148).

Another important chapter of Black-Native history (and one that is not marked by solidarity against a common foe) involves Indian slaveholders in the Southeast. Theda Perdue writes that "by the late eighteenth century, southern Indians increasingly adopted the views of the colonists: Africans were the last human link in the great chain of being, decidedly inferior to both Europeans and Indians." (Perdue 2009, 23) "Between the late 1700s and the end of the Civil War," Tiya Miles writes, "nearly 10,000 black slaves were held in bondage" by enslavers who were members of five southeastern tribes: Choctaw, Chickasaw, Cherokee, Creek, and Seminole (Miles 2009, 149). Brian Klopotek asserts that the enslavement of Africans by Indigenous peoples was a strategic form a survival, as he writes, "in mirroring the peculiar notions of civility held by southern Anglos around race and gender, southern tribes hoped to protect themselves against conquest based on constructions of Indian savagery." (Klopotek 2009, 86) However, historian Barbara Krauthamer argues that Indians did not simply "accept Euro-Americans' ideology of white superiority" or view "their interests as identical to those of white southerners." (Krauthamer 2013, 5) Moreover, adopting chattel slavery did not "stem the tide of white intruders—illegal squatters—on their [Choctaw and Chickasaw] Mississippi lands." (Krauthamer 2013, 6)

While most Indian slaveholding ended as a result of removal policies in the 1830s (Perdue 2009, 23), some Indians did enslave Africans until the end of the Civil War, after which time a new population, whose descendants live on today, emerged: freedmen. In subsequent chapters, I elaborate on the reality of life for freedmen after Emancipation, but broadly speaking, the treaties signed by the Seminole, Creek, Cherokee, Choctaw, and Chickasaw Nations with the U.S. Federal government stipulated that formerly enslaved people in these tribes would be granted citizenship, land, "a share in federal annuity payments," education, "and the right to vote and serve on juries." (Smith 2007, 86) However, in reality, many freedmen were unable to obtain tribal citizenship and suffered under anti-Black laws in Indian Territory and in the United States. In her study of slavery in the Choctaw and Chickasaw nations, Barbara Krauthamer writes that "[r]ecalcitrant slaveholders, Indian and White vigilantes, and intractable lawmakers sought almost any opportunity that arose to keep black people as close to enslavement as possible." (Krauthamer 2013, 120) Although the Curtis Act of 1898 stipulated that freedmen from the Five Tribes would receive land allotments, the tribal rolls used to determine citizenship failed to take into consideration the complex and specific understandings of identity, race, and belonging in Indian Territory, which "resulted in a census that often reflected arbitrary decisions that did not accord with enrollees' self-identification and family histories." (Krauthamer 2013, 149) Creating separate, mutually exclusive rolls for "Indians" and "freedmen" left many in limbo. In his study of Creek slavery and freedom through the lens of a family with Black, white, and Indian heritage, Claudio Saunt poses the question: "Should a woman of Indian descent, fluent in Muscogee, yet a slave be enrolled as a free person or a Creek by blood?" (Saunt 2006, 157) Without clear answers to such sticky questions, "commissioners relied on racist impressions" to make these determinations, thereby obscuring important familial and cultural connections (Saunt 2006, 157).

While the Civil Rights Movement of the 1960s might seem to be a natural crucible for rekindling Black-Native solidarity, such connections were tenuous and localized. In *Custer Died For Your Sins*, Vine Deloria, Jr. cites the two very different aims of these groups as an obstacle to coalition-building (Deloria 1969, 168–196). Whereas Blacks sought integration into American institutions, "Indians wanted recognition of the sovereign rights of native nations." (Perdue 2009, 33) Many people who live at the crossroads of African-American and Native American cultures have recently been at the center of a storm around the status of the descendants of freedmen, whom Robert Keith Collins describes as "slaves, or descendants of slaves, owned by Native American masters" who "possess varying degrees of Indian blood." (Collins 2009, 188) In particular, the Cherokee Nation made headlines in 2007 when its "citizens voted to approve an amendment to the Cherokee Constitution that require citizens to be Cherokee by blood," (Agent 2009, 122) a piece of legislation that would effectively expel many descendants of freedmen who lack Cherokee blood but whose ancestors were on the

Dawes Roll of 1887, a list that "would become the basis for determining membership in the Cherokee Nation" (Hirsch 2009, 119). Citizens had "to prove descent from a person listed on the Dawes Commission 'blood roll,'" which effectively threatened citizenship status for most Black members of the Cherokee Nation, since the Cherokee blood quantum of freedmen was not recorded by the Dawes commissioners (Hirsch 2009, 120). After several years of court battles, in August 2017 U.S. District Judge Thomas F. Hogan ruled that Cherokee freedmen possess citizenship rights (Chow 2017). This struggle over Cherokee citizenship highlights the complicated relationship between the U.S. government and federally recognized (and putatively sovereign) Indigenous nations as well as the ways in which the struggle for those who straddle Black and Native communities continues into the twenty-first century. Because the Black-Indian communities and individuals in this book have a variety of tribal affiliations, in each chapter I contextualize these experiences in light of the histories of the specific Indigenous nations represented.

Despite the generic, temporal, and geographic differences among these primary texts, all of the autobiographical actors in this project engage with discourses of authenticity. These discourses mainly pertain to racial and ethnic authenticity, though gender authenticity plays an important role for some. The metaphor of blood is central to these paradigms of Black and Indian authenticity. Historically, racial authenticity has resided in the body, particularly in the blood. Interestingly, it is usually Indian authenticity that is being claimed, though in some cases Black or African authenticity becomes important to perform. This is not surprising given the very different ways in which Black identity and Indian identity have been constructed in the United States. Angela Gonzales explains that: "But where *hypo*descent assigned racial identity based upon any known black ancestry, Indian identity followed the logic of *hyper*descent, which required a minimum amount of Indian blood, usually one-quarter or more." (Gonzales 2009, 64) In both cases, "blood" determines racial identity, but the algorithm differs. This racial logic is rooted in the historical particularities of the United States, as Adrian Piper asserts:

> A legally certifiable Native American is entitled to financial benefits from the government, so obtaining this certification is difficult. A legally certifiable black person is *disentitled* to financial, social, and inheritance benefits . . . so obtaining this certification is not just easy but automatic. (Piper 1992, 18–19)

Often Indian "blood" has been valorized over Black "blood." As Pauline Turner Strong and Barrik Van Winkle write, "'White blood,' especially of Northern European ethnic groups, is the most valued in discussions of mixed ancestry. In contrast, other kinds of racially construed 'blood' may be used derogatorily in arguments, insults, and comparisons." (Strong and Van

Winkle 1996, 567, footnote 13) Although Strong and Van Winkle make this claim in the course of discussing the Washoe Nation of Nevada, such beliefs are not limited to this tribe. While some of the subjects I discuss here invest in the notion of blood-based authenticity, others create new ways of defining authenticity.

Narratives of authenticity remain salient in Black and Native American communities today. The pejorative terms "oreo" and "apple" represent the ways in which "realness" remains a heuristic for measuring ethnoracial identity. Whereas "oreo" refers to a person who is "Black" on the outside and "white" on the inside, "apple" refers to a person who is "red" on the outside and "white" on the inside. As Richard Thompson Ford writes, "Every racial group (with the telling exception of whites) has a derogatory term for people who fail to exhibit their assigned racial culture: there are African American 'Oreos,' Latino 'Coconuts,' Asian-American 'Bananas' and Native Americans (you guessed it) 'Apples.'" (Ford 2005, 84) These terms suggest that many still believe that there is a true racial essence that can be measured by outward signs, such as skin color, dress, speech, and behavior. The accusation in some Black and Native communities that a person is "acting white" because she listens to country music/uses Standard English/plays water polo reinforces this belief. Yet it also highlights the performative nature of identity, and the ways in which performativity has been (mis)understood as a form of pretense. In fact, we are performing identities on a daily basis, even if we are not passing or cross-dressing.[4] Some of the subjects of this book are doubly performative because they are not only performing identity in the way that we all do, but they are also performers. Long Lance, Jimi Hendrix, and Radmilla Cody have literal stages on which they act out their different identities, a fact that complicates our understanding of their racialized and gendered identities.

In the introduction to their edited collection of essays *Authentic Blackness/"Real" Blackness: Essays on the Meaning of Blackness in Literature and Culture*, Martin Japtok and Jerry Rafiki Jenkins assert that "Questions about authenticity tend to arise when culture is under assault—as it is everywhere as a consequence of economic globalization and the commercialization of every area of life that is one of globalization's major consequences." (Japtok and Jenkins 2011, 1) They discuss the ways in which Blackness in the New World has been defined not only by the colonizers but also by Black people themselves. While citing Stuart Hall's assertion that Blackness is determined by the other's gaze (Japtok and Jenkins 2011, 10), they also assert that a "feisty intrablack dialogue" on authentic Blackness has existed for decades (Japtok and Jenkins 2011, 13). This dialogue was heightened during the Harlem Renaissance, when many Black artists and writers (notably Langston Hughes[5]) saw the "folk" as embodiments of the authentic

spirit of Black people (Johnson 2003, 21). Although such class-based definitions of authentic Blackness perpetuate divisions within Black communities
that narrow instead of broaden the picture of the Black experience, they
remain entrenched today, supported by corporations that promote the myth
that "real" Blackness is rooted in the ghetto (Japtok and Jenkins 2011, 43).
Japtok and Jenkins cite the work of Robin D.G. Kelley and Bakari Kitwana,
both of whom suggest that "corporatized culture is largely responsible for
making ghettocentricity synonymous with black authenticity." (Japtok and
Jenkins 2011, 43) Even within some Black communities, this notion that real
Blackness comes from living in the "hood" persists.

As Eric Michael Dyson writes, this sense of authentic Blackness is rooted
in struggle. That is, a sense of "we" was established to fight "them." (Dyson
2011, xiv) But when group cohesion translates into a narrow sense of identity, then it becomes dangerously narrow: "[O]ur efforts to define who 'we'
are cut against the complexity of our Blackness and sacrifice the depth of
variety for the breath of unity." (Dyson 2011, xiv) Black writers, artists, and
intellectuals in the early twenty-first century are questioning received narratives about authentic Blackness in a variety of ways. For instance, visual
artist Kehinde Wiley "envision[s] . . . Blackness beyond abjection and racial
trauma." (Touré 2011, 51) And Dave Chappelle's subversive comedy "dives
into the cross-pollinization of contemporary Black and white culture, i.e., the
ways that cultural Blackness and whiteness are fungible and fluid." (Touré
2011, 59) In his book *Who's Afraid of Post-Blackness?* journalist Touré uses
the term *post-Blackness* (coined by artist Thelma Golden) as a way to liber-
ate Black people from stultifying discourses of authenticity (Touré 2011, 16).
He emphasizes that post-Black is not the same as post-race (Touré 2011, 12);
rather, post-Blackness offers a way of approaching individual and collective
identity that does not rely on pecking orders like the ones Roland Martin
articulates (Touré 2011, 153)[6]. To be post-Black is to be "rooted in but not
restricted by Blackness." (Touré 2011, 12)

Questions of authenticity have loomed large in American Indian communities as well, though the stakes are different. In her 2003 book *Real Indians:
Identity and the Survival of Native America*, sociologist Eva Marie Garroutte
discusses the four major ways in which Native American identity is measured
and then theorizes a new approach to understanding Indian identities that she
terms "Radical Indigenism." Garroutte places her study within the context
of "American's shifting norms of racialization" in the late twentieth century,
namely the ways in which the newly available option to identify with more
than one race (legally, politically, and socially) has shaped discussions about
"Who, in short, has a legitimate claim on specific racial identities." (Garroutte
2003, 7, 9) Garroutte discusses four definitions of American Indian identity
that are used in various contemporary contexts: legal, biological, cultural,

and personal (Garroutte 2003, 11). Legal definitions function both individually and collectively: they may determine "who is a citizen in the eyes of a specific tribe, or who is an Indian person in the eyes of the federal government" or they "defin[e] what groups constitute an Indian tribe." (Garroutte 2003, 14–15) Perhaps the most ubiquitous symbol of legal Indian-ness is the Certificate of Degree of Indian Blood, or CDIB. As the name implies, this card, issued by the federal government and conferring certain rights to the holder, is a legal marker of Indian identity that is rooted in blood quantum, which varies from tribe to tribe (Garroutte 2003, 34).[7] Biological definitions of Indian-ness, which Garroutte describes as "close biological connections to other Indian people—and the distinctive physical appearance that may accompany those connections," continue to be important in many Native communities (Garroutte 2003, 51). Elizabeth Cook-Lynn asserts that while the Lakota reject narrow solely blood-based definitions of belonging, "biology is *never* dismissed categorically. On the contrary, it is the overriding concern of the people who assiduously trace their blood ties throughout the generations." (Cook-Lynn 1998, 94) But blood quantum has also been imposed on Natives as a metric of identity. Kim Tallbear writes that "racializing the tribe (naming that identity as only a biological entity) undermines both tribal, cultural, and political authorities." (Tallbear 2003, 84) In addition to undermining a tribe's ability to determine its membership, blood quantum was also used by the U.S. government during the allotment era to "support the systematic removal of Native people from their land." (Teves 2015, 200) Garroutte writes that the "original, stated intention of blood quantum distinction was to determine the point at which the various responsibilities of the dominant society to Indian peoples ended." (Garroutte 2003, 42) That is, the fewer people counted as Indian, the fewer resources (including land) needed to be distributed. Moreover, this blood-based biological understanding of Indian-ness "reflected nineteenth-and early twentieth century theories of race introduced by Euro-Americans." (Garroutte 2003, 42) These theories, which "correlated intelligence and character traits with racial background," were at the root of legislation that adversely affected non-white Americans (Teves 2015, 200).

Garroutte discusses the third set of definitions of Indian-ness, cultural definitions, in her wonderfully titled chapter "What If My Grandma Eat Big Macs?" For some, grounding Indian identity in behavior and lived experience rather than "legal fictions" or "genetic 'credentials'" seems like a more "meaningful" way of defining Indian-ness (Garroutte 2003, 74). But too often culture or tradition is construed as unchanging, uniform, and timeless (Garroutte 2003, 67). Such an expectation of homogeneity belies the fact that many significant cultural differences exist within tribes, and that culture itself is fluid and dynamic (Garroutte 2003, 67).

The final definition of *Indian-ness* that Garroutte discusses is what she calls self-identification. Under this definition, "Indians are simply those who *say* that they are Indian." (Garroutte 2003, 82) Immediately one thinks of non-Indians (like Margaret Jones/PeggySeltzer) who appropriate Native or pseudo-Native traditions, names, and practices, often for personal or economic gain (Garroutte 2003, 84–85). Indeed, there are some "born-again Indians" who are exploitative in ways that hurt Indian people and communities, as Garoutte quotes Tewa anthropologist Alfonso Ortiz who asserts: "We resent these people who just come in when the going's good and skim the riches off the surface." (Garroutte 2003, 86) But Garroutte points out that those who engaged in "ethnic switching" do not always have nefarious motives (Garroutte 2003, 94). For many Indians, the agency to define oneself is a matter of personal dignity. Garroutte cites Cherokee scholar Russell Thornton who argues that "a definition of self-identification represents not only a genuine respect for individual human rights, but also a proper submission to the constant reality of Native communities." (Garroutte 2003, 94–95) Indeed, those who claim an Indian identity and become committed to Indian communities may, in some cases, "allow[] for the introduction of new resources into tribal communities." (Garroutte 2003, 97) Yet ultimately the unsatisfactory nature of these four ways of defining Indian identity leads Garroutte to formulate a new paradigm for thinking through what it means to be Native in the twenty-first century: Radical Indigenism.

Garroutte acknowledges the pain that occurs in many Indian communities as a result of attempts to determine who is a "real Indian" and suggests that the answer to healing this pain lies within Native traditions and value systems:

> In response to the present level of anger and argument over issues of tribal belonging, we can usefully remind ourselves that, in our various tribes, we *do* have traditional teachings concerning such questions—that we must continue to rediscover them and, in this way, bring them alive. (Garroutte 2003, 114)

This Radical Indigenism requires active engagement with Native communities and asserts that "American Indian cultures contain tools of inquiry that create *knowledge*." (Garroutte 2003, 107) Garroutte concludes that Radical Indigenism provides a framework for rethinking Indian identity beyond the legal, biological, cultural, and personal definitions that have been so frequently (and unsuccessfully) used to determine "Indian-ness." Without being prescriptive, Garroutte offers a different view of the Native identity which various Indian communities might discuss and evaluate: "individuals belong to those communities because they carry the essential nature that binds me to The People *and* because they are willing to behave in ways that the communities define as responsible." (Garroutte 2003, 134) Both flexible and specific, this definition of Indian identity offers parameters that something like "post-Blackness" does not. In many ways, this makes sense, since historically Indian-ness has been exclusive, while Blackness has been inclusive. And this may explain why those who straddle Black and Native communities often struggle to define identity and to find a sense of belonging. The subjects of this book find different ways to navigate that liminal space. In some cases, they capitulate to prevailing discourses of authenticity while in others, they rewrite their own narratives of racial or ethnic "realness."

Moving in chronological order, this project spans the turn of the twentieth century to the present and explores a wide range of autobiographical modes. In chapter 1, I examine the meticulous scrapbooks (currently housed in the University of Calgary Archives and Special Collections) kept by Sylvester Long, also known as Chief Buffalo Child Long Lance. Born to a Lumbee family in North Carolina who identified as "colored," Long Lance escaped what he saw as the limited options for a Negro man in the early twentieth century by taking on a series of Native identities throughout his short but fascinating life as a writer, athlete, and actor. Though Long Lance published a memoir in 1928, a piece entitled *Long Lance: The Autobiography of a Blackfoot Chief* that was later discovered to be derived from the life stories of a close friend, the scrapbooks he maintained serve as the primary texts in this chapter. Through a close reading of these scrapbooks, I argue that Long Lance's manipulation of this autobiographical mode that is at once public and private gestures toward the ways in which he not only bought into but also manipulated discourses of authenticity around Indian manhood and Black manhood that permeated North American culture in the early twentieth century.

In chapter 2, I move to the slave narratives of people who straddled Black and Indian communities. Collected by the field workers employed by the Works Progress Administration in the 1930s, these oral testimonies reflect an important and often hidden chapter in American history and in the history of relations between African Americans and Native Americans. As examples of collaborative life writing, these narratives demonstrate the importance of considering the complex relationship among teller, writer, and editor. Despite the tendency to view oral testimony as more "basic" than written autobiographies, the narratives by Black Indians that I examine here illustrate a complex negotiation of discourses around racial authenticity and belonging. These formerly enslaved people of African and Native (and often European) heritage define racial authenticity not solely in terms of blood ties but also in terms of cultural practices and political affiliations.

Chapter 3 examines the legacy of one of the most famous Americans of African and Native descent: the legendary guitarist Jimi Hendrix, who claimed African and Cherokee ancestors. Rising to fame during a time of social upheaval, Hendrix strove for self-inscription that resisted the racial essentialism that tended to define the Black, Red, and Brown Power Movements of the late 1960s. I read his songs as autobiographical acts that illustrate his attempt to operate outside of a paradigm of racial and ethnic belonging that was absolute and blood-based. Through a close look at the music and lyrics of a handful of Hendrix's songs, as well as the public persona that he cultivated, I argue that he drew on and recast the musical and political traditions of African-American and Native American communities while striving not to be defined by those affiliations and influences.

Chapter 4 moves forward three decades to the early twenty-first century, when the effects of the multiracial movement of the 1990s meant that many more people—including those of African and Native American ancestry—had the language and the community support to embrace their mixed heritage. Valena Broussard Dismukes's 2003 exhibit of portraits by Black Indians entitled "The Red-Black Connection" testifies to the vast diversity of phenotypes, perspectives, and tribal affiliations of this small subgroup of the multiracial population. Another example of collaborative autobiography, these photographs and accompanying verbal narratives written by the subjects themselves illustrate the continuing navigation of discourses of racial and ethnic belonging even (or especially) in a putatively post-racial era.

In chapter 5, I move to the beauty pageant as a site of autobiographical inscription. The crowning of the first Black Miss Navajo Nation in 1997, Radmilla Cody, brought to the surface tensions within the Navajo community in particular and Indian communities in general. Though most in the community supported Cody's crowning, some found a Navajo woman with African ancestry to be an unfit representation of the Navajo Nation. I argue that Cody used her year as Miss Navajo Nation, as well as her subsequent fame as a musician and activist, to reformulate narrow definitions of Black and Indian racial authenticity. Informed by the framework of Radical Indigenism, Cody uses the teachings of the Navajo Nation in which she was born and raised to suggest ways of thinking about racial and tribal belonging that do not rely solely on legal, biological, or cultural definitions.

Within African-American Studies and American Indian Studies, respectively, questions about the nature of Blackness and Indigeneity persist. This project, in its trickster-like straddling of academic disciplines, offers further insight into defining these terms. While I recognize the value of defining a Black-Indian scholarly tradition, I follow Michele Elam's lead in her discussion of mixed-race texts. She calls for positioning

> texts called mixed race narratives within, rather than as a reinvention of, literary history. The latter approach would allow us to see how such literature can be

situated, and how it participates, in respective ethnic literary traditions; it also, importantly, invites closer attention to the ways hybridity is narrated already within these traditions and where it can be more fully articulated and elaborated. (Elam 2011, 50)

More broadly, this project's focus on various iterations of self by members of an underrepresented ethnoracial group resonates in a historical moment when taxonomies of race and genre have become increasingly elastic.

In the past decades, there has been an explosion of scholarship on Black-Native identities and histories. Historians such as Tiya Miles, Claudio Saunt, Celia Naylor, and Barbara Krauthamer have contributed to our understanding of antebellum connections between African Americans and Indigenous people in the United States. The work of Circe Sturm provides an anthropological lens through which to understand historical and contemporary formulations of different iterations of Native identity, including Black-Native identity. Literary scholars Robert Warrior, Sharon P. Holland, and Jonathan Brennan have illuminated intersections between Native and Black literary traditions. And the 2012 exhibition at the National Museum of the American Indian, "IndiVisible: African-Native American Lives in the Americas," brought together voices of the past and the present to shed light on "the history and contemporary perspectives of people of African and Native American descent." ("IndiVisible: African-Native American Lives in the Americas") While drawing on this extensive archive of Black-Red scholarship, I offer a new methodology for understanding the experiences of Black-Native Americans. I expand the notion of autobiography beyond the written word to consider how people who straddle these two cultures represent themselves across different media. This analysis of various modes of Black-Indian self-inscription since the beginning of the twentieth century is anchored by a close reading literary approach that also pays attention to the historical realities of the texts and the people who produce them. I hope that this project will contribute to broader conversations about self-representation, racial authenticity, and cultural belonging.

I will use the terms Red-Black, Black-Indian, or African-Native American when speaking generally about people who straddle African and American Indian communities and ancestries, but whenever possible I will honor the artist or author's choice of self-identification and be as specific as possible. Much of Black-Red history has been suppressed not only because of historical forces, but also because of deceptive terminology and the fact that the meanings of words (especially in relation to issues of race and culture) are constantly in flux and must be understood within their historical frameworks. Jack Forbes, an historian with a keen understanding of language in relation to African-Native history, writes at the beginning of his book *Africans and Native Americans*:

> Finally, I hope that this study of interethnic contact and racial classifying will lead to progress in the field of human rights by highlighting and clarifying a major area of abuse: the arbitrary and often racist practice of defining identities of other human beings by powerful outsiders, as well as by governments and nations. (Forbes 1993, 5)

By attending to the linguistic dimension of Red-Black identity, I hope to underscore the importance of defining oneself as a sovereign subject.

NOTES

1. One of the most notorious literary racial hoaxes of the late twentieth century is the scandal surrounding Forrest Carter, the author of the apparently autobiographical story of his Cherokee childhood entitled *The Education of Little* Tree. Published in 1976, this tale was read as an authentic example of American Indian life until the 1991 revelation that the text was a fictional story written by Asa Carter, a former card-carrying Klansman and author of George Wallace's infamous "Segregation today, segregation tomorrow, segregation forever" speech (Gates 1991). The element of racial imposture in this case was particularly disturbing for many Native people whose life stories have often been excluded from mainstream publishing venues and/ or been eclipsed by images of Indianness that trade on European-American stereotypes of American Indians, including "the Noble Savage, the Indian Princess . . . the Squaw . . . [and] the Vanishing Indian" (Justice 2000, 32). As Daniel Heath Justice puts it: "This fictionalization of Native lives and histories poses a very real threat to Native America, for it creates powerful stereotypes of Indians (what Anishanaabe writer and critic Gerald Vizenor calls 'interimage simulations') that take on a white cultural reality that is seen as more 'authentic' than the realities of living, sovereign American Indians" (Justice 2000, 30).

2. Lynching was one of the many extralegal forms of racial intimidation practiced in the South after federal troops left the region in 1877 (Earle 2000, 96). "Between 1880 and 1930, 3,220 blacks and 723 whites were lynched in the South, with the greatest numbers taking place in Louisiana, Mississippi, Alabama, Georgia, and Texas" (Earle 2000, 96). In 1892, two years after Sylvester Long was born, the number of African Americans lynched peaked at 235 (Earle 2000, 96). Black activists such as journalist Ida B. Wells led the fight against lynching in the early twentieth century, and "in 1952, for the first time, no lynchings were reported in the United States" (Earle 2000, 97).

3. Paul Cuffe (1759–1817) was the son of an African slave and a member of the Wampanoag nation who worked as a whaler and trader. Brennan notes that "from 1811-1812, Paul Cuffe wrote an autobiographical travel narrative in a ship's journal that details his trading practices travel to Sierra Leone, and political dealings"

(Brennan 2003, 22). William Apess was born in 1798 in Massachusetts of Pequot, European American, and African-American parents. Raised in Connecticut, he later became a Methodist minister and wrote several works critiquing the treatment of Indians and African Americans in nineteenth-century America, including an auto-biographical piece entitled *Son of the Forest: The Experience of William Apess, a Native of the Forest, Written by Himself*, which was published in 1829 and then revised and republished in 1831 (Brennan 2003, 22). Born Warner McCary to a black enslaved woman and her master (whom many scholars assume was European American, though Brennan asserts that it is not out of the realm of possibility that he was Native American [169]), he later changed his name to Dr. Okah Tubbee and claimed to be the long-lost son of Choctaw chief Moshulatubbee in order to escape his enslavement (Brennan 2003, 25). Tubbee established a career for himself as a traveling preacher, healer, performer, and musician, capitalizing on his claim to Native blood and forswearing any African ancestry. Tubbee narrated this version of his life story to his Delaware wife, Laah Ceil, in *A Thrilling Sketch of the Life of The Distinguished Chief Okah Tubbee*, the first edition of which was published in 1848 (Brennan 2003, 25).

4. Judith Butler is most closely associated with this notion that the "body becomes its gender through a series of acts which are renewed, revised, and consolidated through time" (Butler 2004, 53). However, this sense of identity as always being created can extend to other vectors of identity, including, but not limited to, sexuality and race.

5. E. Patrick Johnson notes Hughes' problematic "romanticizing [of] black folk culture as the impetus for all black aesthetic and cultural production" (Johnson 2003, 23). In his 1926 manifesto, "The Negro Artist and the Racial Mountain," Langston Hughes ostensibly celebrates the "common people [who] will give to the world its truly Negro artist, as one who is not afraid to be himself" but also portrays the "folk" as primitive people whose "joy runs, bang! Into ecstasy" and who "work maybe a little today, rest a little tomorrow" (Hughes 1926, 692). As Johnson puts it: "Hughes' persistent references to black working-class people as 'common,' alongside the implications that they are lazy . . . undermines his valorization of these same 'folk' as the site of racial authenticity" (Johnson 2003, 23).

6. In Touré's interview with CNN commentator Roland Martin, Martin explains the four levels of blackness: "The platinum-level authentic Negro . . . is you grew up in public housing, crime, drugs, poverty. The gold level is you grew up in a middle-class Black neighborhood and you went to public schools and maybe to a Black college so you got a pretty good Black experience. Silver is you lived in a neighborhood that was really diverse where you had a mix of educated African-Americans and whites and you may have gone to a black church but it wasn't a Black Baptist Church, it probably was Episcopalian or something on those lines. . . . And then there's bronze. You grew up in the suburbs and you didn't really see many of us. You went to a prep school and an all-white college and your experience of Blackness is really third person, something you heard and read about versus what you know and experienced" (Touré 2011, 153). As Touré points out, these levels of Blackness depend on "proximity to the ghetto experience," which problematically implies that

"blackness requires us to stay poor in order for it to survive and it dies as more of us become economically successful" (Touré 2011, 153).

7. As Garroutte notes, some Indians "feel that the issuing of CDIBs is an intrusion by the federal government into tribal affairs" (Garroutte 2003, 32). Many of the people she interviewed for the book assert that the audience for these cards is white people, not Native people (Garroutte 2003, 32, 34).

Chapter 1

Rogue Self-Inscription

The Scrapbooks of Long Lance

In 1915 a young man who was deemed "colored" by the racial logic of the Jim Crow North Carolina community in which he grew up wrote a letter to President Woodrow Wilson claiming to be a full-blooded Cherokee and asking for a spot at the coveted military academy West Point. He was accepted as a presidential appointee to West Point; but just before taking his entrance exams, he fled North to Canada, the first of many flights to escape possible inquiries into his past (Smith 1999, 51). He instead pursued a different life path, one that would include serving in the Canadian army, working as a journalist, advocating for Indigenous peoples in Canada and the United States, and starring in Douglas Burden's 1929 documentary *The Silent Enemy*. This North Carolina native was born Sylvester Long but was later known as Chief Buffalo Child Long Lance, or Long Lance for short. His audacious request to be admitted to West Point presaged the multiple ways in which Long Lance, both publicly and privately, performed an American Indian identity in order to escape the Black identity that was imposed upon him from the moment he was born.

Yet Long Lance was not simply another example of a non-Indian "playing Indian," to cite the title of Philip Deloria's highly influential 1998 work about the appropriation of American Indian identities, histories, and cultural practices. Long was, in fact, Indian, as records indicate that his family were members of the Lumbee tribe, a North Carolina nation that has a long history of mixture among European, Indian, and Black folks, a history that, as I will explore in this chapter, has hindered the Lumbees' search for federal recognition by the U.S. Government. Long Lance's autobiographical acts throughout his short life indicated his attempt to carve an identity when few options existed. In this chapter I offer a brief biography of Sylvester Long Lance, address how he negotiated discourses of manhood and Indigeneity in the early twentieth century, discuss the history of the Lumbee tribe that his family belonged to, and then analyze excerpts from his scrapbooks, paying attention to the ways that he inscribed for himself an authentic Indian identity through cultural practices, proximity to other Indians, and political allegiances.

Although Long Lance wrote a traditional autobiography (which reflected not his own life but the life of a friend of his on the Blackfoot reservation, Michael Eagle Speaker), I am more interested in the scrapbooks that he maintained throughout his life. Housed at the University of Calgary Archives in Alberta, Canada, these scrapbooks contain articles by and about Long Lance throughout his public life, and reflect a different mode of self-inscription. The moments in which Long Lance has returned to earlier articles to change his tribal affiliation to reflect whatever nation he claimed at the time are especially intriguing. One of the peculiarities of Long Lance's story is that he changed his tribal affiliation and blood quantum throughout his life. As a boy, he claimed to be one-fourth Cherokee, but by adulthood, he claimed to be a full-blooded Blackfoot chief. His investment in maintaining a consistent identity in the seemingly private genre of the scrapbook raises questions about audience. Was this meant for public consumption? And if not, why did he need to make sure that the public persona was reflected in the private scrapbook? Through a close reading of these scrapbooks, I argue that Long Lance's manipulation of this autobiographical mode gestures toward his investment in and manipulation of discourses of authenticity around Indian manhood and Black manhood that permeated North American culture in the early twentieth century. For Long Lance, masculinity and Indian-ness were two strategically constructed and intersecting identities that he manipulated in order to create a public identity that would allow him to escape life as a Black man in a segregated society. Long Lance manipulated both the racialized discourse about gender and the gendered discourse about race in North America in the early twentieth century, operating as a trickster figure who both reinforced and unsettled cultural norms.

Despite Donald B. Smith's tendency to frame Sylvester Long Lance as a tragic non-Indian who was passing for Indian, his 1982 biography is useful as the only full-length study of Long Lance's life. Smith relies on numerous sources, including the archives in Calgary, to reconstruct a life. He explains that Long Lance and his family lived as Black people in Winston-Salem, North Carolina because, according to the logic of the one-drop rule, anyone who was not fully white was considered Colored. Smith writes that, "Sallie and Joe Long [Sylvester's parents] lived as blacks but maintained that they were white and Indian, a not uncommon occurrence at the time in the South, where racial origins were difficult to know and still more difficult to prove." (Smith 1999, 23) As a boy, Sylvester was inspired by Benjamin Franklin's *Autobiography*, the archetypal story of the self-made American man (Smith

1993, 54). Yet his parents taught him that in order to survive in the South, he had to abide by the written and unwritten laws of Jim Crow culture. For young Sylvester, this meant being submissive to white people in all contexts, a behavior he deplored. Smith asserts that "he could not swallow the platitudes, and he could not wait for the rewards in the hereafter." (Smith 1999, 28) Early on, Sylvester looked for a way to escape life as a Black man in the South, and his first opportunity came when he applied to and matriculated at Carlisle Boarding School by claiming that he was part-Cherokee and part-Croatan (Smith 1999, 41). Although rumors swirled at Carlisle that Long had some Black ancestry, he was generally accepted as Indian and well-liked by his peers and teachers (Smith 1999, 51).

Instead of matriculating at West Point as a presidential appointee, Long moved to Canada, where he earned a reputation as an excellent journalist in Calgary, Alberta doing field research and writing articles about various Native American tribes, including the Sarcee and the Blackfeet (Smith 1999, 109). Yet even as he faithfully documented the lives of Native Americans, some Indians were suspicious of Long Lance's version of his own life story (Smith 1999, 157). The Blackfoot were put off by "[h]is easy friendliness and his enthusiasm to write about the sacred ceremonies. . . . He knew nothing about tepee etiquette, and inevitably he made mistakes. . . . To the Blackfoot he talked and behaved like a white man." (Smith 1999, 159) It is important to note, however, that a Native from elsewhere would not necessarily know the cultural practices of another Native tribe. In other words, Long's ignorance about Blackfoot traditions cannot be read simply as a betrayal of his "inauthentic" Indian self. Nevertheless, it is clear that Sylvester consistently made attempts to legitimate his identity as an Indian. For instance, in 1928 he published an autobiography entitled *Long Lance*, which was an elaborate fabrication of his life growing up as a Plains Indian (Smith 1999, 206–207). His life story (the details of which were borrowed from Indians he had met in Canada) was well-received. One British critic wrote that, "this book rings true; no outsider could explain so clearly how the Indians felt." (quoted in Smith 1999, 206) Sometimes, however, his attempts to play Indian were transparent. In one publicity photograph, he wore a mishmash of tribal regalia. Smith describes the image as: "The pants probably came from the Crow in Montana, the tobacco pouch from the Bloods, the vest from the Blackfoot. On his head Long Lance wore a wig and the headdress used in the Chicken Dance." (Smith 1999, 148) Long Lance was quite adept at lying to himself as well. He kept scrapbooks (which will serve as my primary texts in this chapter) in which he kept newspaper clippings of his achievements. Each time he publicly changed his tribal affiliation, Long Lance simultaneously changed the name of his tribe in each newspaper article (Smith 1999, 221).

By the 1920s, Long Lance was a prominent figure in New York society, primarily because he "acted the modern noble savage, the twentieth-century Hiawatha" so convincingly (Smith 1999, 213). The next logical step seemed to be Hollywood, and in 1929, Long Lance starred in the film *The Silent Enemy*. Douglas Burden's goal in this film was to ennoble Native Americans (Smith 1999, 228–229). Smith writes that: "For years Burden had objected to Hollywood's inaccurate and demeaning portrayal of the Indian as a wicked savage of the plains. He knew the reality was different and wanted to record it on film before both Indian and the wilderness vanished." (Smith 1999, 228) Long Lance was chosen to portray the Ojibway hero in the film, and he gave a riveting performance. Yet Long Lance's success in the film was marred by doubts about his authenticity as a full-blooded Indian (Smith 1999, 242–243; 267–268). After the release of *The Silent Enemy* and the accompanying scandal, Long Lance became depressed, which drove him to begin drinking heavily. In 1932, Long Lance died from a single gunshot to the head, and the death was deemed a suicide, though conspiracy theories abound (Smith 1999, 312–313). In his final analysis of Long Lance's life, Smith asserts that within Long Lance "burned two fires: one the desire for boundless celebrity, the other a genuine urge to employ that celebrity in the service of Indian rights." (Smith 1999, 313) Although Long Lance's performance of an Indian identity is the focus of my analysis, his desire for racial and ethnic authenticity must be understood in relation to his performance of gender.

In her book *Manliness and Civilization: A Cultural History of Gender and Race in the United States, 1880–1917*, Gail Bederman outlines how manhood was remade in the late nineteenth and early twentieth centuries. She states the three questions which drive her project: "What do we mean by 'manhood?'"; "What was happening to middle-class manhood at the turn of the century"?; and How is the "discourse of civilization" deployed "to tie male power to racial dominance"? (Bederman 1995, 5) Particularly relevant to my discussion of Long Lance is her last question, as the cultural and political trends of this time period demonstrate the link between imperialism and white manhood that allowed for a refashioning of gender roles and ideals. Bederman identifies the 1910 Jack Johnson–Jim Jeffries fight as an important moment in popular culture that revealed the anxieties of Americans in the early part of the twentieth century. Johnson's win was seen as a blow to white supremacy. The race riots that followed his triumph (and the animosity toward Johnson shown by mainstream press and average white Americans that followed him for years) destabilized the prevailing binarism of the fighting, primitive Negro versus the rational, brainy white man (Bederman 1995, 2–3). Jack Johnson, who not only beat the so-called "Hope of the White Race" in the ring but also openly consorted with various white women, represented a threat to white dominance (Bederman 1995, 2,

10). The link between manhood and whiteness was articulated on a larger scale by Theodore Roosevelt, who, around the same time as Jack Johnson's victory, established a public persona as a civilized white man that was intended to serve as an archetype for white American manhood (Bederman 1995, 171). Particularly in his writings, Roosevelt created the national narrative of unmanly, savage Indians overcome by virile, civilized white Anglo-Saxons (Bederman 1995, 181). As Bederman writes, imperialism was "a prophylactic against effeminacy and racial decadence." (Bederman 1995, 187) While turn-of-the-century discourse linked Blackness with physical and sexual aggression, discourse during the antebellum era associated Blackness with weakness, as Paul Gilmore wrote in his article "The Indian in the Museum."

In his discussion of the case of Okah Tubbee, a man of mixed (most likely white, Black, and Native) heritage who was born enslaved around 1810 in Mississippi but created a public identity for himself as the son of a Choctaw chief, Gilmore outlines prevailing attitudes about Blackness and Indian-ness. Gilmore argues that Tubbee's construction of a Native identity relied upon "racial distinctions between Indians and blacks [that] already circulated in the museum and in the writings of people like Thoreau." (Gilmore 1998, 43) The racialist thinking of the time went something like this: while Blacks were happy-go-lucky submissive creatures who "were content to dance and sing on Southern plantations," American Indians were "stoic" figures who refused to submit to the "advance of a white civilization." (Gilmore 1998, 26) Not only was there a supposed "natural" distinction between Africans and Indians, but each group was also explicitly gendered. Gilmore argues that the antebellum museum "mapped race along a gender axis—blacks represented effeminate submission, Indians manly resistance." (Gilmore 1998, 26) Like Okah Tubbee, Long Lance fled from Blackness by asserting his manhood—and he articulated his distance from Blackness by embracing rugged masculinity.

However, as historians and cultural critics have argued, the link between gender and race/ethnicity was more complicated than a "White equals manly" and "Black or Native equals effeminate" formula might suggest. While some white men did see manliness as a quality that was inextricably tied to whiteness, others acknowledged that men of all races have a primitive sense of survival that must be nurtured (Bederman 1995, 22). As a result, the turn of the twentieth century saw the growth of groups such as the "Improved Order of Red Men" and other clubs that encouraged white middle-class men to get in touch with their inner primitive selves (Bederman 1995, 25). Shari Huhndorf has written extensively about the ways in which Indian-ness was fetishized by white men in the late nineteenth century. She describes how "Indian-inspired men's and boys' clubs began to spring up around the middle of the nineteenth century and proliferated in the decades that followed." (Huhndorf 2001, 65)

European American men belonged to social organizations that "sponsored Indian-type activities." (Huhndorf 2001, 65)

Citing the work of John Hugham and Gail Bederman, Huhndorf makes an important link between public displays of manliness and nation-building: "What physical strength accomplished for the individual, imperialism (as a form of physical and racial dominance) accomplished for the nation." (Huhndorf 2001, 68) Appropriation of Indian (or pseudo-Indian) cultural practices and military techniques by male organizations such as the Boy Scouts were attempts to instill a sense of masculinity in young American men. As Huhndorf points out, though, using Indian life as a model for young European American boys who would grow strong and contribute to the imperialistic activities of the United States seems quite contradictory (Huhndorf 2001, 71). One of the ways this contradiction was resolved was that Boy Scouts were taught both to emulate *and* to conquer Indians (Huhndorf 2001, 72). In a broader cultural context, mimicking Indian cultures was viewed as an important stage in the development of civilization: "This regression into savagery, however, was not an end in itself but instead a means of playing out and finally overcoming boys' savage instincts as they grew into manhood, a process that parallels and confirms white society's rise to civilization." (Huhndorf 2001, 74) That is, playing Indian as a youngster could regenerate what many saw as a decaying and stagnant European American civilization around the turn of the twentieth century, but the goal was not to become Indian or embrace their cultures. "Playing Indian" was a vital but finite phase in the development of a virile, strong, white civilization.

While Bederman, Gilmore, and Huhndorf refer to the literal performances of Indians and Africans in public venues such as museums, minstrel revues, and Wild West shows, their studies also call attention to the performative quality of raced and gendered identities. Poststructuralist theories of the performative nature of identity have sometimes been misunderstood in fairly narrow terms. Performing gender is conflated with being in drag, and performing race is conflated with racial passing. Although gender and racial passing are important modes of performance, they are not the only modes of performance. Judith Butler puts it thus:

> The act that one does, the act one performs, is, in a sense, an act that has been going on before one arrived on the scene. Hence, gender is an act which has been rehearsed, much as script survives the particular actor who makes use of it, which requires individual actors in order to be actualised and reproduced as reality once again. (Butler 2004, 160)

All identities are constituted by a series of actions, actions that are always already informed by cultural norms, values, and practices. Although we have the power to exchange old identities for new ones, there is a limited number of identities to choose from, and those identities cannot be constructed from scratch. While Sylvester Long Lance's identity may appear to be analogous to a series of outfits that he donned at different times for different purposes, in fact his identity as an Indian man was much more complex.

The reasons for Long Lance's unusually complex relationship to Indian identity are numerous; but one of the most important factors is the history of the Lumbee tribe of North Carolina, about which Karen Blu, Gerald Sider, and Malinda Maynor Lowery have written extensively. Despite this large body of work, the origins of the Lumbee people remain in question, and Anne McCulloch and David Wilkins assert that "these conflicting origin theories have contributed in no small part to some of the identity questions Lumbees have confronted internally." (McCulloch and Wilkins 1995, 376) I would further argue that these different origin stories have also made the Lumbees' quest for federal recognition more challenging because the perceived lack of unity among the tribal members does not mesh with constructed images of "real Indians." (McCulloch and Wilkins 1995, 369)[1] Citing the work of Adolph Dial, David K. Eliades, and Jack Campisi, McCulloch and Wilkins offer three possible theories of origin for the people now known as the Lumbee. Some assert that the Lumbee are descended from "several small Southeastern tribes: the Hatteras, Saponi, and Cheraw, who from the 1780s through the 1840s worked their way into Robeson country where they intermarried and gradually developed a distinctive tribal identity." (McCulloch and Wilkins 1995, 376) Another theory (and perhaps the most widely known) is that Lumbee descended from the "Hatteras Indians living on the Outer Banks of North Carolina [who] intermarried with John White's 'Lost Colony' of Roanoake Island sometime in the late 1500s." (McCulloch and Wilkins 1995, 376) This theory of origin was developed and publicized by North Carolina state legislator Hamilton McMillan in 1885 after interviewing Indians in Robeson County, and it explains why the term "Croatan" was used to apply to Lumbee people in the late nineteenth century. Malinda Maynor Lowery explains that the term "Croatan" referred to "the name of the place to which the English colonists are said to have gone after they abandoned Roanoake Island." (Lowery 2010, 26) Yet another account of the genesis of the Lumbee people "asserts that the Lumbees are primarily descended from the Cheraw tribe of South Carolina and related Siouan speakers who were said to have inhabited the area known as Robeson County since the later eighteenth century." (McCulloch and Wilkins 1995, 376) This account of the origin of the people now known as Lumbee reflects the history presented on the official website of the Lumbee Tribe of North Carolina ("History and Culture").

These multiple origin stories also help to explain, in part, the numerous names by which the Lumbee have been called by state and federal governments. In 1885, North Carolina acknowledged the Lumbee "as Croatan Indians of Robeson County." (McCulloch and Wilkins 1995, 378) But "Croatan," which was shortened to "Cro," soon became a pejorative term used by whites in Robeson County (Blu 1980, 78). Karen Blu explains the term's connotations as:

> "Cro(w)" is, of course, a White term for Blacks (as in "Jim Crow"). When I asked one of my Indian friends what kind of bird a crow is, he replied "a nasty black thieving bird." Another explained that Whites used the term "Croatan" to mean "half-breed, mixed-blood someone with Negro blood." (Blu 1980, 78)

Because of the name's negative associations, in 1911, the "Croatans" successfully lobbied to change their name to "Indians of Robeson County." (Blu 1980, 79) However, this shift did not help their bid for recognition, as "the federal government does not recognize 'Indians,' it recognizes particular Indians with historically documented 'tribal' names and affiliations." (Blu 1980, 79) Two years later in 1913, the legislature once again changed the name to "Cherokee Indians of Robeson County," though the Eastern Cherokee balked at this name change because they feared it would diminish their share of federal benefits (Sider 2003, 3). Yet the Lumbee continued to be referred to as Cherokee (a historical fact that legitimates Long Lance's claim that he was part-Cherokee, the claim that earned him a spot at the Carlisle School) until the 1930s, when the federal government considered designating them as Siouan or Cheraw Indians but was defeated by the BIA who opposed this change (McCulloch and Wilkins 1995, 379). Over the next two decades, tension brewed regarding the proper name for the Indians of Robeson County. In 1953, community leaders successfully lobbied the North Carolina government to acknowledge them as "Lumbee Indians of North Carolina," a name "derived from the Lumber River that flows through the county." (McCulloch and Wilkins1995, 379) The Lumbee Act of 1956 acknowledged the Lumbee as Lumbee in the eyes of the federal government, but made them ineligible for federal services (McCulloch and Wilkins 1995, 379). Incredibly, "the tribe was recognized and terminated in the same legislation." (McCulloch and Wilkins 1995, 379) Since then, Lumbee have worked hard to change the legislation to obtain the rights and protections of all other federally recognized tribes. But as of December 2020, the Lumbee Recognition Act, authored by Richard Burr, a Republican senator from North Carolina, appeared to be "stalled in the U.S. Senate." (McGrath 2020)

Long Lance's scrapbooks offer an opportunity to understand how he constructed a public persona that would resonate with early twentieth-century Anglo stereotypes of Indian men. Although the market for scrapbooks is relatively recent,[2] the practice of scrapbooking is centuries-old. Susan Ott,

Katherine Tucker, and Patricia Buckler note that the "genealogy of memory keeping" stretches back to Ancient Greece (Ott, Tucker, and Buckler 2006, 4–5). According to the *Oxford English Dictionary*, the word "scrapbook" was first used in 1825, and was defined as "a blank book in which pictures, newspaper cuttings, and the like are pasted for preservation. Hence occas. as the title of a printed book of miscellaneous contents." Different iterations of the scrapbook include the commonplace book, the friendship album, and the Grangerized book, in which readers were invited to illustrate a text (Ott, Tucker, and Buckler 2006, 7). Despite the different kinds of scrapbooks that have existed over the years, the impulse to record and collect remains constant (Ott, Tucker, and Buckler 2006, 1–2). Moreover, Amy Mecklenburg-Faenger notes that, "Scrapbooking often, although not always, was continued as a communal activity. That is, the scrapbooks were not understood as private documents but as artifacts to be shared with others." (Mecklenburg-Faenger 2012, 11) The assertion that scrapbooks always have an implied or actual audience is especially relevant to our understanding of the ways in which Long Lance constructed and conceived of his scrapbooks.

While people today still keep old-fashioned scrapbooks, which may contain news clippings, personal and family photos, mementos, and other material markers of life events, the explosion of social media since the turn of the twenty-first century has led to a variety of digital forms of self-inscription and memory-making. Facebook, founded in 2004 by Mark Zuckerberg,[3] is a social network in which users can post photos, links to articles, and personal statements that will be seen by a chosen group of friends. A key element of Facebook is the social exchange that it facilitates: users can post on each other's walls, tag each other in photos, and chat with each other in real time. Narrower in focus is Pinterest, founded in 2009, which allows users to create various boards around certain themes on which they post relevant digital content. There is also a communal dimension, as "pinners" may follow each other, suggest new pins, and repin items on others' boards onto their own boards (Wortham 2012). Pinterest taps into both the scrapbooker's desire to collect and curate information and the onlooker's curiosity to view what others find interesting or beautiful. As Katy Good argues, both traditional scrapbooks and digital fora such as Facebook and Pinterest reflect a "private or personal desire to preserve that media for the future" as well as an "impulse to perform through media in public and social ways." (Good 2012, 569) Indeed, any act of self-inscription is never purely about the self; there is always an audience, whether imagined or "real," supportive or hostile. This element is particularly salient in relation to Long Lance's scrapbooking practice.

The story of Long Lance's "hoax" is an intriguing one, especially given the scandal that arose while he was filming *The Silent Enemy,* a docudrama by Douglas Burden whose main selling point was that it starred "authentic

Indians." Placing his performance within the context of a long tradition of self-making in the United States, as Laura Browder does in her book *Slippery Characters*,[4] yields important insights about the nature of race, identity, and performance in America. But I am less interested in separating the "truth" from "fiction" and more interested in how (and why) Long Lance created a personal narrative through this ancient autobiographical mode of collage. Unlike the other subjects in this book, Long Lance did not claim the Black part of his Black-Native identity. Yet it is precisely through his disavowal of Blackness and his embrace of Indian-ness that he demonstrated an engagement with discourses of racial authenticity and belonging.

Long Lance's two scrapbooks are housed at the University of Calgary Archives, and I had access to one of them. This scrapbook contains a variety of items, including newspaper clippings by and about Long Lance, typewritten letters, photographs, and ephemera such as his railway press passes. All of the newspaper clippings are yellowing with age. While some have been neatly clipped, some are torn. There are a few handwritten notes throughout. The scrapbook is roughly chronological, with the earlier items focusing on his life as a student at Carlisle and St. John's Military Academy and the later items highlighting his film debut in *The Silent Enemy*. The aim here seems to be documentation not aesthetic production. That is, the point of his scrapbook is not to be beautiful. The question of authorship is a troubling one: while Long Lance appears to have assembled most of the scrapbook, there is at least one document that must have been included posthumously.

Ott, Tucker, and Buckler affirm the subversive possibilities of scrapbook-making, citing Michel de Certeau's work on the "creative tactics that people use to maintain control over their lives in the face of the power of the state and society." (Ott, Tucker, and Buckler 2006, 20) The freedom that scrapbook creators exercise allows them "avoid the external editing process that would squeeze their creations into narrative and prose forms acceptable to mass audiences. Instead, each album is a rogue and renegade that both parries with and parallels popular forms." (Ott, Tucker, and Buckler 2006, 20) Long Lance could be described as a "rogue" fashioner of self who uses these clippings to reinforce the persona that he presented to the world. They provided material proof of the narrative that he fabricated (Smith 1999, 88). The scrapbooks also instilled confidence in his achievements, as suggested by the fact that he showed them to his brother Abe (Smith 1999, 196). They further served as a job portfolio, as he used his scrapbooks, which included several of his published articles, to obtain a job with a newspaper in Vancouver (Smith 1999, 126–127). These scrapbooks provide evidence of his investment in presenting a seamless, "authentic" Indian identity to a majority non-Indian audience, and they demonstrate his understanding of what it meant to be an Indian man in the early twentieth century. I assert that Long Lance defined his identity as an Indian man according to three metrics: cultural practices, association with and endorsement by other Indians, and political allegiances. These measurements of Native American "real-ness" continue to be relevant well into the twenty-first century, as the subjects in the following chapters of this book demonstrate.

Long Lance's tribal affiliation and blood quantum were moving targets. Blood has often been a marker of racial belonging for both African Americans and Native Americans: one "drop" of Black blood makes one Black, while the more "drops" of Indian blood one has, the more Indian one is. Long Lance, however, could not rely on blood to authenticate his Indian identity. While he is referred to in various articles pasted in his scrapbook as a full-blooded Indian and his body is often described in terms that are associated with Native phenotypes (copper skin, high cheekbones, straight black hair), Long Lance had to rely on other criteria to create his Indian identity. He often did this through a deliberate performance of "Indian" cultural practices, as his scrapbooks attest.

Long Lance drew upon popular conceptions of Indian-ness in order to shore up his Native identity. Although he was admitted to Carlisle by claiming to be Cherokee, by the time he was a young man he had established a public identity as a full-blooded chief of the Blackfoot tribe. Perhaps his most powerful vehicle for doing so was the film *The Silent Enemy*. Materials related to the film take up much of the second half of the scrapbook. Indeed, it was through this film and the images associated with the film that Long Lance "proved" himself as an Indian (though it also meant that he was subject to a great deal of scrutiny).

Although "authentic" Indians, according to European American mainstream culture, practiced traditional lifeways that stood in contrast to the technological innovations of the early twentieth century, "authentic" Indian identity was, ironically, also defined by a successful assimilation into European-American modern culture. That is, Long Lance's ability to exchange his "tomahawk" for a "typewriter," as one newspaper headline puts it, marks his authenticity as a twentieth-century Indian who understands that his noble race is vanishing and thus gracefully acquiesces to modern life among non-Indians, retaining only some of the quaint qualities of Indian-ness that make him a curio.

For instance, in a comic strip from the Tuesday, August 18, 1925 issue of *The Evening World* that has been reproduced in Donald B. Smith's 1982 biography of Long Lance and in the National Film Board of Canada documentary about Long Lance released in 1986, we see Cicero Sapp dressed in full cowboy regalia at the Banff Springs Hotel (Figure 1.1).

He is telling a woman, presumably another employee, that he wants to be dressed appropriately to meet a "Real Indian chief" whose arrival at the

Figure 1.1   Fred Locher, "When in Rome," *The Evening World Comics*, August 18, 1925. Clipping from scrapbook in Chief Buffalo Child Long Lance Collection, University of Calgary Archives and Special Collections.

hotel is imminent (Chief Buffalo Child Long Lance Collection). The woman warns Sapp that his attire is ridiculous for the occasion, but Sapp insists on the appropriateness of his outfit, saying "I want the chief to know I'm a man of the wide open spaces." In the final frame, a formally dressed bespectacled man introduces Sapp to Chief Long Lance who is wearing an elegant tuxedo. His hair is slicked back, and his facial features are striking, almost effeminate. He is smiling in a genteel sort of way. In the same frame we see Sapp holding his side with one hand and scratching his head with the other hand, his mouth agape, his hat hovering above his head. The cartoonist has drawn droplets of sweat and a question mark above Sapp's head to underscore his utter disbelief. This short cartoon says a great deal about how Chief Long Lance must have been perceived by the general public in the 1920s when he was a prominent celebrity. Sapp's vision of a "real Indian" reflected the images of Native Americans that Hollywood was just beginning to produce: "noble savages" dressed in loincloths and feathers, armed with arrowheads, and equipped with a deep connection to the natural world. Yet upon meeting Long Lance, Sapp's prejudices are clearly exposed as mistaken assumptions. Long Lance's ability to serve as an "authentic" symbol of the disappearing Native American and to simultaneously inhabit the white mainstream world was a huge part of his appeal. Long Lance appealed to the average American's desire to know the "real" Indian experience, yet he was palatable enough to be a member of high (white) society. As this cartoon suggests, Long Lance was able to use his "exotic" Native background and looks to his advantage, but he also knew how and when to present himself as the exquisitely packaged Native who has assimilated completely into Anglo-American cultural values.

An alternative rendering of Long Lance's presence among white socialites appears in an undated cartoon clipping more than halfway through his scrapbooks. The image features six figures: Long Lance, who is dancing wildly,

Inside image: "Drawing above is artist's conception of how Chief Long Lance danced his war dance on the quivering carpet of a polite Park Avenue drawing room."

"The question now on many lips is whether or not Chief Long Lance will choose to marry a white girl and remain a figure in white civilization, or whether he will return to the Western plains to wed an Indian girl."

Figure 1.2 **Unattributed clipping from scrapbook in Chief Buffalo Child Long Lance Collection**, University of Calgary Archives and Special Collections.

and five white partygoers whose faces and bodies betray various reactions to his performance (Chief Buffalo Child Long Lance Collection) (Figure 1.2).

Long Lance is at the center of the drawing, and though he is wearing formal dress, he has lost his jacket and shoes and his cuffs have been loosened. His stockinged feet are in motion and he holds objects in each hand that appear to be tomahawks. The expression on his face is hard to discern, though his teeth are prominent and contrast with his hair, which is shaded in almost completely black (except for a few white spots that perhaps represent droplets of sweat), and his face, which is cross-hatched to indicate a darker skin hue than the partygoers who are watching him. On the right is a young woman in an evening gown who is clasping her hands together but has a neutral facial expression and an older man with a full beard and mustache and spectacles. On the left is a more animated couple who appear to be smiling at Long Lance and raising their hands, perhaps keeping time to the dance. And in the background is another guest with furrowed eyebrows who is scratching his head and whose disbelief is indicated by an exclamation mark above his head. The caption below reads: "Drawing above is artist's conception of how Chief Long Lance danced his war dance on the quivering carpet of a polite Park Avenue drawing room." The image and accompanying caption highlight Long Lance's charm among white elites: he could blend in with them enough to be invited to their parties, but he also provided spice, a bit of "primitive" flavor to their events. The reactions of the guests at the party in this cartoon reflect a wide range of reactions: befuddlement, faint admiration, and excited engagement. Long Lance's decision to include this in his scrapbook reflects how he manipulated white society. He knew how to "play Indian" in a way that would rely upon and reinforce stereotypes held by non-Indians.

Just as intriguing as the image and caption here is another clipping that is placed below the cartoon's text. The font is different in this clipping, so it seems that this second clipping came from another source, although it is possible that the periodical used different fonts for captions and articles. The two paragraphs highlight the gossip around Long Lance's romantic partners. The author indicates that Long Lance is seen around New York with "some of the lovely Indian dancers" and that he is "[m]uch sought after by white women of wealth and position." That is, Long Lance has his pick of women, Indian and non-Indian. But the anonymous writer states that if Long Lance does marry, it will be an Indian girl, because he considers Indians "easier to live with" than whites: "He feels there would be too many things he could not make a white woman understand about his people and their ancient traditions." Here Long Lance's choice of mate is framed as an either-or decision that inheres a particular cultural affiliation. The author writes that: "The question now on many lips is whether or not Chief Long Lance will choose to marry a white girl or remain a figure in white civilization, or whether he will return to the Western plains to wed an Indian girl." Ultimately, Long Lance did not marry, though he had no shortage of lovers in the 1920s when he lived in New York, as the 1986 documentary *Long Lance* asserts. In an undated article included in Long Lance's scrapbook entitled "Why I Never Married," columnist Betty Brainerd presents a biographical sketch of Long Lance and quotes his own thoughts on the topic (Chief Buffalo Child Long Lance Collection). Long Lance writes that: "I suppose the reason I have never married . . . is because I have never seen a woman I wanted badly enough to marry. . . . But when I see how most marriages turn out I am very grateful that I am single; that I have never disappointed anyone and that no one has ever disappointed me. For after all disappointment is about the worst and most souring jolt that life can give one." (Chief Buffalo Child Long Lance Collection) Knowing about Long Lance's elaborately fabricated persona makes his statement about wanting to avoid being the disappointer *or* the disappointed quite poignant. Despite his public swagger, he feared that he would not meet expectations, his own or others'. His insecurity and inadequacy are striking but perhaps not surprising. But the fact that Long Lance could choose to marry an Indian woman or a white woman distanced him from a Black identity. If he identified as a Black man, it would have been socially difficult and legally impossible for him to marry a white woman. Perhaps it was the fear of discovery of his African heritage that kept him from making a formal lifetime commitment to another person.[5]

The newspaper clipping from *The Chicago American* dated Friday, January 7, 1927 highlights the transformation of Long Lance. The headline reads "Big Chief Writes History," and the clipping features two images of Long Lance: on the left is Long Lance in full headdress and Plains tribe regalia. On the right is Long Lance looking dapper in a smart black suit, bow tie, and fedora. His right hand is in his pocket, and his left foot is up on a stool. In his left hand, draped over his left leg, are an overcoat and a scarf. He is looking directly at the camera with a kind of suave nonchalance, whereas in the photo on the left, he is looking stoically to his left, creating an arresting profile. The blurb beneath the photos read: "Chief Buffalo Child Long Lance, Blackfeet leader, is going back to his 'teepee,' near Banff, Canada, to write the history of his tribe. The chief has achieved considerable honor on his own hook—as a West Pointer, a war hero and a writer. He has broken in to the literary field by Hearst's International-Cosmopolitan Magazine." (Chief Buffalo Child Long Lance Collection) The description reinforces the notion that Long Lance epitomizes a bicultural success story: he is committed to his people and will write their history so that the rest of the world will know about the Blackfoot Nation, yet he has also succeeded in the "white man's world" as a military man and author. As Donald Smith, Long Lance's principal biographer, has discerned, Long Lance did not, in fact, attend West Point, but many of the articles in his scrapbooks indicate that he did, and he did nothing to set the record straight.

The photos are reminiscent of the before and after photos of Native Americans who attended boarding schools in the late nineteenth and early twentieth centuries. In the "before" photos, the young people often have long hair and wear traditional clothing from their respective nations. In the "after" photos, the children wear Anglo clothing and the hair of the males is short. "[Richard Henry] Pratt [founder of the Carlisle School] termed such paired portraits 'propaganda' and consciously employed them to demonstrate the change from 'Indian' to man, from barbarism to civilization." (Margolis and Rowe 2004, 207) To supporters of Indian boarding schools, these dyptichs were proof of the "civilizing" effects of these military-inspired schools in which children were forced to abandon their Indigenous languages, spiritual beliefs, and cultural practices, separated from their families, and sometimes subjected to emotional, physical, and sexual abuse.

Yet another article included in his scrapbooks that emphasizes Long Lance's ability to navigate between worlds is a piece by Gladys Baker from the *Birmingham News-Age Herald*, dated October 7, 1928 (Chief Buffalo Child Long Lance Collection) (Figure 1.3).

Entitled "Blackfeet Chief is Polished Man," the article was published soon after the release of his well-received autobiography. Despite Baker's essentialist statement that "it is an Indian characteristic to enjoy hours of deep silence among themselves," she notes that Long Lance "contributes richly to any conversation." She goes on to say that "[h]e speaks without a trace of an accent. His words attest to a wide and tastefully acquired vocabulary. . . . His laugh is wholehearted and charmingly contagious." That is, he comports himself like a (white) educated gentleman who can socialize successfully and make others feel at ease. Yet his body hints at his "difference." Baker describes him in great physical detail:

> He rises to more than six feet of sturdy brawn and muscle. He is faultlessly groomed, but not the least foppish in his attire. Were it not for his straight black hair, which is cut close to his head, and his skin, which is not red but more the color of an ivory-toned parchment, he might be taken for a Wall Street broker.

Long Lance's difference is eroticized but contained. He is sexy and alluring without being threatening. Baker's troubling statement that he could "pass" for a "Wall Street broker" (which is a coded way of saying a privileged white man) if his hair and skin color were lighter is framed as a compliment. The images that accompany the article highlight the "miraculous" transformation of Long Lance, from Carlisle School boy to chief to "civilized" man. The top photo features Long Lance in full regalia seated on a horse in front of teepee, and the caption reads: "The top picture shows him as a member of the Blood Band of the Blackfeet Indians, in full ceremonial attire."[6] Below this image are two pictures: one of Long Lance with his hair slicked back and wearing a jacket and tie ("wearing the clothes of the white man's civilization"), and another of Long Lance in "Indian" garb as a teenager, "The first photograph the Indian ever had

Figure 1.3 Gladys Baker, "Blackfeet Chief is Polished Man," *Birmingham News-Age Herald*, October 7, 1928. Clipping from scrapbook in Chief Buffalo Child Long Lance Collection, University of Calgary Archives and Special Collections.

taken . . . as he appeared when he entered Carlisle." These contrasting photos heighten the contrast between the "Blackfeet Chief" and "Polished Man" of the article title. Thus Long Lance moved between "the noble savage" and the "assimilated Indian," aware of the currency of these two archetypes for white audiences. In his public persona, he played on the trope of transformation that was associated with Indigeneity in the early twentieth century.

Long Lance also authenticated his Indian identity through his association with and endorsement of other Natives. One article written by Emma Newashe McAllister comes from a 1925 newspaper whose name is absent from the clipping. The title reads: "Chief Buffalo Child Long Lance Indian 'Sister' Tells Story of Red Man's Voice At School." (Chief Buffalo Child Long Lance Collection) There is a picture of McAllister embedded in the article in the left-hand column, and the middle column features a photo of a young Long Lance in military uniform above a caption that reads "Sylvester long lance, otherwise Chief Buffalo Child Long Lance, as he served the Canadian army in the World War." McAllister begins the article by emphasizing that Long Lance has chosen a sister across tribal lines:

> In pride we parade our chiefs with the same pomp that the other races offer their royalty and it is seldom that one of these stops by the wayside to pick a sister from another tribe, yet that is what our Chief Buffalo Child Long Lance . . . has done for me.

She lists some of Long Lance's accomplishments as an athlete, a soldier, a writer, and a tribal leader, but she also gives a more intimate glimpse into Long Lance's demeanor at Carlisle. Curiously, although during his time at Carlisle Long Lance claimed to be Cherokee, McAllister makes no mention of this tribal affiliation. Instead, she calls him a "full-blood Indian author and Chief of the Blood Band of the Blackfeet in Alberta." McAllister writes that Long Lance's personal qualities are tied to his Indian identity: "There is no Indian I know who carries the traditional dignity of his race more becoming than Long Lance. It is his natural makeup. He is proud to be an Indian, prouder than of all the fame that has come to him." She notes that he was a serious student who was focused on his academics, but still managed to be personable: "There were times that he seemed to be cold, but he was intensely Indian. That is characteristic of our men and Long Lance is typical of our glorious manhood." He serves as representative for Indian manhood, a role model who is worthy of praise. McAllister's depiction of Long Lance and of the "Indian race" as a whole reinforced the idea of the noble, emotionally opaque but dignified Native American that circulated in the early twentieth century (and still does today, I would argue). She writes that, "There is no nobler race than the American Indian, and many have attempted to write our virtues but there is always that lack of understanding." However, Long Lance "portrays the Indian's cults, superstitions, and customs with a full meaning and an understanding, giving to the world for the first time the true aborigine as he wished to be known." Newashe's glowing description of Long Lance as the epitome of Indian manhood serves to authenticate his Native identity.

Long Lance's friendship with legendary athlete Jim Thorpe also legitimates his Indian-ness. Halfway through his scrapbook, there is an autographed photo of Jim Thorpe pasted next to a verbal endorsement for Long Lance's shoe. The photo features Jim Thorpe in a New York Giants uniform and has the following inscription: "High Chief—Remember the mile runs. Was great training for the Olympics Jim Thorpe." (Chief Buffalo Child Long Lance Collection) And the lengthy written endorsement to the right of the photo on this page was entitled "The Greatest All-round [sic] Athlete in Modern History Adds A Word." In this testimonial, Thorpe recalls his days at Carlisle with Long Lance in which they "used to kick about the rubber-soled shoes [they] had to wear in [their] athletics." Thorpe attributes his success at the 1912 Stockholm Olympic Games to the "stiff competition" Long Lance gave him and says that no one is better suited to design a shoe, for he knows what athletes need. Thorpe says that although he has been asked to endorse "hundreds" of products before, this is the first time he has actually "given permission for [his] name to be used in a testimonial which . . . shows [his] wholehearted sincerity in endorsing the Chief Long Lance Shoe as the best [he] [has] ever seen."

Yet another reference to Jim Thorpe appears on page 23 in the second half of his scrapbook. Long Lance includes Thorpe's page from Long Lance's Character Book, in Thorpe's own writing, alongside several news clippings about Thorpe. The largest one on the page is the engagement announcement of Thorpe and his first wife, Ivy Miller. Above a photo of the couple is the headline "James Thorpe and an Indian Girl He Will Marry in The Autumn." The short news item indicates that the couple met at Carlisle and that their former Carlisle classmates will play an important role in the Roman Catholic wedding ceremony. The page also features a reproduction of a photo of Thorpe posing with a football in his Carlisle days and four additional news clippings, all of which highlight Thorpe's success in the 1912 Stockholm Olympic Games. Among these clippings is a letter from President William H. Taft, dated July 20, 1912, congratulating Thorpe on his "note-worthy victory" at the Olympics. Taft does not allude to Thorpe's Indian heritage; instead he emphasizes his suitability as a role model for all Americans: "Your victory will serve as an incentive to all to improve those qualities which characterize the best type of American citizen." (Chief Buffalo Child Long Lance Collection) Another clipping on this page from the *Boston Post* includes the famous compliment Thorpe received from the king of Sweden when he delivered Thorpe's gold medals for the Pentathlon and Decathlon: "You, sir, are the greatest athlete in the world." This page in the scrapbook had the heading "To 'Jim'" in fancy font. It appears to be typed, though it could be carefully handwritten. In any case, it suggests that Long Lance was paying homage to his friend from Carlisle and celebrating his personal and professional success. Long Lance seems to be authenticating his Indian-ness through his association with one of the most prominent Indians of the early twentieth century, a man who proudly represented both his tribal affiliation and the country of his birth in international competition.

Long Lance also includes in his scrapbooks pictures of himself with chiefs from various Indigenous tribes. A photo from the *Calgary Daily Herald* dated Saturday, February 7, 1925, with the headline "Unique Welcome Group" shows Long Lance in full regalia shaking hands with a young smiling man in a pea coat and cap. Next to him is an older man wearing a wide-brimmed hat and carrying what looks to be a shield. The caption reads: "Maori, Sarcee and blood chiefs came together when the all Blacks arrived here Friday. The Maori is Nepia of the all Blacks, and the others are Jim Starlight of the Sacrees and Chief Longlance [sic]." (Chief Buffalo Child Long Lance Collection) It is unclear whether the author is using the word "chief" broadly, to include not only tribal leaders but also team leaders. But Long Lance is clearly making the most of this photo opportunity to align himself with other Natives. Long Lance also appears with other Blackfoot chiefs in a photo featured in the July 8, 1926 issue of the *Calgary Daily Herald*. Long Lance is standing next to the chief who is anointing a young boy with what appears to be a feather. The caption reads:

> Bob Hunt, son of Frazier Hunt, associate editor of the *Cosmopolitan* magazine, is adopted by the Blackfoot tribe at an impressive ceremony. He was given the name of Onista-poka, meaning Calf Child. The Indians in the picture, left to right: White Headed Chief, Boy Chief, Calf Child, Buffalo Child Long Lance, Water Chief and Spring Chief. (Chief Buffalo Child Long Lance Collection)

These images situate Long Lance as a member of a special brotherhood of Indigenous men with status not just from North America but also from New Zealand.

In addition to shoring up his Native identity by performing a version of Indian-ness that appealed to a largely non-Indian audience and associating with other Indigenous people, Long Lance also solidified his public Indian persona by showing his support for Native causes, often through his journalism. As his scrapbooks show, he amassed a remarkable dossier of published articles about Natives, especially in Canada, where he began his writing career. After being fired in 1922 by the *Calgary Herald* for a prank in which he threw a fake bomb into the mayor's cabinet meeting, Long Lance went to Vancouver, where, armed with his growing collection of newspaper articles in his scrapbook, he was hired by the *Vancouver Sun* (Smith 1999, 126). Although "many Indians refused to speak to journalists in British Columbia," lest their lifeways be ridiculed and misrepresented, "Long Lance, as an Indian journalist with splendid credentials, broke through this barrier of distrust." (Smith 1999, 128) He made several connections with Indians in British Columbia, conversations with whom served as the basis for a series of articles for the *Vancouver Sun* in the summer of 1922 (Smith 1999, 135).

In one of these articles, dated June 19, 1922, Long Lance defends the Indian custom of the potlatch, which had been criminalized by the Canadian Department of Indian Affairs and deemed a "'wasteful, heathen' custom." (Smith 1999, 131) He writes that a local club in Vancouver, the Gyro Club, was planning to call its carnival the "Tyee Potlatch," and the Methodist Church was attempting to get them to change the name of celebration (Chief Buffalo Child Long Lance Collection). Long Lance asserts that the potlatch

> has always been the most respected custom among the British Columbia Indians. Previous to the advent of civilization they had no social life apart from the Potlatch, which supplemented the white man's courts, his written laws and his documental records. It recorded the birth of their children and their christening; divorce, death and, above all, their marriage.

He further asserts that "the practice is as innocuous as the custom of Christmas-giving, and far less expensive." Moreover, the potlatch, "in which the host gave away huge amounts of food and valuable gifts to all his guests," (Smith 1999, 131) provided "an insurance against poverty, for when an Indian had been very fortunate he held a Potlatch for his friends, which renders them honor-bound to rescue him from any impoverishment which might come to him in future years." The potlatch, then, is not simply a giveaway but a form of solidifying social bonds and ensuring one's personal welfare. Although Long Lance decries the imprisonment of Indians in British Columbia who practice the potlatch ceremony and believes that an Indian should "be allowed to remain a decent Indian instead of being forced into a ragged nondescript," he ultimately presents it as a dying tradition that the modern, "civilized" Indians of the current generation have no use for: "The younger Indians have advanced far enough to enjoy the white man's recreations, but circumstances decree that the older people must die in their native simplicity." Here Long Lance problematically reinforces the dichotomy of the simple, vanishing, primitive Indian versus the complex, vibrant, and civilized white man (or Indian who has imbibed the white man's values). Thus even his support of an Indigenous practice betrays his belief in the superiority of Anglo ideals.

Long Lance also advocates for Natives in an article entitled "Original Americans' First Vote" in *The Literary Digest* dated September 22, 1928. The unidentified author quotes Long Lance in a discussion of Native Americans' participation in the upcoming presidential election, four years after "Congress in 1924 passed a law giving citizenship to all native-born Indians." (Chief Buffalo Child Long Lance Collection) The author writes that Chief Buffalo Child Long Lance "is the first in the field with an appeal to the chiefs of all tribes in behalf of the Hoover-Curtis ticket." Senator Curtis apparently had a Kaw grandmother, which made him more likely to be sympathetic to Indian causes, according to Long Lance. Long Lance also notes in his appeal that "[t]he Indians deserve to aid in the councils of the government, for they had established a democracy on this soil long before the white man came. The great Iroquois confederation was so perfectly formed that their constitution was largely adopted in framing the one under which this country exists today." Long Lance emphasizes that since the foundations of the U.S. government are rooted in American Indian traditions, Indigenous peoples should be especially invested in the American democratic process. There is a single photo attached to the article, which features members of the Blackfoot tribe in full regalia standing in front of a teepee. Interestingly, the author, who draws from a number of news sources about this momentous occasion in American politics, writes that North Carolina has the most Indian citizens of all Southern states. He cites a journalist from the *Charlotte Observer* who writes that: "The Croatans in Robeson County are quite numerous, but the real Red Man inhabits the regions of Jackson and Swain counties." (Chief Buffalo Child Long Lance Collection) As I discuss earlier in the chapter, Long Lance and his family belonged to the Croatan tribe, a tribe whose members, as the *Observer* quotation indicates, were not considered "real" Indians. This must have resonated with Long Lance on some level and perhaps explains why he included this article in the scrapbook. (That he is the only Indian leader directly quoted in the piece may be another reason for its inclusion.)

In addition to advocating for Indigenous people in the United States, Long Lance also spoke on behalf of the First Nations people in Canada. In a piece for *The Winnipeg Evening Tribune* entitled "The Metis" dated Friday, February 2, 1923, Long Lance describes the current life of the Métis, who "formerly lived and roamed in the vicinity of Winnipeg, who launched both of the Northwest rebellions and who set up a provisional government in this city in 1869." (Chief Buffalo Child Long Lance Collection) Having been displaced from their land, now approximately 1,000 Métis live "in the county of Duck Lake, Saskatchewan." Long Lance indicates that he has spent time with the Métis and serves as a mouthpiece for them: "The Metis declare that the main cause of the two rebellions has never been featured." Yet he also refers to them as an "impulsive" and "troublesome little race of French mixed-bloods, who are never referred to as 'half-breeds,' as are those who are descended from Scotch or English white blood." "Intermarry[ing[neither with white nor with Indians," the Métis have maintained a separate identity as a nation unto themselves. Long Lance writes, however, that recently Metis have begun to marry "treaty Indians" in order to "live on the Indian reserve and send their children to the Indian boarding school at Duck Lake." Long Lance makes the following judgment: "The Metis women are very handsome, but the race as a whole does not measure up to the standard of the Scotch half-breed." It is not clear what criteria he is using to determine why they do not measure up to other "half-breeds." But this statement indicates his belief in the racialist thinking that was so common at the turn of the century. Without brushing aside this problematic statement, it is important that Long Lance is writing about the Métis in a paper with a primarily non-Indian readership, and despite his own biases that are reflected in the piece, he does point out that "some of the Metis of northern Saskatchewan are among the most respected citizens of that province."

Long Lance's scrapbooks highlight the different strategies he used to authenticate his public Indian identity: engaging in Native cultural practices, associating with bona fide Natives, and advocating for Natives, often through his work as a journalist. Yet it was also his ability to adapt his identity according to his environment that enabled him to maintain this persona for so long. Included in the second part of his scrapbook and surrounded by numerous clippings about his success in Douglas Burden's film *The Silent Enemy*, is an article entitled "One Hundred Percent American" from the January 19, 1930 edition of the *New York Herald-Tribune* (Chief Buffalo Child Long Lance Collection). The author marvels at Long Lance's protean character: "There is romance always in the man who can play the game and live the life of another race: A Maharajah of India, Ranjit Singh, who becomes the cricket star of England; a McGovern, who becomes priest of Buddha in Japan; or, in fiction, a Leatherstocking who can match the cunning of the forest with the American Indian. We have such a man in New York now." Perhaps Long Lance included this article in his scrapbooks because it unwittingly summed up his life story: he was, indeed, "living the life of another" group, though not that of another race. Despite characterizations of Long Lance as a "fake" Indian, the historical record points to his identity as a mixed-blood Native American, albeit a member of a tribe that was not federally recognized during his lifetime (and still was not federally recognized as of December 2020). Yet he did falsely claim to be a Blackfoot chief and fought hard to maintain that public image, even after his death. Although everyone engages in the act of self-creation, Long Lance's fabrication of self was more sustained, potentially dangerous, and hard-fought than most. The scrapbooks that he carefully maintained throughout his life testify to that commitment to self-inscription.

In 2004, the satirical newspaper *The Onion* published an article entitled "Local Woman's Life Looks Bearable in Scrapbook." The article responds to the wild popularity of scrapbooking at the turn of the twenty-first century by highlighting the selective nature of this genre. A snapshot of a family Christmas gathering framed by the eponymous local woman, a fifty-eight-year-old scrapbooker named Jane Hemmer,

> depicts a traditional holiday gathering of a functional family. However, on the evening in question, a teenage Alex got into a shoving match with his father,

who knocked over the Christmas tree in the scuffle. The tree upset a nearby candle display, which in turn ignited an heirloom quilt sewn by Hemmer's grandmother. ("Local Woman's Life Looks Bearable in Scrapbook" 2004)

Even the most dysfunctional family can appear somewhat functional within the acid-free, archival-quality pages of a scrapbook: "By layering carefully chosen photos with brightly colored paper, elaborately patterned borders, and whimsical stickers, Hemmer has successfully concealed a lifetime of anguish, scorn, and contempt." ("Local Woman's Life Looks Bearable in Scrapbook" 2004) And as the title suggests, the audience for this representation is not simply other people but the scrapbooker herself. The scrapbook allows the scrapbooker to arrange and frame her life in a way that is, if not palatable, then at least "bearable." This impulse also seems to motivate Long Lance's scrapbooking practice. Though he was invested in creating a public identity that exuded authentic Indian-ness, his private view of himself was equally (if not more so) important. Long Lance's shame was doubled: he was ashamed of his "colored" heritage and was ashamed of rejecting that heritage as well. In his biography of Long Lance, Donald B. Smith writes of Long Lance's private anguish about not returning to North Carolina when his brother Walter came to New York City in 1931 to tell him that their parents were gravely ill and needed money to pay for their medical care (Smith 1999, 293). Ultimately he sent money home for his parents, and thanked his brother for keeping his secret, but he knew that in order to maintain the life and the identity he had created for himself, he had to keep his distance from his family—and from any whiff of Blackness (Smith 1999, 292). In a letter written in 1931 after the brief and clandestine visit with his brother, Long Lance wrote to Walter: "I have not yet fully untangled these emotions: my own darling brother whom I used to romp and play with, coming to me after twenty-two years, wondering if I were going to be ashamed of him." (Smith 1999, 292) This is the only recorded glimpse of Long Lance's pain around rejecting his family and his heritage, and it stands in stark contrast to the official version of his life that he depicted in his scrapbooks. Living in this limbo may have contributed to the depression that led to his suicide in 1932 (Smith 1999, 308).

In chapter 2, I move to a different mode of self-inscription: oral history. Just as Long Lance's scrapbooks are interactive and dialogic, so are the oral personal narratives of formerly enslaved people who lived at the crossroads of American Indian and African-American communities communal acts of self-making that must be read within a particular historical and social context. These life narratives collected by interviewed working for the Works Progress Administration in the 1930s are multiply mediated: people of color were telling stories orally about events that had occurred decades ago, and they were written down by mostly European American people who had strict guidelines from their supervisors about how to render the form and content of these narratives in ways that would jibe with often stereotypical notions of how Black people lived and spoke. Despite the heavily edited nature of these transcribed narratives that are part of the historical record of slavery in the United States, the subjects of these narratives do shape their own stories and navigate prevailing notions of authentic Indian-ness and Blackness in sophisticated and sometimes surprising ways.

NOTES

1. McCulloch and Wilkins identify four factors that determine a tribe's chances of federal recognition: (1) "How well the tribe and its members meet social constructions of the image of an Indian"; (2) "How cohesive . . . the self-identity of the tribes' members" is; (3) To what degree the general public finds "moral value" in the tribe's claims of legitimacy; and (4) The extent of the tribe's resources in terms of "population, wealth, land, etc." (McCulloch and Wilkins 1995, 369–370).

2. Scrapbooking became a multi-billion-dollar business at the turn of the twenty-first century. But this does not mean that people did not profit from the interest in scrapbooks before then. Mark Twain patented a "self-pasting" scrapbook in 1872 that became an "instant success" (Helfand 2008, xix). Jessica Helfand notes: "According to an item in *The St. Louis Post-Dispatch* on June 8, 1886, he made $200,000 from all his other books and $50,000 from the scrapbook alone" (Helfand 2008, xix).

3. The founding of Facebook has been the source of a great deal of controversy. In 2004, Cameron and Tyler Winklevoss and Divya Narendra sued Zuckerberg for stealing their idea. They claimed that Zuckerberg agreed to "develop a similar web site for me then – and then, instead, stalled their project while taking their idea and building his own" (Carlson 2010). The two parties settled for $65 million in 2008, though the Winklevoss twins appealed the settlement (Carlson 2010). After a federal appeals court upheld the 2008 settlement in April 2011, the Winklevosses planned to appeal the decision in the U.S. Supreme Court. But in June 2011, "they decided not to seek Supreme Court review" (Stempel 2011).

4. "His [Sylvester Long's] struggle upward, documented by him in the best fashion of success manuals and inspirational literature, offered his audience a vision of the Indian not as aboriginal American but as American in the best tradition of self-fashioning" (Browder 2000, 131).

5. Long Lance biographer Donald Smith also speculates that this was a reason behind Long Lance's eternal bachelorhood. In the late 1920s, he met and fell in love with Bessie Clapp, an eighteen-year-old white dancer living in Greenwich Village who felt a deep connection to Long Lance, in part because she "believed that she was part Indian" (Smith 1999, 303, 304). Yet Long Lance never proposed to Bessie, instead falsely claiming to be engaged to another woman. Smith asserts that "[h]is

inevitable exposure as a fraud and an impostor, when it occurred – whether days, months or years away – would hurt this young, innocent woman, perhaps even emotionally destroy her" (Smith 1999, 306).

6. Donald Smith notes that Long Lance had this photograph taken at the "teepee village in his white buckskins, moccasins and war bonnet, mounted on an Indian pinto" at the 1923 Calgary Stampede (Smith 1999, 156–157).

Chapter 2

Navigating and Reshaping Authenticity

WPA Black Indian Slave Narratives

In the transcript of an interview conducted in Wichita Falls, Texas in October 1937 by Lottie Major, a writer employed by the Works Progress Administration, formerly enslaved man Felix L. Lindsey recalls a conversation with Geronimo in which the Bedonkohe Apache leader insisted that Lindsey was Indian. Lindsey attributes Geronimo's conclusion to the fact that "[he] wasn't as dark as [he] is now, mo' red like." (Minges 2004, 148) Lindsey, however, insists on a monoracial Black identity, one that might be surprising given his three-fourth Creek blood quantum: "My fathah may have been Injun, but my mother's a nigger, an' 'at's the race I chose." (Minges 2004, 148) Despite the cognitive dissonance for a twenty-first-century reader who hears Lindsey's assertion of Black pride through the use of the most potent racial slur in the English language, his embrace of an African-American identity despite his mixed heritage stands in contrast to Long Lance's rejection of his Black ancestry. Not only does this anecdote point to the ways in which "race" is not always just a matter of "blood," but it also shows that Blackness was not always eschewed in favor of Indian-ness. Decisions to embrace a Black, Indian, or Black-Indian identity vary depending on time and place, as the subjects of this book demonstrate. For Lindsey, a man of African and Creek heritage living in the American West during the late nineteenth century, when, despite the entrenchment of de jure and de facto segregation as well as extralegal anti-Black terrorism in the form of the newly formed Ku Klux Klan, more Blacks were gaining access to educational and professional opportunities, particularly through the military, as Lindsey did, and Indians were being exterminated, removed, or assimilated, claiming an African-American identity was the path of least resistance.

In this chapter, I analyze several narratives by formerly enslaved people of Black and Indian ancestry collected by field workers who were employed by the Works Progress Administration in the American South in the 1930s in order to explore how Black Indians telling their life stories reshaped notions of authenticity. While in 1972 the Library of Congress published hundreds of these interviews with the last generation of Blacks who had been enslaved (and much scholarly attention has been given to these powerful oral testimonies), in 2004, historian Patrick Minges collected twenty-seven of these narratives from people who were "both enslaved as Native Americans and enslaved by Native Americans." (Minges 2004, xx) While not all of the subjects of these Black-Indian slave narratives are Black and Indian by blood, their life stories reflect a straddling of Black and Indian communities, histories, and identities. As elderly people of color recalling events from their early lives to white interviewers, the subjects of these narratives navigate multiple discourses of authenticity. Not only are they keenly aware of the burden of proof that has historically been laid on the formerly enslaved person, whose authenticity is always already in question, but they are also aware of narratives of authenticity around Blackness and Indian-ness that inform the perspective of their actual and potential audiences. I argue that the sophisticated self-inscription that occurs in these narratives belies the lack of formal education reflected in the dialect speech used by many of the former slaves and allows us to see how these subjects refashion authenticity on their own terms. I start with a discussion of oral collaborative autobiography, move to an overview of slaveholding in Indian Territory, discuss the scope and goal of the WPA Slave Narrative project, and then analyze some of the narratives from formerly enslaved Black Natives, paying attention to the ways they navigate discourses around racial authenticity.

Although the phrase "slave narrative" usually calls to mind eighteenth- and nineteenth-century accounts of enslavement by people such as Olaudah Equiano and Frederick Douglass, the oral testimony of formerly enslaved people collected in the early twentieth century also comprises an important part of this genre. In the late 1920s, researchers at Fisk University, including Ophelia Settle Egypt, collected over 200 narratives from formerly enslaved people, many of which were published (Spindel 1996, 247). In 1929, students at Louisiana State University also collected interviews from eighty-two formerly enslaved people. And in the 1930s, the Works Progress Administration conducted interviews with hundreds of formerly enslaved people in seventeen states and the Virginia Writers Project "interviewed about 300 ex-slaves, publishing just a few of the transcripts." (Spindel 1996, 247) These firsthand accounts are incredibly valuable to historical studies of plantation slavery in the United States. Prior to the publication of over 2,000 narratives from former slaves in 1972 in the multi-volume worked edited by George Rawick *The American Slave: A Composite Autobiography*, "The black slave usually ha[d] been portrayed as the victim who never enter[ed] his own history as its subject, but only as the object over which abstract forces and glorious armies fought." (Rawick 1972, xiv) But they must also be evaluated with care. John Blassingame, who in 1972 wrote *The Slave Community* without relying on these twentieth- slave narratives, isolated some of the problems with these accounts, as Donna Spindel summarizes: "[Blassingame] located the trouble with the documents in historians' inexperience with oral evidence, the nature of the interview environment, the absence of skilled interviewers, the editing of the interview, and the age of the ex-slaves." (Spindel 1996, 251) Indeed, as Minges and others have pointed out, the dynamics of the interviewer–interviewee relationship must also be considered in any analysis of these narratives: "The ex-slaves were often reluctant to express opinions that would displease their interviewers." (Minges 2004, xxi) Not only do the socioeconomic and racial differences between the field workers and the previously enslaved interviewees shape the narratives but so do the very questions that were developed by the WPA and given to the interviewees, questions that "were framed within their world view." (Minges 2004, xxi) This knowledge contextualizes the words of someone like Louisa Davis, who told her interviewer: "I'd jump wid joy if I could just git back into slavery and have the same white folks to serve." (Minges 2004, 16) Fear of saying anything less than adulatory about her former owners (even decades later) may have been a powerful motivation for such statements, which, though perhaps not always as emphatic as Davis's, are not uncommon in these narratives.[1] However, as I discuss later in this chapter, such comments about the relatively benign nature of enslavement were not always disingenuous.

Lynda M. Hill looks at another important element of these slave narratives: the appraisal sheets that "[r]eveal the choices national FWP officials made when committing the narratives to publication." (Hill 1998, 68) Hill asserts that the criteria that determined whether these narratives were published were inconsistent and not clearly codified (Hill 1998, 68–69). Not only were interviewers relying upon their own biases to assess whether or not a narrative's content and form were realistic, but they were also massaging the narratives to conform to "conventions of popular, sentimental fiction to create what they considered interesting narratives." (Hill 1998, 69) One popular frame of reference was the work of Joel Chandler Harris, collector of the Uncle Remus stories about plantation life (Hill 1998, 69). Questions of authenticity and ownership are inherent in collaborative autobiography,[2] but they are heightened in this case when the differences in power dynamics and cultural viewpoints between the interviewers and interviewees are so great. Sidonie Smith and Julia Watson assert that, "complicated ethical issues arise when one or more people exercise cultural authority over assembling and organizing a life narrative." (Smith and Watson 2010, 68) Although the question of how accurate or truthful these narratives are is an important one for historians and literary critics alike, and the problem of when the coaxer's role becomes "more coercive than collaborative" (Smith and Watson 2010, 68) is not insignificant, I am less interested in determining whether these narrative are true and more interested in how the tellers of these narratives shape their life stories with a keen awareness of discourses of racial authenticity. Most of the scholarship on the slave narratives collected in the 1920s and 1930s has focused on how these life narratives shed light on the everyday experiences of enslaved people in the United States. However, here I aim to examine these narratives through a literary lens in order to understand the rhetorical strategies that these subjects employ to fashion their own definitions of authenticity.

When considering these narratives, we must consider two time periods: the period of enslavement in the mid-nineteenth century and the era in which these were collected in the 1930s. As I mention in the Introduction, although slavery in the United States is almost always considered to be a Black–white affair, American Indians were central to the story of human bondage in the Americas. Indigenous peoples were the first people to be enslaved in the New World. And a small number of Native Americans owned Africans between the 1790s and 1865 (Miles 2009, 149). Despite the danger of creating a hierarchy of oppression by attempting to determine whether enslaved people were better off with European-American owners than with Native American owners, it is important to recognize the differences between the plantation slavery practiced by Indians and the plantation slavery practiced by whites.

In particular, the Cherokee were notorious for holding slaves, and this practice served as the basis for the economic and social growth of the Cherokee Nation. Initially, the Cherokee acquired enslaved people through warfare, and thus they were usually Indians from neighboring tribes (Perdue 1987, 4). In some cases, enslaved people were adopted into the clan, so they were not always doomed to be perpetual outsiders (Perdue 1987, 15). But by the middle of the eighteenth century, Cherokee realized that enslaved people could serve as valuable bartering tools for exchange with Europeans for the goods they brought to the New World (Perdue 1987, 19, 35). Since Europeans preferred enslaved Black people over enslaved Indians, Cherokee leaders shifted toward enslaving Africans, and "by the American Revolution most Cherokees traded almost exclusively in black slaves." (Perdue 1987, 38) Plans for Indian removal around 1820, however, had a large impact on Cherokee slavery. Whites began seizing Cherokee land and labor population, and for the first time Black enslaved people saw their Indian slaveholders in vulnerable situations, giving them the confidence to rebel (Perdue 1987, 65, 78). Cherokee masters attempted to quell slave revolts by imposing stricter Black codes (Perdue 84). Ultimately, many Cherokee were able to keep enslaved Africans when they were forced to migrate to Indian Territory.

After removal, Cherokee slavery more closely resembled white slavery. Cherokee slaveholders implemented the plantation model and used enslaved people as field laborers, house servants, and translators for encounters with English-speaking whites (Perdue 1987, 94, 106). After Emancipation, formerly enslaved people of Cherokee planters had a limited amount of time to return to claim their land allotments. In some cases, freedmen did not make it back to Indian Territory in time, leaving them disenfranchised. But in other instances, newly freed African Americans remained with the Cherokee because they were the people with whom they had grown up.

Some contemporary scholars have asserted that conditions for Africans enslaved by Native Americans were relatively benign in comparison to their counterparts enslaved by European Americans. R. Halliburton, Jr. cites a 1730 treaty between English colonists and Cherokee leaders that provides a metaphor for the distinction between Indian slaveholders and white slaveholders. The Cherokee delegation asserted that:

> This small Rope we show you, is all we have to bind our Slaves with, and may be broken, but you have Iron Chains for yours; however, if we catch your Slaves, we shall bind them as well as we can, and deliver them to our friends again, and have no pay for it. (Halliburton 1977, 8)

The rope of the Cherokee owners was supposedly less restrictive than the iron chains of their European American counterparts. This perception is supported by firsthand accounts of Africans enslaved by whites. One such person was Henry Bibb, a Black American slave who had both Indian and white slaveholders. Bibb wrote in his 1849 slave narrative that: "All things considered, if I must be a slave, I had by far, rather be a slave to an Indian, than to a white man, from the experience I have had with both." (Bibb 1850, 527) The number of Native Americans who owned human beings was relatively small, as historian Tiya Miles writes that "[a]mong the populations of the Choctaws, Chickasaws, Cherokees, and to a lesser extent, Creeks and Seminoles, nearly 10,000 black slaves were held in bondage between the late 1700s and the end of the Civil War." (Miles 2009, 149) Moreover, the fact that some Indians owned African Americans generated the animosity between these two groups that Europeans had encouraged since the conquest of the New World.

However, other historians such as Claudio Saunt and Barbara Krauthamer resist the notion that Indian enslavers were gentler than Euro-American ones. Krauthamer argues that the narrative that

> depicts slavery in Indian nations as benign and inherently different from bondage in the United States . . . has proved remarkably enduring, [and] refuses to see slavery as an institution grounded in race and gender ideologies that justified

the ongoing commodification and brutal exploitation of people of African descent. (Krauthamer 2013, 153)

By the 1850s, Choctaw and Chickasaw leaders created a set of laws restricting enslaved people's mobility and right to assembly; the punishment for breaking these laws could be rendered "by any citizen of the nation," not just the people who enslaved Africans (Krauthamer 2013, 83). Krauthamer also details how Choctaw and Chickasaw enslavers "had little tolerance for runaways and showed faint mercy for those who were captured and returned to bondage." (Krauthamer 2013, 89) And as early as 1818, the Creek Nation had passed anti-Black laws, one of which stipulated that "if a Negro kill an Indian, the Negro shall suffer death." (Saunt 2006, 23) Note that this language here does not distinguish between free or enslaved Negro, demonstrating the ways that the Creek Nation sought to dominate free Africans as well as enslaved ones. By the 1840s, Creek leaders had implemented a more extensive series of statutes that "confirm a general trend of harsher and more oppressive laws aimed at Black Creeks," likely in response to fears of insurrection by enslaved people like the one in 1842 in the Cherokee Nation (Saunt 2006, 74). Indian enslavers were invested in maintaining control over Africans in their territories, and they used both legal and extralegal means to reinforce that domination.

In addition to understanding the conditions under which these people enslaved by Native Americans lived, one must also consider the time period in which these narratives were collected. The 1930s in the United States was marked by unemployment and poverty, social change, and a desire for national unity. Although many Americans were looking at alternatives to American capitalism during this time, and there was a growing interest in Socialism and Marxism (especially among African Americans), there remained a desire to determine what it means to be American (Mangione 1972, 49). As Jerry Mangione writes in *The Dream and the Deal*, the lack of prosperity made people recognize the rich diversity within the country (Mangione 1972, 49–50). Lynda M. Hill asserts that while the Federal Writers' Project, implemented by President Franklin Delano Roosevelt, was intended to provide jobs for unemployed Americans, it also served a larger ideological purpose: "The FWP's primary goal was to document American culture and social life and in doing so, the national directors of the project expected to show that diversity was the defining feature of America's population." (Hill 1998, 64) Despite the possibilities for creating an alternative vision of America's past and present through the publication of these narratives, as Hill argues, these narratives were used to advance an "assimilationist agenda." (Hill 1998, 66) These former slave narratives place slavery in a nearly extinct past and fail "to address the problem of ex-slaves' exploitation in the 1930s." (Hill 1998,

66) On the one hand, the project of recovering the voices of people who belong to historically marginalized groups is a progressive gesture. On the other hand, these narratives can be used to suit a wide range of ideologies. For example, they can be deployed to show how far the United States has come since the era of slavery. Although few of the subjects of these interviews possessed material wealth, most were able to create spiritually and/or culturally rich lives for themselves and their families post-emancipation. Many took refuge in their spouses and children, and most mention that they belonged to a church and/or found strength in their faith. The end of Polly Colbert's narrative demonstrates the succor that family and religion offer, as she give thanks for her son and believes that she "[has] a lot of friends in de other world," and so she will not be alone when she dies (Minges 2004, 174). In some cases, freedmen who had been enslaved by Native Americans were able to obtain allotments according to the 1866 Treaty. Both Colbert, who was owned by Choctaws, and Kiziah Love, another Choctaw freedman, share that they live on forty acres provided by the government (Minges 2004, 169, 183).

But these narratives can also be used to show that Black people in America were still struggling seventy years after the end of slavery,[3] which may explain why some of the interviewees look back on slavery with relative fondness. For instance, Della Bibles notes that "slavery times was hard on some and not so bad on the other. We had a good house to live in, plenty of covers, plenty to eat, and that is more than I can say now." (Minges 2004, 32) As Stephanie Shaw points out, the word "now" creeps into many of these narratives, "turn[ing] the questions about slavery versus freedom into discussions about the depression." (Shaw 2003, 630) To be sure, the kind of suffering and hunger that many of these former enslaved people speak about in these interviews was not unusual during the Depression. Many people of all backgrounds were impoverished and starving during this period. But Shaw charts the ways in which elderly Black formerly enslaved people in rural areas were more vulnerable to its effects. Being older and sometimes disabled, many could not take advantage of work relief programs implemented as part of the New Deal (Shaw 2003, 642). As a result of the Great Migration, some did not have any family nearby to care for them (Shaw 2003, 648–649). And Black women often suffered disproportionately, as they did not have access to federal pensions that some Black men who were military veterans did (Shaw 2003, 637).

A closer look at the motivations behind the WPA initiative and how these narratives were collected highlights the challenges of interpreting these life stories. Between 1936 and 1938, the Federal Writers' Project, a branch of the Federal Arts Project,[4] which was overseen by the Works Progress Administration, conducted over 2,000 interviews of formerly enslaved people (Rawick 1972, xvi). The original aim of the Federal Writers' Project

(FWP) "was to prepare a comprehensive and panoramic 'American Guide,' a geographical-social-historical portrait of the states, cities, and localities of the entire United States. The original idea of a single multi-volume national guide ultimately gave way to the *American Guide Series*, composed of a number of state and local guides." ("The WPA and the Slave Narrative Collection" n.d.) This interest in local histories led to further emphasis on gathering folklore within various communities in the United States, which laid the foundation for the collection of life stories from former slaves: "Project records reveal that a small number of ex-slave interviews had been sporadically conducted, often by a single black employee, in Alabama, Arkansas, Florida, Georgia, South Carolina, Texas, and Virginia without explicit direction or apparent recognition from Washington before the collection of narratives was officially inaugurated by the national headquarters of the FWP in April of 1937." ("The WPA and the Slave Narrative Collection" n.d.) The initiative grew to include formerly enslaved people from seventeen states: Alabama, Arkansas, Florida, Georgia, Indiana, Kansas, Kentucky, Maryland, Mississippi, Missouri, North Carolina, Ohio, Oklahoma, South Carolina, Tennessee, Texas, and Virginia ("About this Collection: Born in Slavery" n.d.). The roughly 2,000 formerly enslaved people interviewed by the WPA represented "approximately 2 percent of the total ex-slave population in 1937." (Rawick 1972, xviii) Rawick asserts that "very often the ex-slaves being interviewed were either volunteers or were known previously by the interviewer." (Rawick 1972, xviii)

The introductory materials of the 1941 publication of a small portion of the WPA Slave Narratives by the Library of Congress provide vital information about the methodology and parameters of the project. A lengthy memo from director Henry G. Alsberg addressed to "State Directors of the Federal Writer' Project" and dated July 30, 1937 lists five "general suggestions":

1. Field workers should aim to interview a couple of "the more interesting and intelligent people," rather than trying to interview a "large number of ex-slaves."
2. The suggested questions "should be only a basis, a beginning. The talk should run to all subjects."
3. The interviewer should remain as neutral as possible, especially regarding slavery, and should "take the greatest care not to influence the point of view of the informant."
4. *All stories should be as nearly word-for-word as is possible.*
5. Interviewers should spend more time on questions "concerning the lives of the individuals since they were freed." (Rawick 1972, 173)

Alsberg then lists ten questions about life after slavery that should be integrated "naturally into the conversation, in simple language." (Rawick 1972,

173) These include queries about formerly enslaved people's expectations for freedom (and whether those expectations were met), attitudes toward Reconstruction, voting practices, employment after emancipation, and the role of "secret organizations such as the Ku Klux Klan in the lives of former slaves." (Rawick 1972, 173–174) A second list of twenty questions follows, and Alsberg suggests that these should be used to get former slaves to talk about life during slavery. He also writes that "A second visit, a few days after the first one, is important, so that the worker may gather all the worthwhile recollections that the first talk has aroused." (Rawick 1972, 174) Notably, Alsberg emphasizes "that it will not be necessary, indeed it will probably be a mistake, to ask every person all of these questions" and that the "worker should not censor any material collected, regardless of its nature." (Rawick 1972, 174) Following these ten questions are twenty more detailed questions intended to elicit information about life in slavery. Interviewers are urged to ask former slaves about the date and place of birth, their family history, the kind of work they did, the food they ate, the clothing they wore, the games they played, the music they sang, how they spent their holidays, whether they learned how to read and write, and how and when they learned that they were free (Rawick 1972, 174–175). While all of the questions could be potentially controversial, the last three seem particularly charged:

18. What do you think of Abraham Lincoln? Jefferson Davis? Booker Washington? Any other prominent white man or Negro you have known or heard of?

19. Now that slavery is ended what do you think of it? Tell why you joined a church and why you think all people should be religious.

20. Was the overseer "poor white trash"? What were some of his rules? (Rawick 1972, 176)

Finally, there are nearly three pages dedicated to the question of dialect in the recording of these interviews, comments that the memo attributes to "an editor." (Rawick 176) This editor[5] emphasizes that "simplicity" is best in transcription and that "truth to idiom is more important . . . than truth to pronunciation." (Rawick 1972, 176) The editor, John A. Lomax, cites Erskine Caldwell, Ruth Coskow, and Zora Neale Hurston as authors who successfully render "the manner of speaking without excessive misspellings." (Rawick 1972, 176) He counsels field workers to avoid "different spellings of the same word as this would cause unnecessary confusion for the reader." (Rawick 1972, 176) Lomax also lists certain word substitutions that should not be made, such as "ah" for "I," "bawn" for "born," and "wuz" for "was." (Rawick 1972, 177) However, "turns of phrase that have flavor and vividness" should be rendered, such as "durin' of de ar" and "outman my daddy."

(Rawick 1972, 177) The editor also cautions against "excessive editorializing and 'artistic' introductions on the part of the interviewer." (Rawick 1972, 178) The aim of the project is to hear the words, stories, and opinions of formerly enslaved peoples with as little mediation as possible. However, this list of directives, while intending to be helpful, can be interpreted in many different ways. For instance, how can one objectively determine whether an interviewer is "interesting" or "intelligent"? And might a phrase that sounds "flavorful" and "vivid" to one interviewer sounds bland and trite to another? Moreover, the attempt to codify the rendering of written speech is inherently biased. Calling for uniform spelling in these narratives might simplify things for a reading audience, but the danger is that "authenticity" is sacrificed for ease of reading.

The successful implementation of these directives varied widely from state to state. The FWP employed "novelists as well as journalists, along with people who had experience in a variety of white-collar occupations." (Hill 1998, 64) Thus most of the interviewers in the WPA Slave Narrative project were educated professionals who were trained as writers (but not trained as collectors of oral histories). The Library of Congress website lists the known races of the interviewers, though it is incomplete; if an interviewer's race was unknown, her/his name is not on the list. Nine of the interviewers listed were Black, while twenty-two were white. Importantly, many of the field workers who conducted these interviewers "had knowledge of their communities" and thus knew where to look for formerly enslaved people who would be suitable informants (Hill 1998, 68). The journey from interview to final published product was highly mediated. "The transcribed texts the interviewers submitted were edited and in some cases rewritten by trained staff with more experience before being sent to national headquarters." (Hill 1998, 68) Despite the strong language in the memo sent to state directors about avoiding "artistic" renderings of the narratives, other writers and editors often altered these transcripts before sending them on to the national office. Once these transcripts reached national FWP officials, they were evaluated according with appraisal sheets, one of which Lynda Hill reproduces in her 1998 article in the journal *Oral History*.[6] The transcripts were evaluated not only for authenticity (and some were rejected because editors thought they contained language or events that were "improbable") but also for "literary excellence." (Hill 1998, 68) Literary merit was often determined based on "conventions of popular, sentimental fiction." (Hill 1998, 69) The inclusion of folklore in a narrative often appealed to national editors whose sense of Black life in the South was colored by the tales of white southern writers such as Thomas Nelson Page and Joel Chandler Harris (Hill 1998, 69).

In many cases, the handwritten notes of the field workers exist alongside the preliminary and final typed drafts of the interviews in the archives at the Library of Congress. These notes may offer valuable information about the field workers' immediate impressions of their interviews. But only the final typescripts of the interviews have been uploaded onto the Library of Congress website. According to the website, there are also twenty-six extant audio interviews with formerly enslaved Americans between 1932 and 1974, but from what I can discern, none of them was collected as part of the WPA project in the late 1930s.[7] The website also contains 500 photographs of former slaves who were interviewed. The audio and visual evidence of these interviews constitute a powerful archive in itself that demands further attention. None of the twenty-six audio files overlaps with the twenty-seven Black Indian slave narratives that are my central focus. But I have been able to locate photographs of the following subjects whom I discuss in this chapter. Only two of these photos, of Lucinda Davis and Spence Johnson, come from the Library of Congress website. The picture of Felix Lindsey was taken by a news reporter in 1937, and the photo of Morris Sheppard hails from the Oklahoma Historical Association.

Despite the highly mediated nature of these texts, these 2,300 WPA slave narratives comprise a rich oral history that reflects the diversity of the experiences of enslaved peoples. Given my focus on people who straddle Black and Indian communities, I am particularly interested in the twenty-seven narratives collected and published by Patrick Minges in 2004 under the title *Black Indian Slave Narratives*. While not inclusive of all of the narratives that address Black and Native encounters in slavery,[8] Minges's collection represents a wide range of voices by people who lived at the intersection of American Indian and African-American identities, cultures, and communities. The racial makeup of the subjects here varies widely: some have African and Native ancestry, at least one has Native and European ancestry (and presumably this narrative was included in the collection because he was enslaved and lived alongside other enslaved Black people), and others have only African ancestry but are connected to Native American culture because they or their parents were enslaved by members of one of the Five "Tribes." Indeed, more than two-thirds of the narratives are from freedmen (people who were owned by members of the Cherokee, Creek, Choctaw, Chickasaw, or Seminole Nations) or their descendants. Similarly, the knowledge about their own blood quantum and family background varies. In some narratives, blood quantum is explicit, while in other narratives, it is difficult to discern the subject's racial background, even if the genealogical narrative is quite clear. While most of the narratives are rendered in dialect, some are not. There are, however, qualities that unify these narratives. Nearly all of the subjects of these narratives are in their eighties, and are thus reflecting on childhood experiences from a distance. Almost all of these testimonies discuss personal, familial, and communal histories, sometimes in great detail. Most of the subjects see slavery (or at least their former slaveowners) as fairly benign, and in some cases, they see Indian slaveholding as a much milder form of bondage than white slaveholding.

The question of authenticity has plagued the genre of the slave narrative since its inception, and the question remains with these WPA narratives. The inclusion of an authenticating preface written by an upstanding white person (usually an abolitionist) who could vouch for the veracity of the story being told is one of the many conventions of what is, in many ways, a formulaic genre.[9] Charges of falsehood were hurled at formerly enslaved Americans by people who doubted the veracity of these narratives.[10] I confess that I am not immune to such doubts, since I, too, have my own assumptions about how an elderly formerly enslaved person with little or no formal education might express himself. One of the most striking narratives in Minges's collection is the first one by George Fortman, as told to Lauana Creel in Evansville, Indiana. One of the few that is not written in dialect, this narrative rings false to my ears, not because of the content, but because of the language, which seems sentimental, overwrought, and literary in a way that none of the others does. From the opening sentence, the reader feels that she is in a nineteenth-century novel: "The story of my life, I will tell you with sincerest respect to all and love to many, although reviewing that dark trail of my childhood and early youth causes me great pain." (Minges 2004, 3) Compare this with some of the other first sentences in the collection: "Well, well, well! You knows my white folks on Jackson Creek, up in Fairfield!" (Minges 2004, 14) and "De nigger stealers done stole me and my mammy out'n de Choctaw Nation, up in de Indian Territory, when I was 'bout three years old." (Minges 2004, 159) Even though these first lines begin in different places in the speaker's life and reflect different relationships to American Standard English, they seem more conversational and less self-consciously performed than Fortman's first sentence and his ensuing narrative. Perhaps George Fortman did frame his narrative according to literary conventions of the time, which even a non-literate person might be familiar with. But one can't help but suspect a significant degree of editorial in this particular narrative.

However, a look at the typescript of the interview on the Library of Congress website suggests that Fortman's words were recorded faithfully. Significantly, in his collection, Minges omits the interjections of the interviewer, perhaps in an attempt to allow Fortman's voice to shine through. However, I would argue that in a collaborative autobiography, evidence of collaboration should be explicit. While one might say that there is a kind of authenticity that comes solely from hearing Fortman's words, I argue that knowing how the interviewer contextualized Fortman's narrative provides a fuller picture of this autobiographical act. A close review of the version of the narrative in *Slave Narratives: A Folk History of Slavery in the United*

States From Interviews with Former Slaves: Indiana Narratives indicates that Lauana Creel's interjections are plentiful. Her first commentary appears after the very first sentence: "So spoke George Fortman, an aged man and former slave, although the story of his life reveals that no Negro blood runs through his veins." (Works Progress Administration 1941) Here Creel emphasizes what may be the most intriguing detail of Fortman's story: he was enslaved but he has no "drop" of Black blood. Even in the twenty-first century, slavery (at least in an American context) is nearly always linked to Blackness, and this perception would have been even more entrenched in the 1930s when the interview took place. Knowing about the process of appraisal of these narratives, perhaps Creel included this detail in order to ensure that Fortman's unusual story would be told. This detail might also explain (in the eyes of an appraiser or supervisor who was assessing the narrative's veracity) why Fortman's language seems both literate and literary. Although he does not indicate whether he had formal schooling, as a mixed-blood Indian he might have had educational opportunities that a formerly enslaved African might not have had. Creel's other comments are mostly descriptive signposts that help to guide the reader. For instance, before Fortman illuminates his genealogy, Creel writes that, "The aged ex-slave reviews tradition" (Works Progress Administration 1941). In other cases, Creel provides an image for the reader of her experience in the interview. After Fortman reveals that he is the result of the rape of an enslaved woman by a white master, Creel writes: "The face of George Fortman registers sorrow and pain, it had been hard for him to retell the story of the dark road to strange ears." (Works Progress Administration 1941) Creel's commentary heightens the pathos of Fortman's story and in particular what he calls his "unsatisfactory birth." Creel's interjections become more numerous toward the end of the narrative, where she appears to summarize details from Fortman's interview but does not include his actual words. For example, she includes his religious affiliation:

> George Fortman is a professor of faith in Christ. He was baptized in Concord Lake, seven miles from Clarksville, Tennessee, became a member of the Pleasant Greene Church at Callwell, Kentucky and later a member of the liberty Baptist Church in Evansville. (Works Progress Administration 1941)

She also says that he has "friends in at Sauson Springs, Grayson Springs, and other Kentucky resorts" and "has had business connections here [in Evansville] for sixty-two years." (Works Progress Administration 1941) The narrative ends with his poignant words about the possibilities open to the current generation of young people: "They can build their own destinies, they did not arrive in this life by births of unsatisfactory circumstances. They have the world before them and grandsons and granddaughters among them."

(Works Progress Administration 1941) The significant differences between the two extant versions of George Fortman's interview point to the difficulty of discerning the "genuine" article and the slippery nature of collaborative, oral, and as-told-to autobiography.

During the 1930s, when the subjects of the WPA Slave Narratives were decades removed from their experiences in bondage, formerly enslaved people were perhaps even more prone to be disbelieved by interviewers. For instance, Chaney McNair offers corroborating witnesses, saying to the interviewer that, "You just talk to some of his grandchildren. They tell you I's tellin' the truth." (Minges 2004, 42) But there are also moments when they talk back to the interviewer, unafraid of any potentially negative consequences. For example, Felix Lindsey says that he can't "tell dese 'ventures at one time" because they "didn't all happen [at the] same time." (Minges 2004, 145) While we do not know what the interviewer, Lottie Major, said, we can infer from Lindsey's response that she is asking him to narrate his life in an orderly fashion. Yet since lived experience is not linear, neither can his own telling of it be. Louisa Davis also asserts control over her narrative in two instances: when talking about her husband's lovemaking skills and when talking about the Union soldiers' treatment of slaveholders and slaves at the end of the Civil War. Even though her husband became more assertive with age, she says that he was "timid as a rabbit" when they first married (Minges 2004, 15–16). As soon as she shares that intimate detail, she says, "Shucks, let's talk 'bout something else." (Minges 2004, 15–16) Her husband's initial "timidity" seems to be a code for his lack of assertiveness in the bedroom. We can see here that Davis is drawing a boundary between her and the white (presumably younger) stranger who is interviewing her. A few pages later, she says, "When de Yankees come they took off all they could eat or burn, but don't let's talk 'bout dat." (Minges 2004, 18) Here Davis says they should talk about something else, but before moving on, she does elaborate, diplomatically stating that perhaps they might have done the same thing if they were in the Yankees' shoes. She seems to shy away from expressing any residual regional animosity from the Civil War. And in Cora Gillam's narrative, she takes control over her story when she asserts that, "Wait a minute, lady. I want to tell you first why I didn't get educated up North like my white brother and sister." (Minges 2004, 20) These moments signal the agency that these interviewees demonstrate in shaping their narratives.

We can also trace in these narratives a preoccupation with racial authenticity. Historically, racial authenticity has resided in the body, and more particularly, in blood. The narratives of Louisa Davis and Cora Gillam illustrate an investment in the authenticating power of Indian blood. Interviewed by W. W. Dixon in Winnsboro, South Carolina, Louisa Davis shares her mixed ancestry early in her narrative: "My grandpappy was a full-blooded Indian;

my pappy a half-Indian; mother, a coal-black woman." (Minges 2004, 14) While "coal-black" skin could indicate a wide range of racial categories, given the context, one can assume that her mother's ancestry is predominately African, which would make Davis herself three-fourth Black and one-fourth "Indian." Unlike most of the other narratives in which subjects specify tribal affiliation, Davis never discloses hers. When playfully suggesting that in her old age she might be able to replicate the smooth dance moves of her youth, Davis attributes her physical stamina to her Indian blood: "De Indian blood in me have hold me up over a hundred years." (Minges 2004, 18) The narrative ends with Davis showing Dixon around her house and telling the story behind it. She attributes house ownership to God and President Roosevelt (Minges 2004, 18). Her grandson, who fought in WWI, worked in a CCC camp and asked Davis if he wanted him to buy her a car with his bonus. She replied, "Son, de Indian blood rather make me want a house. . . . I been dreamin of a teepee all our own." (Minges 2004, 18) This desire for stability, represented by a house (or, as she says, a teepee) as opposed to mobility, represented by a car, is attributed to her Indian heritage.

Like Davis, Cora Gillam attributes certain characteristics to her Indian "blood." When telling WPA field worker Beulah Sherwood about winning first prize for a bedspread she made, Gillam says, "I have never worn glasses in my life. I guess that is some more of my Indian blood telling." (Minges 2004, 25) Once again, physical stamina and health are attributed to Indian ancestry in an essentializing gesture. Yet Gillam's most striking discussion of Indian blood occurs in her discussion of her mother's brother, Uncle Tom. In her narrative, Uncle Tom becomes a legendary figure: "No white man could stand against him in that Indian fighting spirit." (Minges 2004, 21) Tiya Miles writes that: "But even as Gillam's narrative challenges fixed racial catego-ries, it privileges Indianness over Blackness, imbuing Indian 'blood' with an essentialized array of special qualities." (Miles 2002, 154) The irony of a man who "looks" like a full-blood Indian and possesses the "fighting spirit" that is often attributed to American Indians but whose name resonates with Harriet Beecher Stowe's eponymous character from her 1852 novel is striking. It is unlikely that Gillam is referring to Stowe's Uncle Tom; nonetheless, the phrase "Uncle Tom" calls to mind the "epithet for a black person deemed so subservient to whites that he betrays his race." (Spingarn 2018, 1)

While in many of these narratives Indian blood is potent and "telling," in Chaney Mack's narrative, African blood also takes on a kind of authenticat-ing power. The daughter of a "pure-blood Indian" from the Choctaw Nation and a "full-blood African" from "near Liberia," Mack is Black Indian by blood and culture (Minges 2004, 152, 150). She describes her mother, who was enslaved by a white man named Dr. Jernigan, as a formidable presence. Her authority was matched by her stature, as Mack says that she was "Seven foot tall. Dey call her 'Big Sarah,' and nobody fooled wid her." (Minges 2004, 153) Mack's description of her mother is reminiscent of Cora Gillam's description of Uncle Tom. Both are proud, dignified figures who are feared by their community. And those personal qualities appear to be linked to their Indian "blood."

Mack's description of her African father also reflects an investment in the authenticating power of "pure blood." Mack describes how her father was brought to the United States at the age of eighteen after being tricked by slave traders. They were brought to Georgia and then sold: "There was a boatload of them—all stolen." (Minges 2004, 150–151) The use of the word "stolen" reinforces the belief among people involved in the slave trade that enslaved peoples were property, not human beings. Mack recalls her father's memories of life in Africa, where "dey didn't live in houses," had "never heard about God," and "wore . . . skins of wild animals." (Minges 2004, 151, 150) These images have come to signify Africa at its most "primitive." Yet Mack could also be describing American Indian peoples before European conquest. Mack describes how her father struggled with the trappings of "civilization." He hated "having to wear clothes, live in houses, and work" and often ran away into the woods (Minges 2004, 151). He suggests that the strength of his African blood makes him unable to remain enslaved, and here there is a potential parallel between him and Uncle Tom, who for Cora Gillam is the quintessential symbol of resistance. Yet for Mack's father, it is a futile resistance, since he always returns to his (apparently relatively benign) master. Even if we see practicing cultural traditions (such as music and dance) as a form of resistance, the severing of ties to the mother(land) haunts him, as Mack relays how he would "play de fiddle and sing 'bout Africa" and "cry when he thought of his mother back dere." (Minges 2004, 152) Mack last sees her father in 1884 when he boards a boat to Africa, taking part in the post-bellum repatriation effort of formerly enslaved Black Americans. Although Mack is a mixed-blood woman (and thus within the "logic" of eugenics weak, sterile, and/or deficient), she gains moral, spiritual, and cultural strength from the "pure" full blood of her parents. Mack implies what Island Smith, "an Afro-Creek Freedman and herbal doctor," makes explicit in an interview with anthropologist Sigmund Sameth in the 1930s: "Cross-blood means extra knowledge. I can take my cane [a hollow reed used to apply medicines] and blow it twice and do the same as a Creek full-blood doctor does in four times. Two bloods makes two talents." (Miles 2009, 142–143)

But for other narrators, authenticity, belonging, and identity become a matter of practice rather than a matter of blood. Formerly enslaved peoples who live at the intersection of Black and Indian communities redefine authenticity in terms of language, cultural practices, and political allegiances.[11] For Cherokee freedman Chaney Richardson, Cherokee remained a comforting language, because it reminded her of the time when she was "a little girl, before [her] mammy and pappy leave [her]." (Minges 2004, 53) And Lucinda Davis, a Creek Freedman, starts her narrative with lyrics from what she calls "nigger song[s]." (Minges 2004, 116) She claims that she learned them as an adult because she grew up speaking only Creek (Minges 2004, 117). Knowing that her first language was Creek, not English, reframes our understanding of the lived experiences of enslaved Black people in the United States. Throughout the course of her interview, she uses many Creek words, translating them for her interviewer, Robert Vinson Lackey: "*Tuskayahinihih* mean 'head man warrior' in Creek"; (Minges 2004, 117) "his mammy call him *Istifani*. Dat mean a skeleton" (Minges 2004, 118); "We all called him *Istidji*. Dat mean 'little man.'" (Minges 2004, 118) Davis even gives a brief lesson about Creek naming practices (Minges 2004, 119). Here, the ethnographic aspect of autoethnography[12] emerges, and Davis serves as an informant about Creek cultural practices. Yet these practices also ground her in a Creek identity in a way that might be surprising to those who believe that blood defines Indianness.

Davis also redefines Creek identity in terms of cultural practices. She attributes to Creek culture a certain respect for elders, stating that her children "was raised de old Creek way, and dey know de old folks know de best!" (Minges 2004, 128) Similarly, Polly Colbert, a Choctaw freedman, shares how food connected her to Choctaw culture. Colbert recalls how they "cooked all sorts of Indian dishes" and then gives detailed instructions about how to prepare these dishes. (Minges 2004, 171).

The political allegiances of many formerly enslaved Black Indians also serve as indices of their sense of racial and cultural identity. Felix L. Lindsey, with whom I started this chapter, provides a fascinating case study. As he states at the beginning of his interview, Lindsey chose to identify as a Black man, despite his preponderance of Creek blood: "I's mo' Injun mix dan I is nigger, but makes no difference. I's a nigger. You all knows how dat is. I's proud of it." (Minges 2004, 145) This is one of the few moments in these narratives that portrays an open expression of Black pride. Lindsey's proud assertion of his Black identity represents one example of the ways in which claiming an Indian identity was not always preferable to claiming a Black identity. Indeed, historical and political circumstances may have influenced his decision. During the last quarter of the nineteenth century, the U.S. federal government was actively hunting Indians, especially those who resisted removal to Oklahoma and those who spoke out against white oppression. The Wounded Knee Massacre of 1890 is an example of the brutality perpetrated by the federal government against Indigenous peoples who openly practiced their cultural and spiritual beliefs.[13] An important moment in the so-called Indian Wars of the late 1800s was the search for the "leading guerilla warrior"

Geronimo, who participated in multiple raids throughout the American south-west and Mexico, a search in which Lindsey participated. During his con-versation with Geronimo, in which the Apache leader insisted that Lindsey was Indian, not Black, Lindsey told him: "Lessen you s'render, ah isn't goin' to be happy 'til you is daid." (Minges 2004, 148) In fact, Lindsey did participate in the search for Geronimo (Minges 2004,148). Though he does not use the term, Lindsey was one of the "buffalo soldiers," Black men who played an important role in the Indian Wars.[14] Their nickname was bestowed by Indians who "saw a similarity between the curly, black hair and dark skin of the soldiers and the shoulder hair and coloration of the bison, the cultural heart of the Plains people." (Viola 2009, 53) While Lindsey did not have the satisfaction of killing Geronimo, he seems to take pride in his role in fighting American Indians (Minges 2004, 148). Lindsey was later shot and discharged from the military, but he did work for the government once again as a "special 'livery agent foh pos' office in Wichita Falls." (Minges 2004, 149) While it is a stretch to assert that every person who works for the government has an allegiance to that government and its policies, Lindsey's description of his work history on behalf of the U.S. government suggests that he did support its anti-Indian policies. Like many Black men and women before and after him, Lindsey (whether consciously or not) asserted his allegiance to the United States by fighting on its behalf, even though the U.S. legal system was hardly advocating for people of African descent, particularly when Lindsey was coming of age in the late nineteenth century.[15] So although he doesn't use the word "allegiance" to talk about his relationship with the U.S. government, Lindsey's actions demonstrate loyalty to its aims during this time period, one of which was taking care of the "Indian Problem," through removal, assimi-lation, or extermination. In Lindsey's case, he redefines racial and national authenticity. Racial authenticity is measured not by blood quantum but by political affiliation. Similarly, national authenticity or belonging is measured not by citizenship by birth but by political allegiance. He proves that he is both Black (despite his 75 percent Creek blood quantum) and American by fighting against Indians, including one of the most sought-after Indians of the late nineteenth century, Geronimo.

Lindsey's legacy reflects his choice to identify as a Black man. In October 2013, Lindsey was honored at a "military honors ceremony" for his service in the Tenth U.S. Cavalry (McCorkle 2013). Beside his grave in Riverside Cemetery in Wichita Falls, Texas was erected a historical marker commemo-rates Lindsey's military service (McCorkle 2013). Among the speakers at the ceremony was Rosielietta Reed, president of the Texas Buffalo Soldier Association, who said that: "The amazing part of this story is the persever-ance of two white men, the Greenwoods, who helped bring recognition to a black man, Felix Lindsey, who was a slave and became a buffalo soldier. . . . Felix was a humble man, who didn't brag on what he did, such as helping capture Geronimo. He served his country and community with quiet grace." (McCorkle 2013) Celebrating Lindsey's membership in this often-forgotten group of Black soldiers, Reed remembers him as a Black man who served his country by participating in westward expansion. Lindsey's Creek identity is erased and the ethical questions surrounding a Black Indian's defeat and removal of other Indians are rendered invisible. But for Lindsey, there was no room for moral or racial ambiguity. He was a formerly enslaved Black American man who served his nation proudly and created a life for himself and his family, becoming a "respected member of the community." (McCorkle 2013) Rather than being defined by blood quantum, Lindsey defined himself through political allegiance, creating a sense of racial and national belonging on his own terms.

This examination of WPA slave narratives from people who straddle Black and Native communities before, during, and after slavery in the United States highlights the problems of both authentication and authenticity. The slave narrative and its author are always subject to authentication; responding to accusations (whether implicit or explicit) of falsehood is an essential element of any narrative and has shaped the genre from its birth. Authentication becomes even trickier when the author of the narrative is telling her story orally to a person who is racially, culturally, and socioeconomically different and is reflecting on the experience of enslavement from a significant temporal remove. And discourses of authenticity become important subtexts for these elderly subjects who are navigating what it means to belong to a community or communities. Blood, cultural practices, language, and/or political allegiances all shape how these people who straddle African-American and American Indian communities understand themselves. These narratives were collected in the 1930s during a time in which many Americans were returning to the lives of the "folk" in order to craft a national American identity (and to truly apprehend what *e pluribus unum* looks, feels, and sounds like). But by the 1960s, the United States had become deeply splintered along lines of race, socioeconomic class, and age. The various liberation movements led by members of oppressed groups often required people to worship at the altar of authenticity. Fighting against the oppressor called for a sense of unity among those in one's cohort, whether it be Blacks, Indians, Chicanxs, LGBTQ folk, or people under thirty. In chapter 3, I turn to one of the cultural heroes of that decade, Jimi Hendrix, a man of European, African, and Cherokee ancestry who resisted essentialist narratives of racial belonging through his music, lyrics, and public persona.

NOTES

1. In some cases, "interviewers' ancestors were 'owners' of the former slaves" (Hill 1998, 68). This no doubt influenced how some interviewees characterized their experiences in slavery.

2. Sidonie Smith and Julia Watson identify at least two players in collaborative life writing: "the investigator, who does the interviewing and assembles a narrative from the primary materials given" and "the informant, who tells a story through interviews or informal conversations" (Smith and Watson 2010, 67). Yet when there is a language barrier, as was common in many early collaborative autobiographies between Native American informants and non-Native American investigators, there is a third party, a translator who "'edits' the narrative into a metropolitan language, such as English, and culturally familiar story form, such as traditional autobiography" (Smith and Watson 2010, 67).

3. Many formerly enslaved people interviewed by the WPA experienced food insecurity. Shaw notes that "the narratives include many examples of those able to eat only once a day and many for whom even a single daily meal was not guaranteed" (Shaw 2003, 631).

4. "The Works Progress Administration's Federal Project Number One (known as the Federal Arts Project) established programs in art, writing, music, theater, and historical records; it was created in 1935 and ended in 1939" (Shaw 2003, 623, footnote 1).

5. Although the editor is not named in the memo from Alsberg, John A. Lomax served as the "Project's folklore editor" from 1936 to 1938 (Mangione 1972, 263).

6. Hill includes a scanned copy of a 2-page appraisal sheet date 1/9/41 of a narrative from North Carolina entitled "Story of Isabell Henderson, Negro" (Hill 1998, 67, 69). Much of the information provided is descriptive (title, place, field worker, editor, source), but some of it is evaluative. For example, under item 7, "reliability and value of material," the appraiser has written: "Based on first-hand experiences with slight and vague slavery data and personal history of an undistinguished kind. The tone of the statement is honest, but the narrative contains nothing of value." Someone (perhaps the supervisor, who has signed the document beside the appraiser's signature on the second page) has crossed out "nothing" and handwritten "little." Beside item 15, the appraiser ultimately does not recommend the narrative for publication. Typewritten next to "Reasons" is "vague, rambling, and with no precise valuable slavery data." "With no" has been crossed out and "has little" is written above it. There are several lines of handwritten notes after the typewritten text, but they are barely legible.

7. The audio narrative of Fountain Hughes, a 101-year-old former slave interviewed by Hermond Norwood in Baltimore, Maryland in 1949, is one of seven (of the existing 26) featured interviews on the Library of Congress website. It also appears on the North Carolina Digital History website where it is identified as one of the interviews conducted by the WPA in 1949 ("Interview with Fountain Hughes"). However, the Federal Writers Project was established in 1935 and dissolved in 1943 (Mangione 1972, ix).

8. In the collection of slave narratives from Oklahoma alone, I counted at least 30 by people who are of mixed Black and Indian descent and/or were owned by Indians. Yet in Minges's 2004 collection, 18 of the 27 narratives are from formerly enslaved people living in Oklahoma. In his introduction, Minges does not discuss the criteria for a narrative's inclusion in this volume.

9. In his 1984 article "'I Was Born': Slave Narratives, Their Status as Autobiography and as Literature," James Olney asserts that the "conventions for slave narratives were so early and so firmly established that one can imagine a sort of master outline drawn from the great narratives and guiding the lesser ones" (Olney 1984, 50). Slave narratives were preceded by prefatory materials, including an "engraved portrait, signed by the narrator," a "title page" indicating that the narrative was "Written by Himself," an authenticating introduction by a "white abolitionist or friend of the narrator" asserting that the narrative "is a plain, unvarnished tale," and a "poetic epigraph, by preference from William Cowper" (Olney 1984, 50). The narrative is usually followed by an appendix "composed of documentary material . . . further reflections on slavery, sermons, anti-slavery speeches, and poems, appeals to the reader for funds and moral support in the battle against slavery" (Olney 1984, 51). The outline of the narrative itself consists of 12 major items, including an opening sentence that begins "I was born"; "a sketchy account of parentage"; "description of a cruel master, mistress or overseer"; description of a particularly tough slave who "refused to be whipped"; "record of the barrier raised against slave literacy"; "description of 'Christian' slaveholder"; "description of the amounts and kinds of food and clothing given to slaves"; "account of a slave auction"; "description of patrols"; account of "successful attempt(s) to escape"; "taking of a new last name"; and "reflections of slavery" (Olney 1984, 50–51). Not surprisingly, many of the questions posed by WPA interviewers reflect attempts to elicit similar information.

10. Like many theorists of life writing, James Olney asserts that autobiography is not a transparent rendering of a life: "Exercising memory, in order that he may recollect and narrate, the autobiographer is not a neutral and passive recorder but rather a creative and active shaper" (Olney 1984, 47). Indeed, imagination is central to the process of recollection. But the writer of a slave narrative, who is always writing with the burden of proof at her feet, must appear not to shape her text: "To give a true picture of slavery as it really is, he must maintain that he exercises a clear-glass, neutral memory that is neither creative nor faulty—indeed, if it were creative it would be *eo ispo* faulty for 'creative' would be understood by skeptical readers as a synonym for 'lying'" (Olney 1984, 48).

11. Celia Naylor-Ojurongbe discusses the existence of "ex-slaves born and raised in Indian Territory, living among Native Americans for all or a significant part of their lives, who closely identified themselves with Native Americans and their customs yet did not mention a 'blood' connection" (Naylor-Ojurongbe 2002, 165). She discusses how clothing, language, and food and herbal medicine served as "signs of their cultural identification with Native Americans" (165–166). Although Naylor-Ojurongbe views these cultural practices as examples of what A. Irving Halowell calls "the phenomenon of transculturalization," I read them as authenticating symbols of Indian identity (Naylor-Ojurongbe 2002, 165).

12. Sidonie Smith and Julia Watson define autoethnography "as a hybrid term that has gained increasing utility in autobiography studies for its focus on the *ethnos*, or social group that is the project of ethnography, rather than on the *bios* or individual life" (Smith and Watson 2010, 157). Historically, ethnography was produced by anthropologists who conducted fieldwork on "colonized cultures" and then wrote about these cultures according to "Eurocentric discourses and cultural assumptions" (Smith and Watson 2010, 157). In the past forty years, however, scholars such as James Clifford, Clifford Geertz, and Michael M.F.K. Fischer have critiqued traditional ethnographic practices and "rethought the project of field work, and proposed various models of participant observation" (Smith and Watson 2010, 157). Postcolonial critics Mary Louise Pratt and Françoise Lionnet have theorized the ways in which both subjects and observers implicate each other in the "'contact zone' of cultural encounter" (quoted in Smith and Watson 158). The work of writer/folklorist Zora Neale Hurston is emblematic of this process, as Hurston was both observer and participant in her anthropological endeavors in the South and in the Caribbean. Françoise Lionnet argues that Hurston's 1942 text *Dust Tracks on a Road* "amounts to autoethnography, that is, the finding of one's subjective ethnicity as mediated through language, history, and ethnographical analysis" (Lionnet 1989, 99).

13. Led by a Paiute visionary named Wovoka, Ghost Dance was a "late-nineteenth-century messianic movement among western Indian tribes" that offered hope during a time when whites were hastening the end of Native land, customs, and traditions (Keenan 1997, 92). Wovoka prophesied that a "new order in which the Indians would forever be free of the white man's yoke" was at hand (Keenan 1997, 92). Federal officials became concerned at this growing movement and thus occupied the Pine Ridge and Rosebud Agencies in South Dakota in 1890 (Keenan 1997, 252). Attempts at peacemaking between the Sioux and the government officials failed, and at one point on December 29, 1890, "a rifle was discharged" (Keenan 1997, 253). A brutal conflict ensued, and some of the U.S. troops began firing indiscriminately into the crowd. The encounter left 150 Sioux men, women, and children dead and 50 injured, and "Army losses amounted to 25 killed and 40 wounded" (253). This event is commonly viewed as the end of the Indian Wars and the "end of organized resistance to . . . white culture" (Keenan 1997, 253).

14. The Black men who fought on the frontier belonged to the "Ninth and Tenth Cavalry and the Twenty-fourth and Twenty-fifth Infantry Regiments" (Katz 1997, 174). Conditions for these Black soldiers were difficult, as they were given "poor horses, deteriorating equipment and supplies, and often inadequate and unhealthy rations" (Packard 2002, 115). And they were "disproportionately stationed on the Western frontier . . . to ensure that they be posted as far away as possible from the Eastern Southern States, regions of the country where their presence was immensely unpopular with whites" (Packard 2002, 115). Despite these conditions, these soldiers served proudly and "won 18 of the 370 Medals of Honor conferred by the army" (Packard 2002, 115). Yet the fact that some of the buffalo soldiers themselves also had Indian heritage and that these soldiers were participating in the removal of another minority group makes an unequivocal celebration of their legacy challenging, to say the least (Katz 1997, 176).

15. Despite the constitutional protections granted to Blacks by the ratification of the 13th, 14th, and 15th Amendments and the passage of the Civil Rights Act by Congress in 1875, which, in theory, was intended to counteract the restrictive Black Codes that enforced racial segregation, prohibited blacks from "testifying against whites in court of law," and required blacks to have written permission from their employers in order to move from one place to the next, Reconstruction failed African Americans, both in the South and in the North (Packard 2002, 42, 43). The 1896 U.S. Supreme Court case *Plessy v. Ferguson* famously codified the "separate but equal" logic of Jim Crow laws, though in reality, separate almost always was unequal (Packard 2002, 76).

Chapter 3

Red, Black, and Blue
Jimi Hendrix's Musical Self-Expression

The piece begins innocently enough. The electric guitar strums the familiar descending major triad that marks the beginning of sporting events across America. Drums and tambourine shimmer in the background, but the sound of the guitar is the highlight. At the phrase marked by the words "through the perilous fight," the guitar begins to embellish a bit more by trilling and filling in notes at the cadences. At "O'er the ramparts we watched," the first syllable of "ramparts" is extended as the guitar slowly slides a half step down. But at "and the rockets' red glare," all hell breaks loose as feedback and glissandi distort the pitch. The listener is thrust outside the key of C major (appropriate for a piece that celebrates national victory, pride, and unity) as the guitar meanders into a world that is pure sound: no melody or tonic or rhythmic pattern to cling to. The guitar eventually returns to the melody, and the phrase that ends with "that our flag was still there" is followed by another familiar motif: the opening measures of "Taps." Then the guitar returns to the anthem, using a "Wah-wah" effect on the word "wave" at the end of the phrase "O say does that star-spangled banner yet wave." The liberal use of feedback continues through the final phrase, "O'er the land of the free and the home of the brave," and the piece appears to end with a three-chord coda played by the guitar with heavy feedback. But there is one final note strummed on the guitar before the band moves into "Purple Haze," a note that, if played with the major triads that mark most of the anthem, transforms the sonority to a blues sound. The sense of closure and unity (and triumph) that marks the end of traditional settings of "The Star-Spangled Banner" is troubled by that bluesy major second (Hendrix 1969).

Perhaps the most famous performance of the late Jimi Hendrix, this rendition of the U.S. national anthem on the last day of the Woodstock Music Festival in 1969 became an emblem of the counterculture and the splintered reality of the United States in the late 1960s. Not merely a statement of the collective consciousness, Hendrix's performance was also an important autobiographical act that gestured toward his relationship with the country of his birth and his own multicultural identity. In this chapter, I examine Hendrix's negotiation of competing discourses of racial authenticity through a close analysis of selected song lyrics and his public persona. I argue that although he was limited, to a certain extent, by the fierce racial divisions of his era, Hendrix strove to perform a Black Cherokee American identity that resisted notions of racial realness. In order to understand Hendrix's acts of self-inscription, we must consider the multiethnic roots of the blues as well as the racial dynamics of the world he was born and came of age into.

Because blues is so closely associated with African-American culture, it is tempting to view Africa as the sole ancestor of the genre. However, Mwalim reminds us that African-American culture is "a combination of West African, Native American, and European traditions." (Mwalim 2009, 211) In fact, the strong parallels between West African music and "traditional eastern Native American songs" suggest that the blues "merges African and Native American music, played on European instruments." (Mwalim 2009, 212) Paul Pasquaretta cites similarities between a nineteenth-century white missionary's description of a Cherokee dance and African-American music: "We see that many of the things described in the report, including the steady rhythm, the call and response between audience and leader, and the improvised lyrics are also features of African American musical traditions." (Pasquaretta 2003, 284) In *The Creation of Jazz*, Burton Peretti cites the American West as an important contact zone for Black, white, and Native musicians in the twentieth century (Peretti 1994, 42). And Mixashawn Rozie, "an African Algonquian jazz artist and music educator from the Connecticut River Valley . . . [sees] striking similarities between blues shuffle patterns and the two-step rhythms found in some Indian dance music." (Peretti 1994, 284)

In addition to uncovering the Native American flavor of "certain beats, rhythms, and lyrical and syncopation qualities in jazz," it is also important to recognize that many innovative jazz and blues performers were Indian, including Cherokee bassist Jimmy Blanton, Cherokee and Choctaw bassist Oscar Pettiford, and Cherokee and Choctaw trumpeter Adolphus "Doc" Cheatham (Wellburn 2009, 202, 206). In fact, one of the innovators of Mississippi Delta Blues was reputed to have Black, European, and Cherokee ancestry. In their biography *King of the Delta Blues: The Life and Music of Charlie Patton*, Stephen Calt and Gayle Wardlow recall that fans and fellow musicians were "baffled by his complexion . . . and those who knew him drew various conclusions regarding his ancestry." (Calt and Wardlow 1988, 43) Patton's lineage is difficult to trace with any certainty, and even his paternity is unclear. Although he was legally and socially regarded as the son of Bill

Patton, his mother, Annie Patton, had an affair with a man named Henderson Chatmon, "a bearded farmer and square dance fiddler of mixed racial origins whose grandmother, he once related, had been captured by slave traders on the Niger River," and it is conceivable that Chatmon was Patton's biological father (Calt and Wardlow 1988, 49). But his ambiguous phenotype led most people to assume that Patton had African, European, and American Indian ancestry, and music scholar David Evans reads one of Patton's most famous songs, "Down the Dirt Road Blues," as an exploration of Patton's "own racial ambiguity, expressing the problem in terms of racial homelands." (cited in Smith 2007, 92) This triracial ancestry was also claimed by legendary guitarist Jimi Hendrix who, while usually labeled as a rock musician, was a blues man at heart.[1]

Hendrix had a short, brilliant career during a time of immense social and political upheaval in the United States. Popular (and even scholarly) understandings of the mid-twentieth-century struggle for justice by and for people of African descent in the United States tend to divide the period into two sections: the Civil Rights Movement (1954–1965) and the Black Power Movement (1965–1975) (Joseph 2006, 3, 9). Whereas the Civil Rights Movement is understood as the era of non-violent protest in order to fight Jim Crow legislation and obtain "black voting rights," the Black Power Movement is portrayed as the period in which people proposed radical alternatives to the tactics of the Civil Rights Movement (Joseph 2006, 3). Martin Luther King, Jr. and Stokely Carmichael, respectively, often represent these two factions.[2] Yet as Peniel E. Joseph asserts, a closer look at these two movements suggests that "civil rights and Black Power, while occupying distinct branches, share roots in the same historical family tree." (Joseph 2006, 4) In particular, the work of Komozi Woodward and Timothy Tyson encourages us to understand the Black Power Movements in broader chronological terms. Such studies "extend[] the chronology of Black Power beyond the 1960s and delv[e] back into postwar black political radicalism and civil rights militancy whose antecedents included Depression-era radicals who interpreted events in Birmingham and Harlem, Haiti and Ethiopia, as interrelated." (Joseph 2006, 7) Conventional narratives that Black Power sprang from the ashes of the Civil Rights Movement are belied by historical evidence that points both to earlier iterations of radical Black Nationalism as early as the 1930s and to collective understandings that the struggles of Black peoples around the globe were intertwined, particularly in the late 1940s and 1950s when many African nations were mobilizing to free themselves from colonial rule (Joseph 2006, 3).

Although the Civil Rights Movement is often associated with the struggle for equality by and for people of African descent in the United States, its impact was felt by members of various marginalized groups, including women, LGBTQ folk, people with disabilities, Asian Americans, Latinxs, and American Indians. In particular, the Black Power Movement "had some of the most visible influences on the radical activist struggles of Latinos, Asians, and Native Americans, giving rise to a visible movement of racial ethnic nationalism and new constructions of ethnic identity." (Ogbar 2006, 193) Even the National Indian Youth Council, founded in 1961 by a young Cherokee college student named Clyde Warrior, was modeled after the Student Nonviolent Coordinating Committee (Ogbar 2006, 213). Indeed, the Civil Rights Movement bolstered the Indian cause in the mid-1960s by calling attention to the racist dehumanization of people of color (Wilkinson 2005, 130). The nineteen-month occupation of the island of Alcatraz in 1969 by a group called Indians of All Tribes was an important event that brought national attention to the plight of American Indians (Wilkinson 2005, 133–135). Similarly, the tense standoff between the federal government and members of the American Indian Movement in 1973 at Wounded Knee in South Dakota "raise[d] public consciousness" about the struggles for Native American sovereignty (Wilkinson 2005, 144–148). In fact, one poll indicated that "93 percent of all Americans had heard of the takeover, 51 percent sympathized with the Indians, 21 percent with the government." (Wilkinson 2005, 147)

Yet the goals of the Civil Rights Movement and the Indian Movement were distinct. As Charles Wilkinson points out, one must consider the unique histories of these two groups in order to understand their very different aims: "To appreciate the distinction between the civil rights and tribal movements, one need only consider the nature of the wrongs inflicted on each group: Blacks were determined to eliminate segregation and allow integration; Indians sought to overturn forced assimilation." (Wilkinson 2005, 129) While one might argue that some iterations of the Civil Rights Movement also sought to undo the damaging effects of a "forced assimilation," Wilkinson's point is valid. American Indians were fighting for the "protection of sovereign homelands," (Wilkinson 2005, 130) as the 1972 "Trail of Broken Treaties" highlighted. Organized by leaders from groups such as AIM and NIYC, this caravan of cars, buses, and vans that wound its way from the West Coast to Minneapolis and eventually to Washington, D.C. on the heels of the 1972 presidential election was a symbolic act that illuminated the ongoing struggle between American Indians and the federal government. One of the products of the Trail of Broken Treaties was a document drafted by Hank Adams called The Twenty Points, which "emphasized a return to bilateral treaty relations, restoration of 100 million of acres of land, full tribal control of the reservations, religious and cultural freedom, and abolition of the BIA." (Wilkinson 2005, 141) The document was bold but the federal government did not take it seriously, and unfortunately the Trail of Broken treaties ended in chaos when 400 American Indians occupied the BIA in Washington, D.C. and "destroyed furniture, broke windows, graffitied walls . . . smashed classical Indian pottery and slashed Native paintings . . . [and] burned or otherwise destroyed files." (Wilkinson 2005, 142) Despite this setback, American Indian leaders continued to fight for sovereignty, both on a national level (as demonstrated by the occupation at Wounded Knee in 1973) and on a local level (Wilkinson 2005, 148–149).

But what remains absent from the historiography of this dynamic period in American history is the ways in which people who straddled Black and Indian identities understood their relationship to larger struggles for power, equality, and self-determination. One woman who has written about her experiences as a woman "carrying the blood of the Chappaquiddick Wampanoag, African American, and European" is Penny Gamble-Williams (Gamble-Williams 2009, 217). Coming of age in the 1950s and 1960s, Gamble-Williams struggled with her identity, not only because of the "myth that New England Indians had vanished" but also because "no one, including any African Americans, believed that you were Indian." (Gamble-Williams 2009, 219) But her strong connections to the Chappaquiddick people through her maternal grandmother and the recognition of allegiances between Blacks and Indians in The Longest Walk in 1978 empowered her to "join AIM and Women of All Red Nations." (Gamble-Williams 2009, 221) For Penny Gamble-Williams and others living at the intersection of these two communities in the mid-twentieth century, the Black Power Movement and the Red Power Movement, despite their different priorities, both inspired her to "preserve ceremonies and traditions." (Gamble-Williams 2009, 223) As she puts it, "The black power and red power movements unlocked the doors, empowering New England tribes. The history books could no longer dismiss us as the 'so-called' Indians." (Gamble-Williams 2009, 223) It is significant that many New England tribes have received federal recognition since the 1970s, and, as Gamble-Williams alludes, many have had difficulty achieving that status because of the long history of intermarriage with people of African descent.[3] Another voice that contributes to our collective understanding of the connections between Red Power and Black Power is that of Jimi Hendrix. While he was not, strictly speaking, an activist or a historian, his artistry reflects an engagement with the plights of these two communities. Despite his aversion to politics and his assertion that race was not a significant factor in his world, Hendrix was nonetheless implicated in these struggles, and a close reading of a handful of his songs reveals that tension.

The world remembers James Allen Hendrix (1942–1970) for many reasons, including his experimental guitar playing, his rendition of the "Star-Spangled Banner" at Woodstock in 1969, and his untimely death from a drug overdose at the age of twenty-seven. He is generally *not* known, however, as

a Black Indian. Hendrix is usually referred to as a Black man in the numerous biographies[4] that have been written about him over the past five decades,
which is not surprising, given the abiding power of the one-drop rule. But
Hendrix's Cherokee ancestry complicates our understanding of his work
and provides a different lens through which to examine his political and aesthetic choices. Although Jimi Hendrix never wrote a formal autobiography,
in many ways, his songs constitute autobiographical acts that illuminate his
navigation of discourses of racial authenticity, discourses that were especially visible and codified in the 1960s. A closer look at some of Hendrix's
song lyrics and his public persona illustrates how Hendrix redefined notions
of racial belonging.

    While Jimi Hendrix was the first person to be inducted into the Native
American Music Award Hall of Fame and his multicolored full-length leather
coat was loaned to the National Museum of the American Indian in 2010 by
Hendrix's younger sister Janie for a special exhibit entitled "Up where we
belong: Native American musicians in Popular Culture," his Indian heritage
has not been officially documented ("Up where we belong: Native American
musicians in Popular Culture"). In *Electric Gypsy*, Harry Shapiro and Caesar
Glebbeek provide a detailed family tree that traces Hendrix's paternal ancestry to his great-great-grandparents: a "full-blood Cherokee princess" and an
"Irishman named Moore." (Shapiro and Glebbeek 1990, 6) In terms of blood
quantum, this would make Jimi Hendrix one-sixteenth Cherokee (Shapiro
and Glebbeek 1990, 13). Hendrix learned about his Indian ancestry from
his grandmother, Nora Rose Hendrix (née Moore) who was born in 1883 to
the "Cherokee Princess's" son, Robert, and a Black woman named Fanny
(Shapiro and Glebbeek 1990, 6). Shapiro and Glebbeek describe Hendrix's
visits as a child to Nora in Vancouver where she told stories about her life as
a vaudeville performer and recounted "Indian tales of wonder." (Shapiro and
Glebbeek 1990, 34) From a young age, Hendrix knew about his Native heritage and was informed by the version of Indian culture that his grandmother
Nora shared with him. But no documentation of Hendrix's Cherokee blood
has been found, and its absence is potentially problematic, especially given
the history of appropriation of Indian cultures and identities by non-Indians.
The Cherokee Princess syndrome is familiar and offensive to many Native
Americans who can trace their genealogy with certainty and are actively
involved in tribal communities and practices. Rayna Green writes about this
claim to royal native blood:

>   Most simply claim they are 'part-Cherokee,' as often through some distant
>   grandmother who was, as the phrase always goes, a 'Cherokee princess.'
>   Whether a specific tribe or no tribe at all is specified in the claim, onlook-
>   ers are encouraged to validate the claim by noting the 'high cheekbone' of

whites, or the 'straight hair' or 'reddish cast to the skin' of blacks. (Green 1988, 46)

I recognize the problem of "wannabe Indians" and the damage that such acts of imposture can cause. However, I also respect Hendrix's understanding of himself as a multiracial person with European, African, and Indian ancestry. For my purposes, whether he "really" had a Cherokee antecedent is less important than the fact that he believed it and was shaped by that belief.

As mentioned earlier, Jimi Hendrix never wrote a formal autobiography, but the 2013 collection of letters, journal entries, song lyrics, poems, and interviews compiled by Alan Douglas and Peter Neal in *Starting at Zero* provides unparalleled insight into the man and the artist. As John Masouri writes in his article on the *Starting at Zero* website, in 1995, when the "rights to the Jimi Hendrix estate passed to his family" from the two-decade stewardship of Leo Branton and Alan Douglas, a court ruling stipulated that the book and film that Douglas had been working on could not move forward without "mutual cooperation" between the Hendrix family and Douglas (Masouri n.d.). When the family violated this by independently producing a documentary entitled *Voodoo Child* in 2010, an arbitrator gave Douglas "permission to complete the book and the film with royalty-free use of Jimi's music and any other archival material they required." (Masouri n.d.) *Starting at Zero* relies on over 500 audio, video, and print sources, including "reams of Jimi's original handwriting [that] were auctioned in New York" in 1990 (Masouri n.d.). The book, published by Bloomsbury in 2013, also "features illustrations by Bill Sienkiewicz, creator of *Voodoo Child: The Illustrated Legend of Jimi Hendrix*." (Masouri n.d.) For the authors of the book, fidelity to Jimi's words was of utmost importance. Peter Neal says that: "No, I haven't rewritten anything, but then I determined very early on that I wasn't going to interfere with Jimi's sentences or thought patterns." (Masouri n.d.)

But *Starting Zero* is also a heavily mediated text whose authenticity as an autobiographical act demands careful scrutiny. The well-meaning editors seem keen to allow Hendrix's words to speak for themselves. Perhaps in order to facilitate this (as well as to make the average reader's consumption of the book smoother), there are several editorial notes but no citations in the book itself.[5] Some are listed on the book's website,[6] but in his article on the book's website entitled "*Sources*: Print, Audio, Video, and Jimi's Own Hand—the obsessive Task," co-author Michael Fairchild suggests that it was simply impractical to include all of the sources:

> It would take a good size booklet on its own to list the details of all the Hendrix quotes' sources, not to mention breaking down the sources for each quote on each page of this book. A single paragraph might be composed from a half

dozen different sources. A traditional footnotes listing would look extreme in length, and even compete with the book text itself. (Fairchild n.d.)

This may work for a lay audience (and to be fair, that appears to be the target audience) but as a scholar, I expect citation, if not in the book itself, then at least on the website. Moreover, the stylized and constructed nature of the text belies this apparent immediate access to Hendrix's thoughts and feelings. Neal and Douglas play with font type, size, and color (presumably to appeal to an audience that has a short attention span and a high degree of visual literacy) and include illustrations throughout. These manipulations make for an attractive product, but we cannot know what Hendrix would have thought about the choices that Neal and Douglas made in terms of the choice and presentation of material. John Masouri anticipates potential criticism:

> It feels like the real Jim Hendrix is speaking to us yet critics will accuse Peter of rearranging the guitarist's quotes in a way he never intended. The important thing to remember is that he's remained faithful to Hendrix's own words, and not altered them in any way. (Masouri n.d.)

Peter Neal acknowledges that "there is no such thing as a wholly objective book or film. That whole process is manipulation, and you can't avoid it. But you have to treat what you're doing with integrity, and without stamping your own agenda on it." (Masouri n.d.) Neal's acknowledgment of the "manipulation" that is inherent in any work of art is admirable, and only Hendrix scholars can assess whether he has achieved his goal of refraining from using this book to push for his own agenda. I rely on *Starting at Zero* in this chapter and find a great deal of rich material therein, but I remain keenly aware that while this may be the "closest we'll ever get to Jim Hendrix's autobiography that reads like it," it is a posthumous rearranging and reframing of his words (Masouri n.d.).

There is also a danger in conflating the "I" of Hendrix's songs and the "I" of Hendrix's life. Performers often cultivate a public persona that differs from the private person, and the tension between the two can be a source of drama. (Of course, this drama is often deliberately staged so that it can boost record sales.) But there is evidence to suggest that many of Hendrix's song lyrics were deeply personal. In Harry Shapiro and Caesar Glebbeek's comprehensive 1990 biography *Electric Gypsy*, the authors cite a Hendrix quotation from the March 22, 1969 issue of *Disc*, a British music magazine: "My music is my personal diary. A release of all my inner feelings, aggression, tenderness, sympathy, everything." (Shapiro and Glebbeek 1990, 324) This statement certainly confirms Romantic notions of art and music as expressions of deep human emotion, and it is not unusual for Hendrix scholars to read his song lyrics as autobiographical. But what has not been discussed at length is the ways in which Hendrix grapples with racialized identities in his music. While Hendrix engages with Black and Indian themes and sounds in his music, he does so *not* to promote the nationalist agendas of the Black and Red Power movements that were emerging in the 1960s but instead to grapple with the notion that, in the words of cultural critic Robin Kelley, "we were multi-ethnic and polycultural from the get-go." (Kelley 1999, 6) Four of his songs that demonstrate this point are "Castles Made of Sand," "House Burning Down," "I Don't Live Today," and "Black Gold." But I want to begin with an analysis of three of Hendrix's non-verbal musical pieces in order to illustrate how he used sound as a way of inscribing himself against the backdrop of racialized sonorities.

Hendrix's performance of "The Star-Spangled Banner" at the Woodstock Music Festival in 1969 has often been understood as a critique of the U.S. government's involvement in the Vietnam War.[7] In an interview with Dick Cavett (who functions metonymically for the "Establishment," the force against which the counterculture was rebelling) after the Woodstock performance, the talk show host asked the musician to respond to the controversial nature of his rendition of the anthem. Hendrix said that: "I don't know, man. All I did was play it. I'm American, so I played it. I used to sing it at school. They made me sing it in school, so it was a flashback." (Ventre 2009) Anticipating the "nasty letters" that might arrive in Hendrix's mailbox, Cavett pointed out that "this man was in the 101st Airborne." (Ventre 2009) Cavett noted that any "unorthodox" performance of the piece would get "a guaranteed percentage of hate mail." (Ventre 2009) Hendrix responded that, "I didn't think it was unorthodox. I thought it was beautiful." (Ventre 2009) But there is more happening in this performance. I also read Hendrix's signifyin' on the sacrosanct national anthem as a statement about how historically marginalized groups, especially people of color, have left (and continue to leave) their own imprint on American culture.

This performance sparked the imagination of Sherman Alexie, who wrote the story "Because my father always said he was the only Indian to Hear Jimi Hendrix play the 'Star-Spangled Banner' live at Woodstock." In this story, published in Alexie's 1993 collection of short fiction about contemporary reservation life entitled *The Lone Ranger and Tonto Fistfight in Heaven*, the narrator Victor recalls his turbulent childhood with an alcoholic father, who claimed to be the only Indian at Hendrix's performance. Playing the song just as his father comes home drunk and falling asleep at his feet while they listen to Hendrix becomes a significant ritual for Victor, the only way for him to bond with his emotionally unavailable father. Victor muses that: "Music turned my father into a reservation philosopher. Music had powerful medicine." (Alexie 1993, 29) Victor makes a comparison between Robert Johnson and Jimi

Hendrix that highlights not only Hendrix's blues roots and Native heritage but also the Indian roots of the blues which I discuss earlier in this chapter: "The first time I heard Robert Johnson sing I knew he understood what it meant to be Indian on the edge of the twenty-first century, even if he was black at the beginning of the twentieth. That must have been how my father felt when he heard Jimi Hendrix. When he stood there in the rain at Woodstock." (Alexie 1993, 35) Paul Pasquaretta points out that Jimi Hendrix is central to another text by Sherman Alexie, his 1995 novel *Reservation Blues*, in which "Alexie celebrates Hendrix's music by linking it to the lives of his Indian characters and narrators." (Pasquaretta 2003, 285) Even the title *Reservation Blues* suggests Alexie's interest in reappropriating the blues and transplanting them to a contemporary Indian context. P. Jane Hafen writes that: "Alexie has taken these tropes and reinscribed for his own purposes of presenting an American Indian cultural and political view of subversion and resistance." (Hafen 1997, 71) Alexie braids together Native American and African-American cultural practices and histories, recovering connections between the two that have been obscured by Anglo-American attempts to divide and conquer.

Less well known than Hendrix's version of the "Star-Spangled Banner," the instrumental piece "Cherokee Mist" is an explicit nod to his Cherokee heritage. This seven-minute song without words that Steven Roby calls a "beautiful homage to his Native American ancestry" (Roby 2002, 98) was recorded twice: once in 1968 and again in 1970 just months before Hendrix's death. Roby describes the two distinct renditions:

> The early 1968 version has more intensity, with tom-tom and wild feedback embellishments. The June 24, 1970, version, cut at Electric Lady, is a lot more polished, but moves into a rhythm pattern that is used for the song "In the Storm." (Roby 2002, 208)

After a cursory, single listening, one might conclude that "Cherokee Mist" evokes the pseudo-Indian sonorities that Philip Deloria describes in his book *Indians in Unexpected Places*: "The Indian sound, as it crops up in the folklore of non-Indian Americans, had a melancholy, vaguely threatening, minor-key melody and a repetitive pounding drumbeat, accented in a 'tom-tom' fashion: DUM dum dum dum DUM dum dum dum." (Deloria 2004, 183) Deloria suggests that these particular sounds evoke images such as "a row of horseback Indians silhouetted against a ridge" and "Indians dancing around a campfire or plotting a treacherous attack on the wagons." (Deloria 2004, 183) Hendrix's use of this "sonic wallpaper," as Deloria calls it, may have come from popular (mis)conceptions of Indian music in the mid-twentieth century, and his audience would have immediately recognized it as a (pseudo-) Native sound (Deloria 2004, 222).

But multiple listenings of the two versions of "Cherokee Mist" reveal something more nuanced and complex than the Indian sound that Deloria describes. The earlier version of the piece was released on the 1991 album *Cherokee Mist*, and was recorded in 1968 at the Plant. Overall the piece feels quite loose and improvisatory. It begins with the evocative tom-tom drum rhythm that Deloria describes above. Then the electric guitar enters, playing the minor melody theme, which roughly follows blues form, in which two nearly identical phrases are repeated (AA), followed by a different, longer phrase (B). As Roby writes, Hendrix uses his signature feedback throughout the seven-minute piece. As in many jazz pieces, the melody is not always distinctly audible, but the musicians riff on the tune while staying within the key signature. Interestingly, the instruments on this version include a sitar and a vibraphone, both of which add to the otherworldly quality of the piece (Hendrix 1968).

The rendition of "Cherokee Mist" recorded two years later in 1970 at Electric Lady Studio is quite different. This six-minute version, released in 2000 on *The Jimi Hendrix Experience*, is more of an ensemble piece and less of a showcase for Hendrix's guitar playing. The rough AAB form of the melody is still present, though the second A section is more embellished, making it more of an AA'B piece. The melody is repeated throughout the piece in a very loose theme and variations framework. The tempo is faster and there is a greater sense of forward movement, whereas in the 1968 version, the tempo changes throughout, and the listener feels that she is stepping outside the time signature (Hendrix 1970). The tom-tom beat is present throughout some of the 1970 recording, but it does not color the piece as it does in the earlier version. Indeed, whereas the 1968 recording sounds like an after-hours jam among friends, the 1970 version sounds more like a studio cut that is packaged for mass consumption. But both go beyond the hackneyed Hollywood Indian sounds that Deloria defines so succinctly. While some of the elements might be present (including the minor melody and the tom-tom rhythm), neither rendition of "Cherokee Mist" is defined by those elements. The form of the blues, the improvisatory quality of jazz, and the creative manipulation of the guitar that defines so much of Hendrix's corpus all contribute to the creation of a piece that transcends categorization.

This piece is an important nod to Hendrix's American Indian family history, and it may have been one of the few ways in which Hendrix, who was seen as a monoracial Black man, could publicly identify with his Native heritage. Indeed, the title of the piece is quite evocative. Not only does the word "mist" suggest that Cherokee culture is evanescent and hard to grasp, but the pun on the word "missed" opens up new interpretive possibilities. Indeed, Hendrix's relationship to his Cherokee culture is misty, for his sole connection to that aspect of his ancestry was his grandmother, Nora. But there is also a sense that Hendrix has "missed" the opportunity to be part of a Cherokee or Indian community. Although he expressed his solidarity for American Indians through his anthem "I Don't Live Today," which I discuss later in this chapter, Hendrix was not enmeshed in Native community on a regular basis, which, for many Indians, is a more important marker of Native identity than blood quantum or tribal documentation. "Cherokee Mist" is a passing reference to his Indian-ness, a piece that reinforces notions of Native identity through sonic shorthand while also representing (particularly in the freer 1968 version) his experimental genius and his blues roots.

The blues was a vital part of Hendrix's musical coming of age. After an intimate performance of the blues tune "There's a red house over yonder" for friend and journalist Sharon Lawrence following a recording session in Los Angeles in 1968, Hendrix said that:

> When I was a little kid. I heard a song playing at a neighbor's house turned way up. The song called to me, and now I don't even remember which one it was. I left my yard, went down the street, and then the song was over, I knocked on the door and said, "Who was that playing?" "Muddy Waters," the guy said. I didn't quite understand. He repeated it and spelled it out—M-u-d-d-y. I heard more blues, of course, along the line when I was in school, and I fooled around trying to write blues, but it wasn't until I was working the chitlin circuit that I heard a whole mess of blues, usually on southern radio stations. When I was alone, I'd play every riff, every change I could remember from the radio. I saw it as holy music. (Lawrence 2005, 110–111)

Hendrix's primal scene of being enchanted by the legendary blues guitarist Muddy Waters sheds light on the strong blues inflection of his guitar playing. Interestingly, in another recollection of that moment, Hendrix writes that he was attracted to but also frightened by Muddy Waters's playing. The combination of fascination and fear was clearly potent and productive (Hendrix 2013, 21). His description of the blues as "holy music" presaged his formulation of the ensemble called "Electric Church." Hendrix first used the term on a live recording in October 1968 before performing the blues number he wrote called "Red House":

> 'Bout this time, I'd like to present to you the Electric Church—Mitch Mitchell on drums, Buddy Miles on another set of drums, we got Noel Redding playing bass, we gotta whole lotta our friends—we got Lee Michaels on organ, have mercy. We're gonna have a jam right now, we feel very free about these things, we like for you all to have peace of mind, just dig the sounds, it's all freedom. (Shapiro and Glebbeek 1990, 322)

Shapiro and Glebbeek define *Electric Church* as a "loose communion of musicians who would ideally perform untrammeled by the constraints of rote rendition of hit songs." (Shapiro and Glebbeek 1990, 322) The collaboration of like-minded individuals who come together to create something while also honoring their own differences may seem antithetical to some notions of church as a place where ritual, repetition, and routine structure worship. But in some churches, especially Black churches, improvisation, call and response, and spontaneity figure prominently. Though Hendrix did not adhere to any organized religion, as a child he attended Pentecostal Black church services with family members and was mesmerized by the experience (Shapiro and Glebbeek 1990, 34–35).

While the blues is often associated with heartache and despair, Hendrix rejected the notion that human suffering is a prerequisite to effective performance of the blues: "Most people believe that, to be a good blues musician, one has to suffer. I don't believe this. I just like the sound of the blues. When I hear certain notes, I feel real happy." (Shapiro and Glebbeek 1990, 243) This comment reflects a certain abstract affection for the blues: he loves it not because it reflects the African-American experience or because it serves as an outlet for his emotions, but because the sound itself makes him feel good. Yet the blues cannot be taken out of historical context. Indeed, the sound of the blues is, for many listeners, the sound of Blackness. This certainly would have been the case for listeners of Hendrix's music, despite, the fact that many non-Black artists (Bob Dylan, Eric Clapton, and Janis Joplin, to name a few) were using the blues idiom in the 1960s. Hendrix performed blues numbers in some of his shows during his brief career, but in 1994, MCA released *Jimi Hendrix: The Blues*, which featured "mostly previously unreleased material" that pays homage to "nearly every aspect of the style, from country blues (the acoustic *Hear My Train A-Comin*) to the near psychedelic (*Voodoo Chile Blues*)." (Considine 1994) "Hear My Train A Comin'" was an original blues song written by Hendrix that he performed fairly frequently. The first two verses reflect the speaker's despair over the end of a love affair. He is waiting for the train to "Take [him] home, yeah/ From this lonesome place." (Hendrix 1967) His tears are "burning" and he laments that he and his love "had to part." But as is customary in the blues form, the third verse reflects a shift in perspective. The speaker is determined to "leave this town," "make a whole lotta money," "put it all in [his] shoe," "buy this town," and maybe "even give a piece to you." (Hendrix 1967) He will triumph over the heartbreak and find material success that he might deign to share with others. The music is as blues-inspired as the lyrics.

There are several versions of "Hear My Train A Comin'" available. But one of the most moving renditions is his performance of the piece for Joe Boyd's documentary *A Film about Jimi Hendrix*, which was released in 1973 (Lawrence 2005, 36–37). The visual image that accompanies the music is particularly arresting: Hendrix sits on a stool in stark room strumming a "Zemaitis twelve-string guitar." (Roby and Schreiber 2010, 11) He is wearing a brown-black fedora hat adorned with jewels, including a large turquoise stone, black pants with buttons running up the ankle, a brightly colored collared shirt, and an orange, black, white, and blue coat. For the first minute or so, Hendrix is jamming on the guitar, looking down at his instrument intensely, focused on his craft. Then he abruptly stops and says to the cameraman and director, "'No I'd rather do that again. . . . Cause I was scared to death. Can't I just do it one more time? Can I just do it one more time?" (Hendrix 1973) The offscreen voice obliges happily, and after a short guitar introduction, Hendrix begins singing. Although he is being taped, there is something deeply intimate and personal about his lament. The combination of his easy, unforced voice and the raw sound of the acoustic guitar is quite affecting and offers a very different side of Hendrix from the hypersexualized performances on the electric guitar in large sold-out venues that sometimes overdetermine his legacy. After the final chord, he says softly, "Ya think I can do that?" (Hendrix 1973) It is not clear who the referents of the pronouns "you" and "that" are. It may be the people from his early life who didn't believe he would amount to much. By the age of seventeen, Hendrix had dropped out of high school and had been arrested and held in juvenile detention for riding in a stolen car (Shapiro and Glebbeek 1990, 46, 48). One senses that the vulnerable little boy Jimi who was passed around from relative to relative and lacked stability and continuity in his life was still looking for approval as an adult, if not from his family then from his fans. Despite Hendrix's insistence that suffering is not a prerequisite for a good blues musician, the power of his own experiences, particularly during his childhood, may well have provided an emotional depth that, when combined with his talent as a guitarist and his inventiveness as songwriter, made him a consummate blues musician. As David Henderson, one of Hendrix's biographers, points out, Hendrix's genius was marked not only by his "improvisational ability" but also his "ability to range between pure blues and avant-garde jazz forms." (Henderson 1995, 214) Hendrix drew on multiple forms and refused to be hemmed in by labels, whether musical, spiritual, or racial.

One of Hendrix's more explicitly autobiographical pieces,[8] "Castles Made of Sand" comes from the 1967 album *Axis: Bold as Love*, recorded by The Jimi Hendrix Experience. Each verse describes three different scenarios: a domestic dispute between a man and a woman, a young Indian boy who dreams of being a mighty "Indian Chief," and a "crippled" girl in a wheelchair who approaches the edge of the ocean intending to kill herself (Hendrix 1967). After each verse is a simple chorus consisting of one line that reflects on impermanence: "And so castles made of sand fall in the sea, eventually"; "And so castles made of sand melts into the sea, eventually"; and "And so castles made of sand slips into the sea, eventually." (Hendrix 1967) The image of sand castles functions as a metaphor for the ephemeral nature of life.

I want to focus, however, on the three stories that Hendrix portrays in the three verses. Although the first two are perhaps more explicitly autobiographical, the final verse also sheds light on Hendrix's sense of himself in intriguing ways.[9] The first verse, which begins with the lines, "Down the street you can hear her scream you're a disgrace/ As she slams the door in his drunken face," may reflect Hendrix's own tumultuous childhood (Hendrix 1967). According to Shapiro and Glebbeek, when Hendrix was born, his father Al was in the Army and his mother Lucille "was unprepared and unwilling to play the dutiful woman waiting for her man to come home from the war." (Shapiro and Glebbeek 1990, 15) From birth, Hendrix was passed around from one relative to the next, as Lucille was often unwilling or unable to properly care for him (Shapiro and Glebbeek 1990, 16). When Al was discharged in 1945, he returned home to Seattle to live with Lucille and Jimi, but their marriage was volatile and they finally divorced in 1951 (Shapiro and Glebbeek 1990, 22). Although Al became the primary caretaker for Jimi and his younger brother Leon, "Al was out of the house for long periods of time and this severely limited the chances of Jimmy and Leon having a proper family life." (Shapiro and Glebbeek 1990, 27) Clearly disruption and instability colored Hendrix's childhood.

The image of the "neighbors [who] start to gossip and drool" compounds the sense of humiliation that the man feels in this situation (Hendrix 1967). The private has become public as the whole neighborhood witnesses the volatile encounter. The man then asks his partner, "What happened to the sweet love you and me had?" (Hendrix 1967) The image of "his tears fall[ing] and burning the garden green" paints a picture of male vulnerability that is rarely portrayed in popular culture, even today in the twenty-first century, and certainly in the 1960s when Hendrix wrote the lyrics (Hendrix 1967). This desolation and shame reflect, perhaps, not only the feelings of Hendrix's father, as Lucille apparently consorted with other men and often left for several days at a time, but also that of Hendrix himself (Shapiro and Glebbeek 1990, 22). As an adult Hendrix said of his family: "My dad was level-headed and religious, but my mother used to like having a good time and dressing up. She used to drink a lot and didn't take care of herself. She died when I was about ten. But she was a groovy mother." (Roby 2002, 7) One can hear in his comments both a recognition of her flaws and a desire to hold a positive image of her. And his recollection of a dream he had before his mother passed away highlights that abiding sense of loss:

There's a dream I had when I was real little about my mother being carried away on these camels. It was a big caravan, and you could see the shadow the leaf patterns across her face. You know how the sun shines through a tree? Well, these were green and yellow shadows. And she was saying to me, "Well, I won't be seeing you too much anymore, you know, so I'll see you." And then about two years after that she died. I always will remember that one. I never did forget. There are dreams you NEVER forget. (Hendrix 2013, 16)

The second verse about the "Indian brave" is one of the few references to Indians in Hendrix's corpus, and, like the first verse, can be read autobiographically. The narrator describes "A little Indian brave who before he was ten/ Played war games in the woods with his Indian friends." (Hendrix 1967) The word "brave" is an antiquated term for American Indians that conjures up the romanticized image of the Indian popularized in texts such as Henry Wadsworth Longfellow's 1855 poem *The Song of Hiawatha*. Hendrix creates the picture of an Indian community that nurtures this little boy and inspires him to grow up to be a "fearless warrior Indian Chief." This image of the Noble Savage is supported by the dream of "sing[ing] his first war song and fight[ing] his first battle." Even the reference to the passing of "many moons" passing is reminiscent of pseudo-Indian-speak and evokes a world perspective in which time is measured not by clocks but by the natural world. This narrative about a boy wanting to be brave and bold but being thwarted may reflect Hendrix's experience. In a snippet from *Starting at Zero*, he recalls watching the "race riots" and being refused service in certain restaurants in Nashville while he was playing with a group called the "King Kasuals." (Hendrix 2013, 37–38) Looking back on his childhood, he writes that:

I used to have a childhood ambition to stand on my own feet, without being afraid to get hit in the face if I went to a 'white' restaurant and ordered a 'white' steak. But normally, I just didn't think along these lines. I had more important things to do—like playing guitar. (Hendrix 2013, 38)[10]

If we understand this verse as a reflection of his own childhood dreams and sense of himself, it is striking that he casts himself as Indian. This might be because he sees Indians as noble people who fight with dignity and refuse to be subdued. Rayna Green offers a compelling explanation for the reasons that people of African descent might claim Indian heritage: "When Blacks, as opposed to Anglo-Americans, play Indian, perhaps they are connecting to a world that allows them to be first, to be other than Black, other than white, other than victims that did not fight their enslavement." (Green 1988, 48) This is a powerful and troubling statement about the ways in which people of African descent might still understand themselves as actors in the drama of enslavement in the Americas. As formerly enslaved American Cora Gillam emphasizes in her testimony, discussed in chapter 2, Indian-ness is still understood as a symbol of dignified resistance, whereas Blackness is associated with subservience. This remains entrenched even though we know about the many ways in which people of African descent resisted attempts to enforce their physical, spiritual, and mental enslavement.[11] However, the demise of Hendrix's "Indian brave" is anything but heroic, for "Something went wrong, surprise attack killed him in his sleep that night." (Hendrix 1967) This final line rings eerily presages Hendrix's own demise. The circumstances of Hendrix's death have been debated since that September day in 1970. But something did, indeed, go "wrong" for Hendrix. Shapiro and Glebbeek assert that he was depressed during the last several months of his life (Shapiro and Glebbeek 1990, 476). While he was not literally killed in his sleep by enemy fire, death did take him by surprise. The autopsy "attributed . . . [his death] to choking on his own vomit and acute barbiturate intoxication." (Roby and Schreiber 2010, 182) Despite Hendrix's depression, Shapiro and Glebbeek assert that "Nobody interviewed for this book believes Jimi did commit suicide nor is there any real evidence to suggest this." (Shapiro and Glebbeek 1990, 476) This was not a planned exit. Hendrix died just as he was on the verge of new projects and new possibilities, including his new (and expensive) recording studio Electric Lady Studio in New York, whose opening party occurred just weeks before his death (Shapiro and Glebbeek, 1990, 416–417; 442). Hendrix was also working on an album entitled *The Last Rays of the Morning Sun,* which featured strings and the Mormon Tabernacle Choir (Roby 2002, 205).

The final verse seems to depict a figure that is as far removed from Hendrix's own life as possible: a disabled girl. Problematically, the word "crippled," though used as a verb, evokes the offensive noun "cripple"; moreover, the young woman is portrayed as a helpless creature who is confined to a wheelchair and cannot express herself verbally. Disabled and mute, she decides that her life is not worth living and resolves to die by suicide—until she sees a magical image in the sea and says, "Look a golden winged ship is passing my way/ And it really didn't have to stop, it just kept going." (Hendrix 1967) The ending of the verse is ambiguous: does the image inspire her not to take her own life? Or does she kill herself, realizing that the only way to freedom (embodied by the "golden winged ship") is death? It is unclear, but it can be related in fruitful ways to Hendrix's life. Although we might argue that Hendrix was the opposite of this girl, in that he had the freedom to use his body, mind, and voice in ways that she could not, the writings of Hendrix suggest a kind of paralysis, particularly toward the end of his brief life, that made it difficult to live and work on his own terms. In particular, Hendrix's relationship with his manager Michael Jeffery was fraught. Jeffery feared that unless The Jimi Hendrix Experience retained its original person-nel of Hendrix, Noel Redding, and Mitch Mitchell, it would not make money (Moskowitz 2010, 60). However, by mid-1969, Noel Redding had left the band and Hendrix was experimenting with new sounds, new musicians, even a new name. When introduced as The Jimi Hendrix Experience at Woodstock, Hendrix corrected the announcer and reintroduced the group (which on that day consisted of the multiracial crew of Hendrix, Mitch Mitchell, Billy Cox, Larry Lee, Juma Sultan, and Jerry Belez) as the "Band of Gypsys" (Moskowitz 2010, 59). The Band of Gypsys [sic] that produced the self-titled album a few months later in early 1970 consisted of Billy Cox, Buddy Miles, and Hendrix (Moskowitz 2010, 67). But the group lasted only a few months, and by February 1970, The Jimi Hendrix Experience was reformed with Billy Cox replacing Noel Redding on bass guitar (Moskowitz 2010, 71–72). While Hendrix remained with Jeffery until his death in September 1970,[12] Hendrix was increasingly frustrated by his lack of creative control. Although it was written in 1967 at the beginning of his ascent to rock and roll royalty, "Castles in the Sand" presages Hendrix's understanding of the impermanence of exis-tence and the contingency of his fame.

While "Castles in the Sand" depicts intimate moments of despair and struggle, "House Burning Down" reflects a community that is consuming itself with hatred. This song appeared on the album *Are You Experienced*, recorded in 1968 by The Jimi Hendrix Experience. Moved by the "race riots" in U.S. urban cities in the mid-to-late 1960s, [13]Hendrix ruminates on the con-flagrations in urban areas and the rage that oppressed people felt that led them to hurt their own people, as the speaker asks, "I say oh baby why'd you burn your brother's house down?" (Hendrix 2021) The senselessness of the Black-on-Black violence riles the narrator, an interested observer who proposes to uncover the truth that others don't want to see by asking "Where is that black smoke comin' from?" (Hendrix 2021) But his comrade "just coughed and changed the subject and/ said oh I think it might snow some." (Hendrix 2021) Instead of confronting the realities of the situation, this friend deflects any engagement with the violent events. The speaker seems to have a privileged outside perspective as he "jump[s] in [his] chariot" to see where the smoke is coming from and offers the following advice: "I said the truth is right ahead so don't burn yourself instead/ Try to learn instead of burn, hear what I say, yeah, yeah." (Hendrix 2021) This outsider perspective reflects Hendrix's own viewpoint on the racial conflicts of the 1960s: he found violence senseless and believed that fighting one's brother would not solve problems, yet it is not clear that he was actually a part of a "Black community." Shapiro and Glebbeek write that "House Burning Down" marks the "beginning of Jimi's more overtly political stance, particularly on black issues," but he did not support a "by any means necessary" approach (Shapiro and Glebbeek 1990,

319). Although Hendrix was approached by the Black Panthers, he stopped short of supporting them publicly.[14]

Moreover, Hendrix had a challenging relationship with Black audiences, one that he hoped to ease: "He was prepared to offer limited support [to the Black Panthers] . . . particularly if doing so would earn the approval of the black community, which overall had failed to respond to Jimi and his music." (Shapiro and Glebbeek 1990, 369) Hendrix's distance from life in America for Black people (both figurative and literal, for he spent a great deal of time in the United Kingdom and in Europe)[15] may have provided unique insight on the cause of these conflicts and divisions. He writes in *Starting at Zero* that:

> Quite naturally I don't like to see houses being burned, but I don't have too much feeling for either side right now. There is no such thing as color problem. It is a weapon for the negative forces who are trying to destroy the country. They make black and white fight against each other so they can take over at each end. (Hendrix 2013, 100)

Hendrix's statement that he has no "feeling for either side" is striking, given that he was not immune to American racism.[16] Before a concert in Dallas in 1969, a group of white men outside Hendrix's dressing room threatened the singer's life when they informed his booking agent, Ron Terry: "You tell that fucking nigger that if he plays 'The Star-Spangled Banner' in this hall tonight he won't live to get out of the building." (Henderson 1983, 287) No harm came to Hendrix that night, but the threat exemplified the ways in which his stardom did not protect him from racial hatred. And while Hendrix's assessment that the "establishment" is the cause of interracial and intraracial violence may sound like the ramblings of a paranoid conspiracy theorist, the history of the United States reflects a divide-and-conquer approach to oppression. This becomes especially clear when looking at the ways in which European Americans went to great lengths to separate and antagonize Indians and Blacks, fearing that alliances between these two groups would threaten their power (Gross 2008, 19).

"I Don't Live Today" highlights the harsh realities of American Indian life in the mid-twentieth century. It is a manifesto that asks listeners to look at the past, present, and future of Native life in the United States. Shapiro and Glebbeek note the "Indian" themes and sonorities of this anthem, which appeared on The Jimi Hendrix Experience's 1967 album *Are You Experienced?* They call the introduction by percussionist Mitch Mitchum "a Native American drum pattern [that] is the cue for Jimi as the reservation Indian to lay his plight before the world." (Shapiro and Glebbeek 1990, 175) They argue that the song "reflects on the modern-day barbarities of Indian life on the reservation as Jimi might have experienced or heard tell from Grandma Nora Hendrix." (Shapiro and Glebbeek 1990, 175) While it is true that Hendrix dedicated this song to the "American Indian," Shapiro and Glebbeek's description of Jimi as the "Reservation Indian" is a bit fanciful. Although Hendrix claims to have spent time on his grandmother's reservation in Vancouver, which may have heightened his awareness of the difficult conditions for reservation Indians in the mid-twentieth century, he grew up in Seattle in a fairly multiracial environment where racial prejudice did not circumscribe his existence (Hendrix 2013, 21). Hendrix said of his secondary school, Garfield High School in Seattle: "On the whole my school was pretty relaxed. We had Chinese, Japanese, Puerto Ricans, Filipinos. . . . We won all the football games!" (Shapiro and Glebbeek 1990, 17) Shapiro and Glebbeek paint him as someone who puts on his Native American garb figuratively speaking just for this song, and while that may be one way of looking at it, I think that his lyrics tell a different story. In fact, the lyrics make no mention of race, ethnicity, or culture.

The structure of the song reflects blues patterns: there are two AAB verses, a declarative statement that functions as a chorus, and then another final AAB verse, which consists of a verbatim repetition of the first verse that begins "Will I live tomorrow?/ Well I just can't say." (Hendrix 1967) The lyrics reflect a kind of existential agony. The speaker does not know if he will live tomorrow, but he does know that in the moment, he is not living: "But I know for sure/ I don't live today." (Hendrix 1967) Orlando Patterson's notion of social death for people of African descent is also relevant to American Indians. In his review of slaveholding cultures around the world, Patterson articulates a key element of slavery: "Because the slave had no socially recognized existence outside of his master, he became a nonperson." (Patterson 1982, 5) Patterson argues that the enslaved person, "alienated from all 'rights' or claims of birth . . . ceased to belong in his own right to any legitimate social order." (Patterson 1982, 5) This notion of "natal alienation" is particularly resonant for Blacks, Indians, and Black Indians (and their ancestors) in the United States who were enslaved. But it can also describe the ways in which people of color, though nominally "free," have often been severed from their histories and deemed sub-human by the hegemonic majority.

The second verse makes more explicit this notion of living death through the following image: "No sun coming through my windows, feel like I'm sitting at the bottom of a grave." (Hendrix 1967) The description of the lack of sunlight, which is necessary for all living things to flourish, and the image of being at the lowest point of one's grave both illustrate the speaker's desperation. While this is relevant to the discussions of conditions for American Indians in the mid-twentieth century, it also becomes a kind of anthem for the disaffected and disenfranchised, whether they be people of color, young people, or members of the counterculture who questioned the status quo. The B section of that second verse is intriguing: "I wish you'd hurry up 'n' rescue me so I can be on my mis'rable way." (Hendrix 1967) The desire for "rescue" seems ironic, especially since even the rescue will not assuage the speaker's misery. Considered in the context of American Indian communities in the 1960s (and before and after), the line becomes a poignant statement about European American paternalism that was motivated by a desire to "help" American Indians but in fact ended up hurting them. It also resonates with the idea of a Red Power Movement started and led by Indians themselves. Having non-Indian allies can be useful, but no one is going to rescue us except ourselves, the speaker suggests. Hendrix's support of Indian sovereignty, as illustrated through this song, is perhaps his strongest expression of the importance of self-determination. But in typical Hendrix fashion, by using language that is not racially specific, Hendrix allows the lyrics to take on multiple meanings in multiple contexts.

Shapiro and Glebbeek tantalizingly note that in a live performance of this "I Don't Live Today," Hendrix "slipped in an ironic snatch from America's national anthem." (Shapiro and Glebbeek 1990, 369) Citing the U.S. national anthem in a performance of a song about the struggles of American Indians might be an ironic gesture, particularly if we consider the ways in which the ideals upon which the United States was founded—"life, liberty, and the pursuit of happiness"—have not been accessible to (and in many cases have been deliberately denied) people of color, including American Indians. But it may also be an earnest expression of patriotism that can be quite fervent in some Native American communities.[17]

Perhaps the most explicit expression of "Black pride" in Hendrix's corpus comes in his song "Black Gold," one of several solo recordings he made the year before his death. In 1970, Hendrix gave Mitch Mitchell a headband containing seven tapes, as Steven Roby describes: "Mitchell put the tapes in his suitcase and later brought them home to England, leaving them untouched for twenty-two years." (Roby 2002, 196) Tony Brown, a Hendrix archivist, tracked down Mitchell in 1992 and found a treasure trove of material that, except for the track "Suddenly November Morning," as of December 2020, had not been released (Maxwell 2019). The lyrics, however, are available, as the early and final drafts of *Black Gold* were auctioned in 1990 and appeared in Bill Nitopi's 1993 book *Cherokee Mist: The Lost Writings of Jimi Hendrix* (Roby 2002, 197). (Nitopi reproduces Hendrix's handwritten lyrics on National Airlines stationery on pages 91–92, 94, and 96 of his book.) The first tape was *Black Gold*, a series of nineteen interrelated songs recorded by Hendrix "sometime between mid-1969 and the beginning of 1970." (Roby 2002, 197) Alan Douglas, music producer and steward of the Jim Hendrix estate until 1995, describes *Black Gold* as a "kind of phantasmic autobiography about a super stud that goes out on the road becomes famous and goes up in the sky." (Roby 2002, 197) Hendrix himself alluded to the project in a *Rolling Stone* interview: "Mostly cartoon material . . . there's one cat who's funny, who goes through all these strange scenes. I can't talk about it now. You could put it to music, I guess." (Roby 2002, 197) Somewhat fantastic and incorporating themes of outer space that often crop up in Hendrix's writings, the suite does not (based on this description) sound like a politically motivated work. But a closer look at the lyrics of the title song, "Black Gold," suggests otherwise.

The title song of the collection begins as: "Black is gold is pure/ And true kings of this earth." (Hendrix 2021) The equivalency of the first line is fascinating, for Blackness and gold are equated and both are worthy, but they derive their worth from their "pur[ity]," which seems to contrast with Hendrix's refusal to fit into any single community, history, or group. Indeed, he was a culturally hybrid person with eclectic interests and a multiracial audience. The image of the "true king" evokes notions of African royalty that were becoming more and more prominent during the 1960s as African Americans were discovering and celebrating their African heritage and embracing an Afro-centric worldview.[18]

Despite the seemingly revolutionary and racially specific lyrics of "Black Gold," Hendrix's own writings suggest that he was referring to something larger. In a snippet from *Starting at Zero*, Hendrix writes that: "There's this song I'm writing now that's dedicated to the Black Panthers, not pertaining to race, but to the symbolism of what's happening today. They should only be a symbol to the establishment's eyes. It should only be a legendary thing." (Hendrix 2013, 189) The editors of *Starting at Zero* include some of the lyrics of "Black Gold" on the following page, which implies that this piece was dedicated to the Black Panther Party. Yet Hendrix's desire to unhook the lyrics from a discussion of race is curious and belies the direct address to European Americans: "White man, watch your mouth/ because our drums they face the south." (Hendrix 2021) The lyrics continue the warning: "You better adjust your place in this world/ before your hair it starts to curl." (Hendrix 2021) And then end with a threat: "and the yellow, red, and black of this world/ will tear your ass and soul apart." (Hendrix 2021) The explicit juxtaposition of the "white man" with the "yellow, red, and black of this world" makes a non-racial reading of the lyrics nearly impossible. The use of the image of the drums is also racially significant, as the drum is an important instrument in both African and Native American musical traditions. The warning that the white man's hair will "start to curl" may refer to a curling of hair that comes from the fierce opposition that the white man may encounter if he doesn't "adjust [his] place" and "watch his mouth"; but it may also refer to the curling of the hair as a result of miscegenation (especially of the Black-white variety) that may be one consequence of racial progress. The tension between the lyrics and Hendrix's private writings reflects his ongoing negotiation with the sentiment of nationalist movements by people of color. "Black Gold" suggests his frustration with and desire to overturn the white power structure, but he seems reluctant to align himself with the Black, Brown, Red, or Yellow Power Movements.

In addition to examining the music and lyrics of some of Hendrix's songs in order to assess his relationship to discourses of racial authenticity, it is useful to look at his performance persona. Steve Waksman asserts that the ways in which Hendrix thought about race and music are inextricably intertwined:

> Hendrix's understanding of race . . . cannot be separated from his understanding of music. Both musical and racial boundaries (which intersect in the division, say, between "real" blues and "white" blues, or between blues and rock) appeared to Hendrix to be similarly artificial constructs that served to limit the free play of the imagination as well as the ability of individuals to play freely with one another. (Waksman 1999, 88)

In contrast to the leaders of the Black Arts Movement of the mid-1960s who linked the political aims of the Black Power Movement with the effects of a new Black Aesthetic,[19] Hendrix did not see music, and, more specifically, the blues, as emerging from a particular set of historical circumstances: "Whereas for [Amiri] Baraka the blues emerged out of a specific set of social and historical relationships, out of the lived experience of African Americans, for Hendrix the blues seem almost to have a life of their own removed from any specific context." (Waksman 1999, 87) Other interviews with and personal writings of Hendrix suggest that he viewed music as a vehicle for transcending racial, social, and cultural difference.[20] In a snippet from *Starting at Zero*, Hendrix writes that: "Music is a universal language, and if it were respected properly it would have a way to reach people. There should be no barriers. I think it should be brought outside—almost like the evangelists." (Hendrix 2013, 203)

But this does not mean that Hendrix was not aware of his image as a phenotypically Black man and all of the baggage that goes along with it. Not only were his performances influenced by the tradition of his blues forefathers such as Muddy Waters and Buddy Guy (Waksman 1999, 77), but he was also aware of how Black masculinity was understood as something to be feared and admired both by the white mainstream that comprised the majority of his audience and by contemporary white blues guitar players.[21] Hendrix's (in)famous performance of "Wild Thing" in 1967 at the Monterey Pop Festival in which he "simulate[d] intercourse with his guitar and amplifier" and then "'ejaculate[d]' onto his instrument" with lighter fluid represents an extreme example of the sexual prowess that he exuded in many of his live performances (Waksman 1999, 93). But he was not merely capitulating to white conceptions of Black male sexuality; rather, as Waksman asserts, he was "playing upon those expectations using preexisting material to demonstrate his own creativity and virtuosity." (Waskman 1999, 108) Drawing on Henry Louis Gates, Jr.'s theory of "signifyin(g)" Waksman asserts that Hendrix signified on at least two levels: "With his body, he 'Signified' upon the preexisting text of black male potency and hypersexuality; and with his music, he 'Signified' upon the various traditions that contributed to his own unique style." (Waksman 1999, 107) Waksman's reading of Hendrix as a trickster who is both relying on and reformulating mainstream notions about Black music and Black male sexual potency in order to assert his own brand of genius is compelling. But missing from this discussion is any attention to Hendrix's relationship (as a man who claimed Cherokee blood) to popular notions of Indian manhood that circulated at the time. How did those stereotypes about Indian-ness in general and Indian masculinity in particular inform his performance both on and offstage?

The answer to this question lies in the intersection between the accoutrements of the counterculture and Hendrix's sartorial choices. It is always dangerous to claim knowledge of authorial intent, and I have found nothing to suggest that Hendrix was deliberately "playing Indian"[22] through his clothing and accessories. However, these visual cues may have heightened his "Indianness" in the eyes of the audience members who did know of Hendrix's connection to American Indian life. Rayna Green discusses the ways in which "Indian-style fashion" became a trend in the 1920s for modernist bohemians such as Mabel Dodge Luhan, Georgia O'Keeffe, and Martha Graham (Green 1988, 43–44). A few decades later "In the sixties, the counter-cultural hippies put on headbands, love beads and fringed jackets, carrying purses adorned with feathers." (Green 1988, 44) In addition to dressing "like Indians, many of these young white hippies . . . begin to show up on Southwestern mesas and reservation areas, begging to be 'inducted' into the natural way of life." (Green 1988, 44) For many young people, playing Indian offered the chance to "find reassuring identities in a world seemingly out of control." (Deloria 1998, 158).[23] As a leading icon of the countercultural movement, perhaps it is no surprise that Hendrix dressed the part.[24] It is not within the scope of this project to determine what motivated Hendrix's clothing choices. Deloria writes that:

> Sacred pipes, Black Power fists, Aztlan eagles, peace signs, Hell's Angels, beers and joints, Peter Max design—everything fed into a whole that signified a hopeful, naïve rebellion that often had as much to do with individual expression and fashion as it did with social change. (Deloria 1998, 164)

Hendrix's dress might have been a matter of a personal choice, an expression of a political stance, a manifestation of a cultural identity, or some combination thereof. Many of the photos in Shapiro and Glebbeek's biography feature him wearing a headband, bellbottoms, and a brightly colored, busily patterned, and/or intricately embroidered patterned shirt with a broad collar. His shoes are obscured in many of the photographs, but when they are visible, he is usually wearing black or tan boots, though in one dynamic image of him in performance in Sweden from September 9, 1967, he was wearing fringed moccasin-style boots (Shapiro and Glebbeek 1990, 216).

But perhaps the most enduring and iconic image of Hendrix is that of him performing the Star-Spangled Banner at Woodstock in August 1969 (Figure 3.1).

His afro is garnished with a red headband, and he is wearing stud earrings, two rings (one on each hand), and a turquoise necklace. He dons a leather white fringe shirt that appears to be dotted with turquoise blue beads and blue bellbottom jeans. The red, white, and blue of the outfit may represent the colors of the American flag. Despite the fact that some see Hendrix's rendition as a desecration of the national anthem, he did have respect for the United States and those who served in uniform. Similarly, the blue jeans, though not necessarily a patriotic fashion choice then or now (and certainly inflected by the counterculture with the fit and flare style) do represent an all-American sensibility. The fringed shirt is perhaps the most intriguing portion of this outfit. Not only does the fringe evoke Native ornamentation, but the decoration is also reminiscent of Indian beadwork that is the hallmark of certain tribes. Like the tom-toms in "Cherokee Mist," Hendrix's fringed shirt may function as a shorthand symbol of Indian identity for a man who was read as monoracially Black. Yet ultimately the combination of clothing and accessory choices in his Woodstock outfit suggest a kind of integrated, multiracial (or perhaps post-racial) self that Hendrix envisioned himself to be. He could be American, Native, and Black without having to choose one over the other, even though at the time many people did not see those as intersecting identities. His musical, aesthetic, and intellectual influences came from many different sources. Perhaps more than any other subject in this book, Hendrix was attempting to move beyond race by moving through it. In a snippet from *Starting at Zero*, he writes that: "Race isn't a problem, in my world. I don't look at things in terms of races. I look at things in terms of people. I'm not thinking about black people or white people. I'm thinking about the obsolete and the new." (Hendrix 2013, 188) While such a statement could reflect his privilege (he doesn't have to think about race because he is Jimi Hendrix), it might also reflect a desire for a world where one need not make either-or choices. In his writing and his life, he attempted to move beyond binary oppositions, a gesture that was

Figure 3.1 Jimi Hendrix playing "The Star-Spangled Banner" at Woodstock, NY 1969. Photograph by Henry Diltz.

an act of resistance in the increasingly racially splintered U.S. landscape in the late 1960s.

In a snippet from *Starting at Zero*, Hendrix displays his frustration with binary racial classifications of his music: "Sometimes when I come up to Harlem people look at my music and say, 'Is that white or black?' I say, 'Why are you trying to dissect it? Try to go by the feeling of it.' People are too hung up on musical categories. They won't listen to something because it sounds completely alien." (Hendrix 2013, 204) Hendrix sought to transcend racial and musical categories that he found to be stifling, not only for performers but also for listeners. Yet he was not "post-racial" in the twenty-first-century sense of the term. Hendrix understood his own identity as a mixed-race man of color living in a time when nationalist movements erected boundaries between communities. His private writings, song lyrics, and public persona reflect both an awareness of the very real existence of racial hatred and racial divisions and a refusal to succumb to discourses of racial authenticity that stifled him as a human being and as a musician.

Nearly fifty years later, questions of racial authenticity continue to be worked out in popular music. In his 1999 solo debut album *Black on Both Sides*, Mos Def (née Dante Terrell Smith and also known as Yasiin Bey) performs a song that critiques the appropriation of the blues, typically associated with African-American culture, by white artists such as Elvis Presley and the Rolling Stones. Yet his song, entitled "Rock n Roll," begins with a nod to his female ancestors and the ways in which they used music to survive oppression: "My grandmomma was raised on a reservation,/My great-grandmomma was from a plantation." (Bey 2021) He then explains why they sang: "They sang—songs for inspiration/They sang—songs for relaxation." (Bey 2021) And he ends with a gut punch of a line: "They sang—songs to take their minds up off that fucked up situation." (Bey 2021) Whether or not Mos Def's actual grandmother and great-grandmother, respectively, grew up on a reservation and a plantation, his reference to a mixed musical, familial, and cultural background resonates with the view of American history as one that is founded on the land of American Indians and the labor of African Americans. It also suggests the ways in which Black musical modes such as the blues and hip-hop may be more influenced by Indian musical elements than has previously been acknowledged. Although the title of Mos Def's album, *Black on Both Sides*, seems to gesture toward a kind of essentialist Black Pride ideology, the songs therein suggest a renegotiation of ideas of racial authenticity, in particular Black racial authenticity. Being "Black on both sides" does not undermine Mos Def's (and his audience's) inheritance of a multicultural musical legacy in the United States. In chapter 4, I move forward in time to examine how Americans of Black and Native (and often European) ancestry navigate their own multicultural and multiracial identities through verbal and visual texts. Photography allows for the inscription of Black Indian identity in ways that both reinforce and destabilize visual cues that are often associated with both authentic Blackness and authentic Indian-ness.

NOTES

1. Of course, some would argue that the rock 'n' roll *is* the blues, albeit in a slightly different form. In *The Devil's Music: A History of the Blues*, Giles Oakley

asserts that "there is a connecting line extending either side of the blues of the late '40s back to swing and forward to rock 'n' roll, which was itself strongly rooted in the blues" (Oakley 1997, 209).

2. Peniel E. Joseph recalls the first utterance of the phrase "black power" in 1966, when Martin Luther King, Jr. and Stokely Carmichael continued James Meredith's "March Against Fear" after he was "ambushed on the second day of his trek" (Joseph 2006, 1). In contrast to the Southern Christian Leadership Conference's "more mainstream" motto of "Freedom Now," "Black Power" represented a new message. Carmichael stated: "The only way we gonna stop them white men from whuppin' us is to take over. What we gonna start saying now is black power!" (Joseph 2006, 2). According to Joseph, "The national media seized on Carmichael's words as the signpost of a new militancy," and King "distanced himself from the slogan" (Joseph 2006, 2).

3. In 1983, the Narragansett Indian Tribe of Rhode Island received federal recognition ("History" n.d.), as did the Mashantucket (Western) Pequot Tribal Nation ("Tribal History" n.d.). The Mashpee Wampanoag Tribe of Massachusetts was federally recognized in 2007 (Ryan 2007). In her discussion of three mixed groups (Melungeons, Lumbee, and Narragansett), Ariela Gross argues that "when racially ambiguous groups came before courts or legislature, the state demanded that they exercise their claims to citizenship through the rejection of blackness" (Gross 2008, 139). In the case of the Narragansett tribe, their "national identity . . was reinstated only after the Bureau of Indian Affairs approvingly noted the extent of their rejection of blacks in the mid-twentieth century" (Gross 2008, 139).

4. See Sharon Lawrence, *Jimi Hendrix: The Intimate Story of a Betrayed Musical Legend* (2005), Charles R. Cross, *Room Full of Mirrors: A Biography of Jimi Hendrix* (2005), Harry Shapiro and Caesar Glebbeek, *Jimi Hendrix: Electric Gyspy* (1990), Steven Roby and Brad Schreiber, *Becoming Hendrix: From Southern Crossroads to Psychedelic London: The Untold Story of a Musical Genius* (2010), Charles Shaar Murray, *Crosstown Traffic: Jimi Hendrix and Post-War Pop* (1989).

5. For instance, before his reflection on the run-in with the law that led him to enlist, the editors write in brackets: "In May 1961, Jimmy was arrested for riding in a stolen car. He was given a two-year suspended sentence after the public defender told the judge that Jimmy was going to enlist in the Armed Forces" (Hendrix 2013, 25).

6. In the section of the website entitled "Q&A Quote Sources," the authors reprint the four interview portions of the book and list the sources (but not the authors or dates) of the interviews' questions and answers. Based on the book alone, a reader might reasonably assume (as I did) that each interview comes from a single source. However, the website indicates that the questions and answers from each interview section come from dozens of sources. For instance, the "interview" printed on pages 62–65 contains information from 17 different sources.

7. Music critic Steve Sutherland views Hendrix's performance as a musical "blast[ing] of the American Dream to tatters" (Sutherland 1989, 34). Hendrix biographers Shapiro and Glebbeek read the performance on that rainy Monday in August as a revolutionary critique of the Vietnam War, though they point out that Hendrix's attitude towards American involvement in the conflict was surprisingly ambivalent.

In an interview, he said: "The Americans in Vietnam are fighting for a completely free world. . . . Of course war is horrible but at present it's still the only guarantee of peace" (Shapiro and Glebbeek 1990, 387). Charles Shaar Murray's assessment of the performance in his Hendrix biography reflects this more nuanced understanding of Hendrix's politics: "'The Star-Spangled Banner' is probably the most complex, and powerful work of American art of to deal with the Vietnam War and its corrupting, distorting effect on successive generations of the American psyche. . . . It is an interpretation of history which permits no space for either the gung-ho revisionism of Sylvester Stallone and Chuck Norris or the solipsistic angst of Coppola and Oliver Stone; it depicts, as graphically as a piece of music can possibly do, both what the Americans did to the Vietnamese and what they did to themselves" (Murray 1989, 24). And Mark Daley views the performance in broader historical terms, asserting that the Woodstock Festival "increasingly came to symbolize the last hurrah of the love and peace era" (Daley 2006, 57).

    8. See Shapiro and Glebbeek (1990, 226–228).

    9. In an interview with Steven Roby, Leon Hendrix, Jimi's half-brother, claimed that the song was "about my family. The Indian war chief is about me. The first verse is about Mom and Dad fighting and the third verse is about my mom and her dying" (Roby 2002, 77).

    10. Hendrix suggests that being a freedom fighter and being a musician are mutually exclusive, when, in fact, there is a rich tradition of artists who used their visibility to effect social change, especially during the Civil Rights Era, including Nina Simone, Lena Horne, Harry Belafonte, and Sidney Poitier. Missing from Hendrix's reflection is the possibility that being an artist can be a form of liberation, not only for oneself but also for others. While Hendrix was not an "activist" in the strict sense of the word, he did empower others through his performances and served as a voice of the counterculture generation. His 1969 performance of "The Star-Spangled Banner" at Woodstock exemplifies the ways in which he functioned in this role.

    11. Jonathan Earle writes: "Perhaps the most common way slaves protested the continuous forced labor of plantation life was sabotage: slave hands broke tools, stole food, abused farm animals, and burned down buildings. Other day-to-day acts of resistance include slowing the pace of work, feigning illness, or self-mutilation. Slaves also used their culture to protest their situation. Songs, folk tales, and religion all helped slaves find release from hardship and suffering" (Earle 200, 50). In addition to these strategies, some enslaved people ran away and mounted rebellions against their white masters, though most "understood that armed revolt was virtually suicidal" (Earle 2000, 50).

    12. This may be due in part to the fact that "Jeffery met with Warner Brothers executives and secured the loan that would allow Electric Lady Studio to be completed" (Moskowitz 2010, 72).

    13. In his reflection on the fortieth anniversary of the 1967 conflagration in his hometown of Detroit, Kevin Boyle writes: "Detroit was neither the first nor the last great urban upheaval of the 1960s. Los Angeles's Watts neighborhood had burned in 1965, West Side Chicago in 1966, the inner cities of Tampa, Cincinnati and Newark earlier in 1967. After the Rev. Martin Luther King, Jr. was assassinated in Memphis

in the spring of 1968, rioting broke out in more than 100 other cities, including Washington and Baltimore. But Detroit was the worst, a week-long conflagration so fierce it killed forty-three people, injured hundreds and destroyed huge swaths of the city's most impoverished neighborhoods. Standing alongside 12th Street's smoldering ruins on the riot's final day, Detroit's mayor thought the area looked 'like Berlin in 1945'" (Boyle 2007).

14. Hendrix writes in *Starting at Zero*: "They asked us to give benefit concerts for the Black Panthers, which I was really very happy for them to do. I was honored and all this, but we have not done it yet. . . . I just want to do what I'm doing without getting involved in racial or political matters. I know I'm lucky that I can do that, because lots of people can't" (Hendrix 2013, 187). Hendrix never did perform a benefit for the Black Panther Party, but he was pressured into giving money to the group (Shapiro and Glebbeek 1990, 369).

15. In fact, the Jimi Hendrix most people know today was "born" in London in 1966. Chas Chandler, bassist for The Animals and music producer, brought Hendrix to London in September of 1996 and formed the Jimi Hendrix Experience (Shapiro and Glebbeek 1990, 105, 118). Consisting of Hendrix and two Englishmen, Noel Redding and Mitch Mitchum, the band played throughout Britain and Europe in the first half of 1967 and made its U.S. debut at the Monterey Pop Festival in June of that year (Shapiro and Glebbeek 1990, 182–183).

16. Or British racism, for that matter. David Henderson, one of Hendrix's biographers, describes how the press in England depicted him (especially early in his career) in distinctly racialized and racist terms: "One London paper called him a 'Mau-Mau' in banner headlines, while another called him a 'Wild Man from Borneo.' They played to the racism the press was prone to exploit, knowing their readers would not ignore any aspect of the 'race problem'" (Henderson 1983, 128).

17. In his book *Serving their Country: American Indian Politics and Patriotism in the Twentieth Century,* Paul C. Rosier discusses the ways that American Indians have navigated the rhetoric of American patriotism in the twentieth century, especially in the context of the Cold War. He asserts that Native Americans have "imagined an American nationalism that drew upon rather than destroyed their values, and developed an ideology of hybrid patriotism - both Indian and American - to define the heart of 'America'" (Rosier 2009, 9).

18. The term "Afrocentric" was first introduced by W.E.B. DuBois, the great African-American intellectual and activist who spent the last years of his life in Ghana, and was "used by black activists during the late-1960s battles over the character of black and African studies who called for an Afrocentric approach to these subjects" (Bay 2000, 502–503). But according to Mia Bay, it was Molefi Kete Asante's 1980 text *Afrocentricity: The Theory of Social Change* that codified the term as an "Africa-centered consciousness rooted in African ideals and values" (Bay 2000, 503).

19. Playwright and critic Larry Neal (1937-1981) was a leading member of the Black Arts Movement who wrote a foundational essay entitled "The Black Arts Movement" that was published in *The Drama Review* in 1968. Here he articulates the motivation behind the movement: "it is this natural reaction to an alien [Euro-American] sensibility that informs the cultural attitudes of the Black Arts and the

Black Power Movement. It is a profound ethical sense that makes a Black artist question a society in which art is one thing and the actions of men another. The Black Arts Movement believes that your ethics and your aesthetics are one. That the contradictions between ethics and aesthetic in Western society is symptomatic of a dying culture" (Neal 1968, 30–31).

20. Steve Waksman goes even further by asserting that Hendrix viewed the electric guitar and the sounds he could elicit from it as vehicles for "exert[ing] a transformative effect upon the contemporary social landscape" and "allow[ing] Hendrix to escape the restrictions normally imposed upon African-American performers within the music industry" (Waksman 1999, 88).

21. Waksman reads the comments of blues guitarists Eric Clapton, Michael Bloomfield, and John Hammond through a Fanonian lens by which "fetishiziation of black male potency and hypersexuality show the extent to which black man has become the 'mainstay' of the white man's preoccupations and desires.' White males wish to possess such qualities themselves even though they have been taught to associate such bodily excess with 'other'-ness. The desire for the black man must be opaque, beyond easy recognition, so it is turned into fear or otherwise displaced, but the desire persists" (Waksman 1999, 96).

22. Philip J. Deloria's 1998 book *Playing Indian* traces the ways in which white Americans have "engaged racialized and gendered Indians in curious and contradictory ways" in order to "defin[e] themselves as a nation" (Deloria 1998, 5). Deloria charts this American phenomenon of playing Indian from Revolutionary times to the late twentieth century, demonstrating how notions of Indian-ness have been deployed in different ways in different eras.

23. Deloria points out, however, that mid-twentieth-century counterculturalists and communalists valued "a detached, symbolic Indianness" over "real Native people" (Deloria 1998, 163, 159). Such appropriation often rendered invisible the lived experience of Indians: "They [white radicals] devalued words like *Indian* and *nigger* and deemphasized the social realities that came with those words" (Deloria 1998, 164).

24. However, as Deloria argues in *Playing Indian*, the images associated with the countercultural revolt did not have fixed meanings: "Sixties rebellion rested, in large part, on a politics of symbol, pastiche, and performance. . . . That headband might mean Geronimo, but it also meant Che Guevara and Stokeley Carmichael. Indeed, it meant many things, depending on its context and its interpreters" (Deloria 1998, 164).

Chapter 4

Shooting Lives

Black Indians as Photographers and Subjects

In this chapter, I move forward three decades and shift autobiographical modes to examine the photography of Valena Broussard Dismukes, a woman of European, Choctaw, and African heritage who produced a series of photographs about Black Indians entitled "The Red-Black Connection." First shown in 2003, the entire exhibit is reproduced in a book published in 2007 by Grace Enterprises. Although Dismukes sometimes includes verbal narratives written by the subjects themselves, the power of this project derives from her photographic portraits of people of all ages from around the country who straddle Black and Native identities and communities. Both Dismukes and her subjects participate in the creation of visual autobiographical texts that reflect this particular multiracial identity. Photography offers a powerful medium for negotiating discourses of racial and ethnic authenticity. While these photographs represent a small fraction of the lived Black Indian American experience, like the WPA former slave narratives I discuss in chapter 2, collectively and individually they reflect some of the questions about identity, authenticity, and belonging that people of Black and Native heritage face.

The connections between photography and autobiography are more striking than they might appear at first glance, as the work of Timothy Dow and Linda Haverty Rugg demonstrates. Dow's 2000 book-length study *Life Writing and Light Writing* is divided into three sections: "Autobiographies with Few or no Photographs," "Autobiographies that Contain Words and Photographs," and "Autobiographies by Photographers." (Dow 2000) Looking at a range of authors including Maxine Hong Kingston, Michael Ondaatje, and Eudora Welty, Dow presents "a series of case studies exploring the various ways in which text and image can interact and reflect on each other." (Dow 2000, xxi) Rugg, in her 1997 book *Picturing Ourselves*, also takes a case study approach, though she limits her examination to four authors: Mark Twain, August Strindberg, Walter Benjamin, and Christa Wolf. Despite the different scope of these two projects, both Dow and Rugg make similar claims about the problematic relationship to reality that characterizes autobiography and photography. Dow puts it as, "photography and autobiography operate in parallel fashion, both deliberately blurring the boundaries between fact and fiction, between representation and creation." (Dow 2000, 20) Rugg, too, discusses the problem of referentiality in both modes:

> Autobiography, like photography, refers to something beyond itself; namely, the autobiographical or photographed subjects. But both autobiography and photography participate in a system of signs that we have learned how to read—at one level—as highly indeterminate and unreliable. Below that level of doubt rests, in some persons, the desire to accept the image or the text as a readable reference to a (once-) living person. (Rugg 1997, 13)

As readers and viewers, we often want to view the image or text as a fixed and reliable representation of a person. This is supported by our common use photographs as "documentary evidence" that have a privileged legal status in the form of "driver's licenses, bank cards with photographic identification, medical records, crime photographs, and passports." (Dow 2000, 6) But neither photography nor autobiography is transparent. Rugg asserts that theorists like John Berger argue for an "understanding of photographs as both constructed and constructing entities." (Rugg 1997, 15) The same could be said for autobiographical texts.

But what about the use of photography as autobiography? Certainly self-portraiture is an important genre in photography, and Dow highlights some of the more innovative approaches to self-portraiture, including the work of photographers such as Charles Martin and Friedl Bondy (Dow 2000, 234, 236). Citing literary theorists like Charles A. LeGuin, Dow posits (and subsequently complicates) a "connection between word and image through the following analogy: biography is to portrait as autobiography is to self-portraiture." (Dow 2000, 226) In this framework, we might see Dismukes's work as biographical rather than autobiographical, since she is the creator of the photographs and the individuals she captures are her subjects. But I would argue that her work is an example of photographic collaborative autobiography. Indeed, Dismukes is the artist, making decisions about the equipment she uses and how she frames her subjects. Not only does she choose what appears within (and outside) the actual photographic frame, but she also situates her subjects as members of a group of people whose presence in the United States is rich, diverse, and lengthy. Both of these choices inform how we as viewers interpret these images. But her subjects are not passive; in fact, they also make decisions about where they will be photographed, with what objects, and in what clothing. Rugg articulates that: "An individual can forge a photographic self-image through canny manipulation of photographers and the economic and cultural institutions surrounding the production and publication of the photography, thus maintaining a kind of 'authorship' of self-image." (Rugg 1997, 3) Thus these autobiographical acts that I read in *The Red-Black Connection* emerge as evidence of the collaborative process of inscribing the self that has a long history both in African-American and American Indian communities. I argue that both Dismukes and her subjects manipulate a medium that has been historically oppressive in order to represent their experiences on their own terms. In doing so, they demonstrate how photography can become a fruitful medium for navigating narratives of authenticity and belonging. Before closely reading a handful of Dismukes's photographs and accompanying narratives, I discuss the historical context of the mixed-race movement of the late twentieth century and the ongoing importance of photography as a vital mode of self-representation for Native Americans and African Americans alike.

As a result of the Civil Rights Movement and the nationalist movements of the late 1960s and early 1970s, many changes occurred that changed the lived experience of people of color in positive ways. Three frequently cited milestones in the struggle for racial equality are the 1954 *Brown v. Board of Education* decision that rendered school segregation unconstitutional, the passage of the Civil Rights Act of 1964, and the passage of the Voting Rights Act of 1965 (Hall 2005, 1234). The introduction of Affirmative Action opened up professional and educational opportunities for women and historically underrepresented groups. In the 1970s and 1980s, multiculturalism left its imprint on many school curricula. Yet there was also a conservative backlash "by a New Right bent on reversing its[the Civil Rights Movement's] gains," a backlash that continues to this day (Hall 2005, 1234).

Structural inequality did not disappear as a result of these three important legal milestones in the 1950s and 1960s, and the fight against racial oppression continues into the twenty-first century. As many recent events demonstrate, "living while Black" is still a crime in some communities. And the continued controversy over the use of American Indian mascots in college and professional sports points to the dehumanization of Natives that has become so embedded in our culture that "many non-Indians are blind to the inherent racism and stereotyping that is concealed by an ideology of 'honor.'" (Baker 1998, 154) In his documentary on the controversy around University of Illinois' mascot Chief Illiniwek, Jay Rosenstein points out a startling double standard: "While blackface and black caricatures have virtually disappeared from the mainstream, Indian caricatures remain." (quoted in Baker 1998, 155) The persistence of these demeaning Native representations can be explained, in part, by the persistent myth of the "Vanishing Indian" that always places Indigenous peoples in some distant, pre-modern past.

One of the hallmarks of the post-Civil Rights era is the neoliberal focus on personal responsibility. We moved from being a country that valued the well-being of the collective to one that focused on individual accountability.[1] As Susan Searls Giroux writes, while the 1960s was marked by and "quickly reduced to a clichéd set of images—of tear gas, water hoses, dogs, No Knock, napalm and carpet bombs," the first decades of the twenty-first century have their own corollary evils: "rampant racial profiling, mass incarceration, the PATRIOT act, Gitmo, and Abu Ghraib, depleted uranium, and precision bombs." (Giroux 2008, 430) The movement from a commitment to the well-being of all members of society to an emphasis on personal responsibility has led to repressive social policies and the demonization of the "other" that seems antithetical to the hopes and dreams of civil rights leaders such as Martin Luther King, Jr. Jacquelyn Dowd Hall provides her own list of the troubles that beset us several decades after the Civil Rights Movement:

> The resegregation of public schools; the hypersegregation of inner cities; the soaring unemployment rates among black and latino youths; the erosion of minority voting rights; the weakening of the labor movement; the wealth and income gap that is returning the United States to pre-New Deal conditions; the unraveling of the social safety net; the ever-increasing ability of placeless capital to move at will; the malignant growth of the prison-industrial complex, which far outstrips Apartheid-era South Africa in incarcerating black men— those historical legacies cannot be waved away by declaring victory, mandating formal, race neutral public policies, and allowing market forces to rule. (Hall 2005, 1261)[2]

Indeed, the struggle continues, and while many people work to assuage these ills by working in political, legal, and educational arenas, artistic production remains an important vehicle for effecting social change.

Finding the means to represent oneself instead of being (mis)represented or rendered invisible by the majority has always been an important part of the struggle of marginalized and oppressed peoples. One group that has, in the last couple of decades, taken charge of its representation, is mixed-race people. In the 1980s and 1990s, the multiracial movement emerged in order to "allow mixed-race persons to adopt a biracial or multiracial identity." (Davis 2002, 27) One of the movement's major concerns was the question about racial identity on the U.S. Census. Until 2000, Americans had to "check only one" racial box, effectively forcing multiracial people to deny one or more aspects of their heritage (Davis 2002, 27). Thanks to the efforts of the movement, the U.S. Office of Management and Budget, "which defines racial categories for all levels of government in the country," replaced "check only one" with "check one or more" on the racial identification section of the Census form (Davis 2002, 28). While the mixed-race movement is not without its problems,[3] it has given people of mixed heritage a political base and has led to the flowering of mixed-race art, music, and literature that reflects what Michele Elam calls an "aesthetics of mixed race." (Elam 2011, xv) Beyond simply representing themselves, mixed-race artists are challenging the "box fetish" and instead "explor[ing] mixed racial identity not as a special interest but as a performative mode of social engagement." (Elam 2011, xix) While Dismukes's project (and public interest in it) may be aided by the growing visibility of mixed-race people in a variety of media, I do not see Dismukes engaging in the kind of pointed critique of the rhetoric of the multiracial movement in the way that Aaron McGruder, Nate Creekmore, Danzy Senna, Carl Hancock, Dave Chapelle, and the other artists that Michele Elam discusses in her book *The Souls of Mixed Folk: Race, Politics, and Aesthetics in the New Millennium* do. Instead I situate Dismukes's work within a longer tradition of photography being used both as a tool of conquest by the dominant group and as a weapon of liberation for and within Black and Native communities.

Anthropologists and art historians have explored the ways in which photography has historically been used as a tool of oppression against people of color. Susan Sontag argues that photography was an integral part of westward expansion in the nineteenth century: "Faced with the awesome spread and loneliness of a newly settled continent, people wielded cameras as a way of taking possession of the places they visited." (Sontag 1979, 65) Taking pictures of the "vanishing" Native American provided a way for white frontiersmen to document their conquest of Native land and to relegate Indigenous peoples to a static past. Mick Gidley writes that:

> Photography was part and parcel of a colonizing movement which not only took possession of land from Native Americans but also appropriated—or attempted to appropriate—their cultures. Indians themselves do not generally "wield cameras"; and so were almost powerless to keep control of the images made of them as they were of the land they had inherited. (Gidley 2000, 262)

The photography of Edward Curtis, whom I discuss later in the chapter, powerfully exemplifies the ways in which the camera is used as a tool of colonization.

In the twentieth century, many Native Americans have taken cameras into their own hands in order to represent themselves. Prominent Native photographers include Jennie Ross Cobb (Cherokee), Horace Poolaw (Kiowa), Lee Marmon (Laguna Pueblo), and Victor Masayesva (Hopi). Masayesva's decision to embrace photography is particularly intriguing, given the fact that he sees the camera and the missionary as equally dangerous tools in the attempt to decimate Native Americans and their culture (Lippard 1992, 21). He and other Indian artists have reconciled with this painful past by affirming that photography of Natives by Natives can also be a "ceremony, a ritual" that allows people to sustain and preserve their culture." (Lippard 1992, 21) Leslie Marmon Silko, a Laguna Pueblo author whose work demonstrates a deep engagement with the visual, affirms that wielding a camera is a revolutionary act. In her essay, "The Indian with a Camera," Silko recalls how Hopi and Pueblo tribes banned Whites from photographing their religious and cultural ceremonies in an act of "cultural pride and legal protection." (Silko 1996, 176) But writing at the end of the twentieth century, Silko sees how the camera, in the hands of the people who had previously been shot by it (pun intended) can be a tool of self-declaration. Silko asserts that European Americans are frightened by Indians with cameras because that image unsettles the Eurocentric desire to see Natives as dead, as relics of a tragic past (Silko 1996, 177). Seeing Indians as agents of their own representation undermines the European-American fantasy. Moreover, the Native American photographer is an "omen" of the not-so-distant day when Indigenous people will take back the land that was taken from them (Silko 1996, 178). Indeed, the revolutionary and political power of photography is palpable for many Native Americans.

Like Native Americans, Black Americans have reclaimed their images by becoming photographers themselves. In his introductory essay in *Committed to the Image: Contemporary Black Photographers*, Clyde Taylor traces the rise of Black photography during the Civil Rights Movement and the continued development of an African-American photographic tradition (Taylor 2001, 16). Taylor highlights the political implications of Blacks as photographers by pointing out that African Americans' right to look was denied during the Jim Crow Era. The fact that many young Black men were taught from an early age never to look at a white woman if they wanted to avoid being lynched illuminates the life-and-death implications of looking for African Americans. Taylor affirms that collecting the work of contemporary Black photographers "testifies to the liberation of the Black gaze." (Taylor 2001, 15) Instead of being passive objects of a racist photographic gaze that perpetuated stereotypes about Black folk, African Americans challenged those misrepresentations and "provid[ed] an image of black life and community as multi-dimensional and self-sufficient." (Patnaik 2001, 31) Deba P. Patnaik, author of another prefatory essay in Taylor's edited collection, emphatically states that Blacks as artists "composed and projected themselves into being through their imagemaking and imagery." (Patnaik 2001, 34) Indeed, the camera has been used as a tool of liberation and empowerment for Black people, just as it has for many Native Americans. Notable Black photographers include James Van Der Zee, Gordon Parks, and Carrie Mae Weems. Yet the inevitable question arises: Because we see the "same gestures, devices, and references that Arthistory[4] considered its own" in the works of Black photographers, does this mean that African-American photographers are "capitulating" to Eurocentric values? (Taylor 2001, 21) Naturally, there will be some elements of the dominant culture in the artistic production of a group that has been oppressed for a long time. There is no escaping the paradigm in which we are born and raised. But as Patnaik points out, most African-American photographers are not simply mimicking the "white man's" work; rather, they are manipulating Eurocentric forms in order to reflect their cultural reality. In fact, many Black photographers engage in what is known as signifying (Patnaik 2001, 35). As I discussed in chapter 3 in relation to the artistry of Jimi Hendrix, this aesthetic practice that involves subversion of the status quo is the foundation for Black literature, art, and music. While signifying is an ancient technique, only recently have scholars such as Henry Louis Gates, Jr. theorized about signifying in relation to Black culture and to other theories of signification. Gates writes in his 1983 essay "The 'Blackness of Blackness': A Critique of the Sign and the Signifying Monkey": "Signification is a theory of reading that arises from Afro-American culture; learning how 'to signify' is often part of our adolescent education. I had to step outside my culture, had to defamiliarize the concept by translating it into a new mode of discourse, before I could see its potential as critical theory." (Gates 1983, 686) Indeed, uncovering the modes of signifying in Black cultural texts helps us to understand how people of African descent have manipulated the form and language of the dominant culture's discourses in order to critique those very discourses and the paradigms they inhere.

Valena Broussard Dismukes is a contemporary photographer who is producing visual texts in the spirit of both Native and African-American cultural traditions. But one must seriously consider the questions that Gidley raises: Can Indian photography "evade the pervasive and deeply-etched stereotypes that the history of photography bears witness to?" "Is it possible for anyone to create 'authentic' Indian photographs?" and "Should photographs made by Indians themselves have any kind of privileged status?" (Gidley 2000, 264) Of particular interest to me is Gidley's second question about the possibility of "authentic" Indian photography. While none of the subjects featured in Dismukes's photo essay utters the word "authentic," many do discuss their own struggles with being accepted by others as Black Indians, whether by African-Americans or American Indians or both. And the photos themselves indicate the ways in which the subjects either consciously or unconsciously engage with discourses of authenticity, particularly around the Indian aspects of their identities. The visual element of these narratives offers additional insight into these negotiations with ethnic and/or racial belonging.

Like many people of Black and Native descent, Valena Broussard Dismukes also has European blood, and she claims "African, Choctaw, French and Scotch-Irish ancestry." ("At Southwest Museum" 2001) Her interest in photography was sparked by a desire to "document her son's growth" in the early 1970s, and since then she has "explored the human condition via her camera's lens." ("At Southwest Museum" 2001) Compiled over a two-year period, the photographs in *The Red-Black Connection* feature "portraits of African Native Americans in settings ranging from their homes to pow-wows." ("At Southwest Museum" 2001) Dismukes notes that she was motivated by the corpus of Edward Curtis, a European-American photographer and ethnologist who documented American Indians at the turn of the twentieth century. This is intriguing, especially since some contemporary Native American scholars and artists have critiqued Curtis's work as "patronizing, even racist." (Durkin 1997, 21) Hopi photographer Victor Masayesva has called the works of Curtis and other white photographers who documented Native American life in the early twentieth century "colonization by camera." (Durkin 1997, 22) And what is troubling to Vine Deloria, Jr., is how Curtis created a palatable, "romanticized, sanitized Native World that simply did not exist." (Durkin 1997, 22) Deloria suggests that Curtis wanted to package his Indians for Anglo consumption, and therefore he staged his subjects in stereotypical and/ or unrealistic poses without regard to tribal specificity.

One artist who is responding directly to Curtis's legacy is Matika Wilbur, a member of the Tulalip and Swinomish tribes in Washington State. While traveling through South America taking pictures of Indigenous peoples there, Wilbur had a dream in which her late grandmother told her "to go home to photograph [her] own people." (Fiege 2012) Wilbur borrowed money to purchase a camera and began shooting. Her work was first displayed publicly in 2006, and her photographs have appeared in museums and galleries around the world, from the Kittredge Gallery at the University of Puget Sound to the Museum of Fine Arts of Nantes in France (Fiege 2012). In 2012, Wilbur embarked on her most ambitious project yet: photographing members of all 562 federally recognized tribes. Entitled Project 562, Wilbur envisions her work as a response to the stereotypical Indians presented in Curtis's photography: "[He] showed some Indians as the public wanted to see them at the time, stereotypes out of the 18th century. But it isn't even that Curtis sometimes took artistic license. . . . It's just that it's time for non-Indians to stop romanticizing the American Indian. It's not 'Dances with Wolves' or 'Twilight.' We need a shift in consciousness." (Fiege 2012) Capturing thriving contemporary American Indians on their land in stunning black and white photographs, Wilbur says that: "My objective is to unveil the true essence of contemporary Native issues, the beauty of Native culture, the magnitude of tradition, and expose our vitality." (Walker 2013)

There are some Natives, however, who praise Curtis's work and view his corpus as an important link to the past. In her introduction to *The Heart of the Circle*, Pat Durkin includes the perspectives of six Native women and their reactions to Curtis's photographs of Native women in particular. For instance, Lark Real Bird Paz, a Crow woman who grew up on a reservation in Montana and currently lives in Phoenix, Arizona, sees Curtis's photos as embodiments of her ancestors and relics of a past that she is trying to hold onto: "I'm glad Edward Curtis took these photographs. . . . They make me think of home. I can look at them for hours and be there." (Durkin 1997, 16) At a historical moment when many Natives live in urban areas and have largely assimilated to Anglo culture, these images may allow people to reconnect with their roots. Papago-Pima-Cherokee Janelle Sixkiller recalls that: "I look at these women who could be my grandmother, my aunts—actually, they are my relatives. . . . I wonder at what allowed them to survive, to keep it together. . . . I look into their eyes and say, 'Oh, yes. I'm here because of you.'" (Durkin 1997, 21–22) Both Paz and Sixkiller imply that no matter who took these photographs, their very existence provides reminders of traditional values and symbols of perseverance.

Curtis himself was an energetic, passionate, and idealistic white man who wanted to document the lives of people who were supposedly members of a "vanishing race." (Durkin 5) He saw himself as a scientist or ethnographer first, and his own assessment of his 1907 photography collection *The North American Indian* demonstrates his belief that he was capturing the truth: "[*The North American Indian*] is a comprehensive and permanent record of the important tribes of the United States and Alaska that still retain to a considerable degree their primitive customs and traditions." (Curtis quoted in Durkin 1997, 16) Curtis viewed himself as a recorder of history, yet he was also an artist. As theorists such as Roland Barthes and Susan Sontag in the late twentieth century articulated, there is no such thing as a neutral relationship between photographer and subject. In fact, Sontag argues that the relationship between the photographer and the photographed can be seen as "predatory." (quoted in Wells and Price 1997, 40) And Barthes identifies another figure in the dance between photographer and subject: viewer. Barthes is especially interested in the person who looks at the photograph (Wells and Price 1997, 44). The meaning of a photograph is not inherent; rather, it is contingent on the spectator (Wells and Price 1997, 45). These basic tenets of photography theory inform Christopher Lyman's balanced critique of Curtis's work. Lyman documents how Curtis manipulated putatively "authentic" images of Native Americans by doctoring his photographs to remove evidence of contact with Whites (Lyman 1982, 63, 76). Like many European Americans in the early twentieth century, Curtis believed that "real" Indians were static, primitive, and untouched by the modern world, and this belief dictated his artistic choices (Lyman 1982, 63). Thus in looking at Curtis's work in particular and documentary art and film in general, it is important to question the traditional dichotomy between "documentary" and "artistic" in photography (Lyman 1982, 148). Lyman asserts that: "All art *documents* the subjective perceptions of the artist, and all documents present the *subjective* perceptions of their creators – at least in the selection of what has been documented." (Lyman 1982, 148)

Like some Americans who rediscovered *The North American Indian* in the 1970s, Valena Dismukes was inspired by the photography of Edward Curtis. Dismukes's collection of over seventy photographs of Black Indians has been displayed at "thirteen museums, galleries, and libraries across the country," including the Eiteljorg Museum of American Indian and Western Art in Indianapolis, Indiana between July 17 and October 24, 2004 (Dismukes 2007, 96). I first viewed the exhibit on a trip in September 2004 to Indianapolis, where I met with Tricia O'Connor, the project's exhibit developer for this project, and James Nottage, Vice President and Chief Curatorial Officer at the Eiteljorg. Nottage noted that the Eiteljorg was in the process of compiling a larger exhibit entitled "Allies and Adversaries" that dealt with the history of African Americans and Native Americans. He also mentioned that other museums had attempted similar exhibits but then backed off because of the sensitive nature of the subject. Indeed, the construction of a narrative of Black-Indian relations in the Americas remained a controversial endeavor at the dawn of the twenty-first century. However, the Eiteljorg seems to have succeeded in exposing the general public to this rich history, and the Black Indians exhibit demonstrated an understanding of the complex and long history of these two groups.

The exhibit at the Eiteljorg contained seventy photographs and their accompanying texts, some historical information about Black-Native contact, and a few artifacts that provided context for Dismukes's work. These artifacts included a dress helmet worn by the all-Black Ninth Cavalry (also known as buffalo soldiers) between 1881 and 1902, an elaborate chief's turban worn by Black Seminoles, a picture of First Sergeant Charles Daniels, a Seminole Scout, with his family, and an oil painting of Chief Billy Bowlegs, the famous Black Seminole Chief. The exhibit also had an interactive aspect. Specifically, there was a handout in the gallery that explained how to trace one's genealogy, and Native American ancestry in particular.

While James Nottage described the photographs themselves as somewhat "journalistic" in nature, there is a remarkable amount of diversity among the black and white photos. Some are headshots, while others are full-body shots. Some appear to be candid shots taken at pow-wows, while others are obviously posed portraits. In addition, Dismukes's subjects range in age from toddlers to octogenarians. The sheer number of photos is quite powerful, and the exhibit as a whole implies that Black Indians are alive, well, and much more common than most people think. Moreover, these portraits illustrate the variety of ways in which Native identity, Black identity, and Native-Black identity are represented visually.

According to Nottage and O'Connor, the overall response to the exhibit was positive, based on feedback from visitors. Visitors were given a two-sided sheet. On one side was a survey that contained Yes/No questions about the exhibit, and on the other was a concept map. In the center of the page was the phrase "Black Indians" in a circle, and in the top left-hand corner was a list of "Ideas to get Started": "Mixed heritage, Identity, African Americans, Native Americans, Politics, Culture, Economics, Stories, Tribal Membership and History." Although I only looked at twenty responses, these sheets reflect the various ways in which Black Indians are perceived in twenty-first-century American culture. One woman had a very personal response to the concept map and the exhibit. A note from the program coordinator of the exhibit indicates that this "participant offered that her paternal grandmother was 1/2 Cherokee and 1/2 black, and because neither culture had good access to doctors, her grandmother became a healing figure in the community. She is interested in those medicines and how some of those medicines found their way into mainstream culture." In this case, this exhibit may have validated this viewer's identity and perhaps encouraged her to share information about her family background and heritage that she might not have divulged otherwise. Another respondent wrote beside the phrase "Black Indian," "fry bread and greens for dinner!" and "me-Cherokee, Choctaw, African-American." One viewer expressed the idea that many scholars of Black-Native history have discussed: this long history of interaction between African and Indigenous peoples in the Americas has been obscured, and some people cannot imagine such an identity. One viewer wrote: "Where are they? Who are they? No Black Indians that I am aware of. Never seen any." Still others recognized that Black Indians do exist but that their story has been suppressed in the "mainstream."

In a 2004 phone interview with *Indy Star* reporter S. L. Berry, Dismukes noted the popularity of the exhibit among various groups when it was first shown: "When this exhibition was first shown in a gallery in the heart of the African-American community in Los Angeles, people lined up to see it. . . . It was also popular among Indians when it was displayed in a Native American community center." (Berry 2004) It seems clear that this is a chapter of American history that people are interested in learning more about, and Dismukes's photographs make that history accessible. It is significant that both Black and Native communities alike appreciated this exhibit. Perhaps

for some Black people, Dismukes's photographs validated the Native blood-
lines in their family trees that had previously been repressed or unrecognized.
And maybe American Indians responded positively to this exhibit because
it provided a more complex and nuanced composite image of contemporary
Native Americans who, in the collective American psyche, are often imagined as either extinct, dressed in feathers and moccasins, or drunken and
impoverished on the reservation.

Based on the popularity of the exhibit, Valena Broussard Dismukes published
the photographs and accompanying narratives in 2007 with the hope of promoting solidarity between the two groups. Dismukes writes in her Introduction to
The Red-Black Connection that: "The Red-Black people depicted here and others like them represent the best chance for African-Americans and American
Indians to be united in celebration." (Dismukes 2007, x) As a scholar I am
grateful to have had the chance to hold in my hands the exhibit that I visited in
person over a decade ago, and Dismukes provides a great deal of supplemen-
tary material, including a bibliography, related resources for further research
(including relevant websites, films, and organizations), a historical overview of
Black-Indian encounters in the United States, and a list of "Historic Red-Black"
people (which includes Jimi Hendrix). But the reproduced images in the book
are much smaller and less detailed. Therefore in some cases, I have sought out
larger versions of these images online and relied on them in my analysis.

Dismukes's 2007 book features fifty photographs with accompanying verbal narratives and fifteen additional photographs without narratives that are
captioned only by the subject's name and tribal affiliation. I will focus primarily on selections from the photos with verbal narratives, especially since
I am interested in the intersections (and tensions) between image and text.
Some trends in the fifty photographs with accompanying personal statements
are worth noting. In twenty-six of the photographs, the subjects are wearing
Native jewelry or clothing, including traditional regalia from various Indian
tribes. While most of the subjects are photographed inside their homes, eight
are photographed outside or in a natural setting, and seven appear to be posing at pow-wows or other Indigenous celebrations. The vast majority of the
subjects (37) are affiliated with one of The Five Tribes (Creek, Cherokee,
Chickasaw, Choctaw, and Seminole), though other tribes are represented,
including Northeastern nations (Narangansett, Wampanoag, Abenaki) and
Plains tribes (Comanche, Kiowa, Cheyenne, Sioux). And in terms of phenotype, the subjects of these photographs represent a wide range of skin colors,
hair textures, and facial features that indicate varying degrees of European,
African, and Indigenous heritage. Most of the subjects would likely be perceived as Black, at least in a U.S. context.

Without using the word "real" or "authentic," many of the subjects of
Dismukes's collection are nonetheless engaging with a politics of authenticity

through their words and images. Like the formerly enslaved people who straddled Black and Native communities and whose narratives I discussed in chapter 2, these subjects both implicitly and explicitly understand racial belonging in terms of blood, cultural practices, and/or political allegiances. The struggle to belong to one or more communities is evident in their visual and verbal narratives, but in many cases, these individuals can weave these multiple identities together into a cohesive whole. This ability to integrate multiple parts of one's identity is due, in large part, to a changing social climate in the late twentieth and early twenty-first centuries in which people of mixed racial and ethnic heritage can more freely and fully accept all of their ancestors. A close reading of these portraits shows that Native, Black, and Black-Native identities are negotiated and performed in a number of ways. Dismukes's subjects demonstrate their multilayered identities through their affinity for cultural practices, Native languages, community involvement, and material objects such as dress, art, and sacred objects. As a literary scholar, I tend to be drawn to the word, and I do attend to the verbal narratives that accompany these photographs. But my analysis in this chapter is guided by the visual, especially the juxtapositions and contradictions within these photographs and what they suggest about racial authenticity.

I begin with Boe Bvshpo Lawa (Many Knives) Glasschild, whose image and narrative is frequently featured in articles about Dismukes's exhibition in the early 2000s (Figure 4.1).

In his portrait, Glasschild, a shamanic healer of Choctaw, Cherokee, and Blackfoot heritage, is standing in what appears to be his living room and is looking directly at the camera. Behind him is a painting, (most of which is obscured), feathers, and what appears to be a dream catcher. His black curly hair is shaved into a mohawk and he wears a Native-inspired beaded choker. His arms are crossed and he holds an object in each hand: a feather in his left hand and a beaded rattle in his right hand. Glasschild wears a t-shirt that reads "Malcolm" and depicts a picture of Malcolm X, as well as additional writing. Most of the objects in the picture "read" as Native American, even to an audience that sees only stereotypes of American Indians in the media. (What could be more "authentically" Indian than a mohawk and a feather?) The African-American part of Glasschild's heritage is represented through the image and name of one of the most revolutionary Black leaders of the twentieth century. For many people Malcolm X is Black Nationalism incarnate (Frady 1994, 300). His slogan "by any means necessary" is often contrasted with Dr. Martin Luther King, Jr.'s plea to "love your enemy" and "turn the other cheek." Indeed, Malcolm X embodied the alternative to the non-violent movement that many young Black people in the 1960s began to view as futile. It is this militant, uncompromising Malcolm X that most viewers would associate with the image on Glasschild's shirt. One might find it ironic that Glasschild, a mixed-race

Figure 4.1 Boe Bvshpo Lawa (Many Knives) Glasschild, Choctaw/Cherokee/Blackfoot, Midland, Texas, Shamanic Healer, ANASCA Co-founder. Photograph by Valena Broussard Dismukes.

person, is idolizing Malcolm X because during the 1960s and 1970s, there was little space for multiracial people in the Black Nationalist movement. To claim a Black biracial identity was viewed by many as a negation of Black pride. Yet here Glasschild reclaims Malcolm from essentialist Black Nationalist rhetoric. On the other hand, it is important to recognize that Malcolm X did undergo a significant change in his thinking about racial justice and equality. While he had previously called white people "devils" and asserted that there was no role for them in the movement, after going on hajj in 1964, Malcolm X developed a more inclusive worldview. Worshiping with Muslims of all colors transformed him. Malcolm X experienced the possibility of brotherhood between Blacks and non-Blacks (Natambu 2002, 303). While he still felt that people of African descent should be the leaders of their own liberation, Malcolm X was more open to working with white people who shared a desire for justice for African-Americans. Perhaps it is this Malcolm X that Glasschild is identifying with in this portrait. Perhaps as a multiracial Black Indian in the twenty-first century, Glasschild commemorates the Malcolm X who saw the possibility and power of unity across racial and color lines.

Glasschild does not discuss his visual nod to Malcolm X in his verbal narrative, though his statement suggests that he might support the more inclusive, post-hajj Malcolm X. Raised by his Choctaw grandmother in a "household that honored both [his] African and Choctaw lineage," Glasschild was taught to valorize both aspects of his heritage from a young age (Dismukes 2007, 23). He speaks fondly of his Choctaw relatives, many of whom were medicine people (Dismukes 2007, 23). Like many of the subjects in *The Red-Black Connection*, Glasschild is anchored by his Native beliefs: "I live in a state of ceremony with the Earth Mother during every waking moment. I hold everything to me that respects my Earth Mother as a sacred being." (Dismukes 2007, 23) He is also committed to keeping these traditions alive and passing them on to his children (Dismukes 2007, 23). On his Amazon.com author page (no date given, but some time after Dismukes's book was published in 2007, since he mentions the organization that he founded in 2009), Glasschild writes that he has walked a number of "diverse paths" toward healing, including "Choctaw and Amerindian spirituality, Tawepiki (Lightning Dance) shamanism, Kundalini and Hatha yogas, Hawaiian Huna, Qigung, Tuva throat singing, Buddhism, Tribal drumming." ("Boe Glasschild" n.d.) He is also the founder of Nature's Own Wisdom, a non-profit 501(c)(3) organization that sponsors workshops that draw on "Amerindian, Eastern and aboriginal philosophies that serve as the starting point for the greatest journey of all- the journey inward." ("Boe Glasshild" n.d.) Glasschild represents the amalgamation of Indian and African, past and future, "traditional" and "modern."

Like Glasschild's photograph, the portrait of Melanie Midget underscores the movement across and between Black and Native identities, although Midget's connection to her Choctaw heritage arrived only as an adult. A Choctaw physician living in Los Angeles, Midget appears in Dismukes's portrait sitting on white carpeted steps, presumably in her home, and there is a plant behind her. Midget is a relatively dark-skinned woman with braids who is looking directly at the camera. She is wearing light wash jeans and a white t-shirt with some writing on the front. Some of the words are obscured, but I can make out the words "Kaniyo Kiya." Based on the other letters on

Midget's shirt and some Internet sleuthing, I ascertained that the phrase emblazoned on her chest is "Chahta Annopa Ik hapi kaniyoh kiya." According to the website of the Mississippi Band of Choctaw Indians, this is "the battle cry of the Department [of Chatha Imi] against the dangers of language loss." ("Choctaw Language Learning Resources" n.d.) This focus on language as a vital element of Choctaw identity is an important one in American Indian communities, as language facilitates a connection to "the associated cultural knowledge stored in an undocumented oral tradition." (Kroskrity 2012, 12) According to linguist and anthropologist Paul D. Kroskrity, "90 percent of Native American languages are either dead, moribund, or in desperately threatened conditions." (Kroskrity 2012, 11) While most Indian communities "verbally support efforts at heritage language renewal," resources to execute these plans are often scarce (Kroskrity 2012, 11). Choctaw, however, is more widely spoken than some Indian languages that have much fewer speakers.

But what really drew me to Midget's portrait are the multiple books that keep her company. She holds a book in her hands, whose title is hard to make out, though I can see the words "red and black" and a historical photograph of a man and a woman in nineteenth-century Euro-American garb on the cover. To her right is a stack of nineteen books, among which I could discern the following titles: *Black Indians, Cherokee Americans, Black Genealogy, Black Frontiers, The Chickasaw, Creeks and Seminoles, Black People Who Made the Old World, Choctaw Language Dictionary, After Removal, Idiot's Guide to Genealogy,* and *The Five Civilized Tribes*. Midget's multiple identities are represented through books, most of which pertain to Black, Indian, or Black-Indian history. Some of these are scholarly studies that are central texts in the growing field of Black-Native Studies. Yet as the books about tracing one's genealogy indicate, Midget has spent time tracing her roots. Her investment in Black-Indian identities, histories, and communities is both intellectual and personal. Her personal statement reads:

> My great-great-great grandmother is first identified as Choctaw. . . . My family has a tribal number that made them quasi-citizens of the nation, but as descendants we do not benefit or enjoy the same rights as other citizens of the Choctaw Nation. (Dismukes 2007, 43)

Here Midget puts a face on the history of slaveholding among the Choctaw in the 1800s as well as the second-class treatment that many descendants of Choctaw slaves received. The challenges she faced getting information from the Choctaw Nation as a Choctaw freedman speaks to the ongoing tensions between Choctaw who trace their ancestry to people enslaved by Choctaw slaveholders and Choctaw who claim tribal membership based on blood (Dismukes 2007, 43). As recently as August 2020, the Choctaw Nation has actively resisted "federal efforts to require that descendants of the tribe's former slaves, called Freedmen, be given promised rights before the tribe can receive federal housing funds," arguing that "any such requirement infringes upon tribal sovereignty." (Carter 2000)

Midget's relationship to her multiple identities is also performative. Like many of the subjects in Dismukes's work, she expresses her Black and Native identities through various cultural practices, including "food, history, song, language" as well as pow-wows (Dismukes 2007, 43). Her participation in Choctaw community events and her commitment to speaking Choctaw are two markers of Midget's Native identity that she has only discovered as an adult. Midget says that when she shares her mixed heritage with Black people, she often encounters resistance (Dismukes 2007, 43). Midget asserts that "they need to learn that there are African Americans who celebrate many aspects of their different heritages. There is not a monolithic African American culture that overshadows or envelops heritages." (Dismukes 2007, 43) Indeed, this sentiment seems to undergird Dismukes's project. Neither Blackness nor Indian-ness is monolithic. Those who identify as Black or Native often have much more complex histories than those signifiers imply. But the negative reaction that Midget receives from African-Americans may also point to an underlying issue: that those who simply identify as "Black" or "African-American," even if their ancestry includes other racial and ethnic groups, are perceived as thinking of themselves as superior to their putatively "undiluted"[5] Black brothers and sisters (Bates 1993).

As in the photograph of Midget, Black-Native identity seems deliberately constructed in intellectual terms in the image of Richard Procello, a Muscogee/Creek professor who poses in his office surrounded by books. He is a light-skinned, handsome, middle-aged man who is smiling directly at the camera. Procello is pointing to a manuscript on the desk in the foreground, a manuscript of his mother's life that he recently researched and wrote. Behind him is a map of Creek territory, a large family tree, what appears to be a walking stick, and several shelves of books. The two titles that can be read in the picture are *Black Men* (author unknown) and *The Greatest Generation* by Tom Brokaw. In no uncertain visual terms, Procello pays homage to his Native identity, his Black identity, his identity as Baby Boomer, and his family identity. His photograph projects a sense of ease with his multiple identities, an ease that is reflected in his personal statement.

This sense of ease has been hard-won, however, as Procello begins his narrative with an account of the year-long process of enrolling in the Creek Nation. He states that, "[a]lthough I am an enrolled Creek, I identify myself as Black." (Dismukes 2007, 51) Just as Midget participates in the Choctaw community, Procello engages with Creek community and continues to learn about his history: "I attend powwows, and have joined an organization that celebrates our two cultures. I read books about the Creek Nation and culture and wear a cap that reads 'Creek' or Muscogee.'" (Dismukes 2007, 51) The juxtaposition of modernity and tradition by wearing a baseball cap that verbally indicates Procello's tribal affiliation is a wonderful example of the various ways that American Indian identity is marked in the twenty-first century. Procello's connection to his Indian identity has also come through genealogical research, which is a theme for many of Dismukes's subjects. The possibilities for genea-logical research (especially thanks to the Internet) in the new millennium have transformed many individuals' understanding of themselves. But particularly for Black-Natives, whose authenticity is often questioned (by Blacks, Indians, and/or federal and tribal governing bodies), having access to these documents and being able to form a narrative about their history is an important authenti-cating gesture. Procello notes that as a child he knew about his Indian heritage but did not "identity [sic] . . . as part Indian." (Dismukes 2007, 51) But when he traced his maternal family history "starting around 1835," he gained "new insights and a new understanding of [his] Indian heritage. To know who you are and where you came from is very empowering and exciting." (Dismukes 2007, 51) This knowledge of his past allowed Procello to claim his Muscogee Creek identity in a way that he had not before. Interestingly, there is no discussion of blood in his narrative. In fact, blood quantum is rarely expressed in these narratives. This absence gestures toward an understanding of American Indian identity that is based not on blood but on cultural practices, language, and community involvement. Indeed, Procello's pride in his family history reflects the centrality of kinship that Eva Garroutte articulates in her theory of Radical Indigenism, a framework for thinking about tribal belonging that encourages Natives to rely on the "Original Instructions" as expressed by elders, oral narratives, and "records of historical practice and forms of community life or social structure" practiced by the ancestors (Garroutte 2003, 117–118). Garroutte points out that social scientists' definition of *kinship* is quite differ-ent from Indigenous peoples' definition of *kinship*: "The consistent orientation of kinship studies . . . has understood 'true' kinship as founded exclusively on biological relationships. Such an assumption clearly implies a kind of essential-ism, in that it posits a fundamental substance connecting relatives." (Garroutte 2003, 123) Historical and contemporary definitions of *kinship* among Natives, however, operate according to a "sacred logic to which notions of genealogical distance and blood quantum are foreign and even irrelevant." (Garroutte 2003, 125) Moreover, in many tribal communities, kinship is not necessarily inher-ited; "it can also be created ceremonially." (Garroutte 2003, 125) Procello's focus on ancestry and kinship rather than blood reflects historical understand-ings of Choctaw identity.[6]

In one of the few full-length portraits in the series, Don "Little Cloud" Davenport appears in full regalia. I could not identify the tribal affiliations of his regalia, but he is identified as Seminole/Muskogee, Creek/Chickasaw (Bird Clan). A dark-skinned, phenotypically Black man, Davenport carries a large feather in his right hand and a wooden stick in his left hand. He wears moccasins and stands behind the trunk of a large tree. In the background, peeking out from behind the tree are two late-model cars. Davenport does not explain his dress in his narrative, though he does discuss various objects that are sacred to him, including a "Walking Stick" with "hieroglyphics" that denote "his great great grandfather's . . . passage to this country." (Dismukes 2007, 7) He also has what he describes as "tribal earrings" from a medicine person and "a beaded sweatshirt decorated with wolves looking up to the sky." (Dismukes 2007, 7) As for many of the subjects in *The Red-Black Connection*, objects of art, family heirlooms, and sacred objects are prized possessions that represent their past, present, and future.[7]

Davenport's expression of cultural pride through this photograph is supported by his extensive verbal narrative. He shares his knowledge of his great-great-grandfather from Sudan who was "captured by Arabs, sold into slavery, and taken to the coast of West Africa to be brought to the New World." (Dismukes 2007, 7) He escaped from a slave ship, and later "immigrated to lower Florida and lived with Black Musogulges, where he met and fell in love with a woman named Koot of the Muskogee Creek/Chickasaw (Bird Clan)." (Dismukes 2007, 7) Knowledge of this family history comes from Davenport's grandmother who was a "medicine person" and had a "spiritual teacher" who was "African and as well as Seminole." (Dismukes 2007, 7) Davenport recalls that growing up, he learned to respect both "Native American and Sudanese cultures." (Dismukes 2007, 7) As an adult, Davenport continues to be actively involved in Native practices: "I participate in powwows, ancestral prayer vigils, sweat ceremonies, rites of passage, pipe ceremonies, corn and ghost dances, Sun dances, and other spiritual ceremonies." (Dismukes 2007, 8) Unlike many of the subjects of Dismukes's work, Davenport shares detailed knowledge of the African (especially Sudanese) aspect of his heritage, knowledge that seems to coexist fairly seamlessly with his Native heritage. But like many of the subjects in *The Red-Black Connection*, Davenport says that while "most of [his] friends are accepting of [his] dual heritage," others are not:

There are some African Americans that think I should only honor the African part of my heritage. When asked about my personal racial identity, I simply say that I am biracial, Black and Native American. I choose to honor both cultures for it makes me feel like a whole individual. (Dismukes 2007, 8)

This sense of wholeness that Davenport derives from embracing all of his ancestries is, interestingly, rooted in his blood: "It is all that I've every [sic] known. It is in my blood and is the essence of my life." (Dismukes 2007, 8) Rare in these narratives, Davenport's invocation of a "blood connection" suggests a link to the past that is rooted in the body and is reminiscent of some of the testimonies of formerly enslaved people discussed in chapter 2.

Dismukes's portrait of Elnora Tena Webb-Mitchell exemplifies the wide range of visual cues of identity that exist in *The Red-Black Connection*. A dark-skinned Black woman who appears to be in her thirties, Webb-Mitchell has microbraids in her hair that extend past her shoulders. The rich, dark hue of her skin contrasts with the white t-shirt she wears. At her neck is a small pin that reads "Support the Stanford Professors!" The image of a black and white feather separates the two halves of the slogan on the pin. She is outside, and a tree is visible in the background. She holds a feather in her hand and wears two beaded necklaces, and on one of them hangs a small pouch. On her white t-shirt is emblazoned an ankh, an "image used in ancient Egyptian art as a symbol of life." (OED) She looks directly at the camera, her head is tilted to one side, and she projects a sense of serenity.

Webb-Mitchell's path to embracing her multiple identities has been complicated not only because she grew up in foster homes but also because "there is much information about our ancestry that is kept secret." (Dismukes 2007, 65) Although some of her family members are either "disinterest[ed]" or "embarrassed" by her exploration of her American Indian heritage, Webb-Mitchell owns her choices and identifies with multiple heritages: "I consider myself to be Black Native American of multi-ethnic origin, I have ancestry from France, Spain, and India as well." (Dismukes 2007, 65) Interestingly, her photograph does not reflect all of these traditions; if anything, it is the markers of Native identity (and, to a lesser extent, African identity) that stand out. The language she uses to discuss her spiritual practices also seems broadly inflected by an Indigenous worldview: "I express, celebrate, and participate in each culture by acknowledging the presence of my ancestors daily, being conscious in all moments with others, all life forms, mediating [sic], praying, and giving thanks to the Great Spirit for allowing me and all aspects of me—other people, the trees, animals, plants, soil, butterflies, water, wind, sky—to be in order for the Source Unconditional Love, the experience being outside of its true nature." (Dismukes 2007, 66) She also takes part in "community prayer vigils," thus engaging with others in her communities, though she doesn't mark these communities in spiritual, racial, or national terms (Dismukes 2007, 66).

But one of the most fascinating moments of Webb-Mitchell's verbal narrative is her alignment of certain character traits or beliefs with her various ethnic/racial/national heritages. For example, she links her African heritage to the Ankh, her Blackfoot heritage to "the intuitive ability to know," and her Cherokee heritage to the "diamond because it symbolizes the four corners of life." (Dismukes 2007, 65–66) She also describes personal qualities that she attributes to her French, East Indian, and Spanish heritage (Dismukes 2007,

65–66). Although Webb-Mitchell appears to integrate practices associated with these heritages in her daily life and in her sense of herself as a "multi-ethnic" woman, this list reads as a compartmentalized and essentialist assessment of her ancestries. She appears to have a paint-by-the-number approach to identity that reduces certain cultures to images or traits or practices. Without using the words "blood" or "authentic," Webb-Mitchell seems to subscribe to earlier notions that blood will "tell." Whereas nineteenth-century understandings of race as a "property of blood" were often used to justify the subjugation of certain groups of human beings,[8] here Webb-Mitchell embraces the qualities that have been bequeathed to her by virtue of her multicultural and multiracial heritage (Gross 2008, 8). But perhaps there is also a desire on Webb-Mitchell's part as a product of the foster system to create a personal mythology. We often look to our biological parents (if we have a relationship with them) to help us understand why we are the way we are. Without access to that knowledge, one might look to what one does know— the various ancestries – and construct an understanding of self that can be attributed to the traits associated with certain racial, ethnic, or national traditions.

While Samuel L. Parker, Sr. does have knowledge of his family's Native history, his relationship to that ancestry is complex, as his verbal narrative and portrait suggest. A legal assistant from Phoenix, Arizona with Comanche ancestry, Parker is sitting in a large wicker chair. A middle-aged Black man, he is wearing slacks and a patterned short-sleeved shirt. In his right hand, he holds a copy of the book *500 Nations: An Illustrated History* by Alvin M. Josephy, Jr. Unlike some of the other subjects in the series, Parker is not dressed in Indian regalia. There is not much that is visibly Comanche in his portrait. But he is cradling this book. The title itself evokes the multiplicity of American Indian identity. As of February 2, 2020, there were 574 federally recognized tribes in the United States, according to the Bureau of Indian Affairs website ("Bureau of Indian Affairs"). Often that diversity is flattened in perception and depictions of "Indian-ness," which usually takes on a vaguely Plains tribe quality. Josephy's book "adheres closely to an eight-hour CBS television film series titled *500 Nations*, narrating the history of the Indian nations of North America and produced by Kevin Costner, Jack Leustig, and Jim Wilson." (Josephy 1994, 440) A substantial, coffee-table tome, *500 Nations* provides an overview of Indigenous cultures in North and Central America and includes paintings, photos, maps, and reproductions of artifacts. Scattered throughout the book are photos of contemporary American Indians identified by name and tribal affiliation and short personal statements. These provide windows into contemporary Native American life, but the narrative of the main text ends with the Wounded Knee Massacre, described in a chapter entitled "The End of Freedom." While I respect Josephy's decision to delimit the vast history that he is narrating, this problematic framework implies that the history of North American Indians (and the history of their fight for sovereignty and self-determination) ends in 1890.[9] Despite this issue, Josephy's book does provide an overview of the vast diversity of Indigenous cultures in North America, and as one reviewer suggests, would "work well in the classroom in tandem with the film series." (Osborne-McKnight 1995, 496)

Parker's connection to this diverse history is reflected in his lengthy narrative, in which he shares the history of his great grandfather, Quanah Parker, "the last Chief of the Comanche people" and the founder of the Native American Church (Dismukes 2007, 48). Parker speaks with apparent pride about his forebear, who was born around 1850, to Cynthia Parker, a white woman who had been captured by Comanche raiders at the age of nine, and the "renowned" Comanche Chief Peta Nocona (Neeley 1995, 9, 13). Quanah "became a noted war chief in his own right, leading his tribesmen in fierce opposition to white settlers, the buffalo hunters in particular." (Keenan 1997, 164) He was "forced to surrender in 1875 following the U.S. Army's prosecution of the Red River War, or Buffalo War" and settled on the Comanche reservation (Keenan 1997, 164). Bill Neeley describes Quanah Parker's legacy as: "Not only did Quanah pass within the span of a single lifetime from a Stone Age warrior to a statesman in the age of the Industrial Revolution, but he accepted the challenge and responsibility of leading the whole Comanche tribe on the difficult road towards their new existence." (Neeley 1995, 151) He died near Fort Sill, Oklahoma in 1911 (Keenan 1997, 165). Samuel L. Parker notes that his family name is "descended through Topay, one of Quanah's wives," but after that the narrative is unclear (Dismukes 2007, 48). Despite the lack of genealogical information, Quanah Parker's legacy as a mixed-blood Indian who served as an intermediary between Whites and Indians seems to resonate strongly with his Black Comanche great-great-grandson.

Parker's relationship to this Indian ancestry, however, seems tentative. He mentions that he considered enrolling in the Comanche Nation in the 1970s but says he was dissuaded by his uncle who thought it might "raise resentments." (Dismukes 2007, 49) His honesty is striking and contrasts sharply with other verbal narratives in Dismukes's series in which people express the connection between certain traditions and their tribal affiliations: "I don't know enough about my Native Culture to say that any or all of the rituals I perform or the traits that I express are derived from Native, or for that matter, African, culture, rather than popular culture." (Dismukes 2007, 49) Parker asserts that popular culture, which may stand in for American/Western culture, is the biggest influence on him, not Indian culture or even African culture. His observation raises the issue of tribal affiliation. While many of the subjects in Dismukes's series can identify their American Indian tribal affiliations with some degree of certainty, hardly any of them share their African tribal affiliations. In general, most African Americans who have been in the United States for a few generations have ancestry from West Africa, the origin of most of the transatlantic slave trade, but do not know from which tribe or tribes. This lack of knowledge about tribal affiliation is one of the effects of slavery: the severing of people from their land, language, and customs and traditions. As Parker says at the beginning of his narrative, he identifies as African-American because that is how the world perceives him (Dismukes 2007, 48). In other words, Parker's understanding of his Blackness comes from other people and in some cases other people's cruelty and ignorance. He recalls a painful childhood incident: when he told his teachers and classmates that Quanah Parker was a relative, some of his Black peers "were quick to remind [him] that [he] wasn't nothing but a n****r." (Dismukes 2007, 49) For Parker, his Blackness is rooted in being a target of anti-Black racism and is cemented by the assumption that others make about him based on his phenotype. His Indian identity comes from knowledge of his family history, but he is hesitant to claim it openly by, for example, enrolling in the Comanche Nation.

The subjects of Dismukes's project that I have discussed here highlight some of the issues of belonging and racial identity that regularly arise in various narratives of Black-Native identity from the early twentieth century to the present. The visual self-inscriptions provide a new lens through which to understand Black-Native identities. Although they are not, strictly speaking, self-portraits, Dismukes gave them latitude in their self-expression. As many are marked phenotypically as African, they rely on other visual markers to inscribe their Indian heritage. And their accompanying verbal narratives complement rather than describe their visual narratives, thus reminding us that the modes of photography, autobiography, and photo-autobiography are hybrid, mediated, and opaque. Indeed, these complex negotiations of identity unfix notions of authentic Black or authentic Indian identity.

The ways in which African-American identity and Native identity are read in Dismukes's photographs stem from the very different ways in which Blackness and Indian-ness have been constructed in the United States. As I discuss in the introduction, the law of hypodescent has determined Blackness ever since Africans first came to North America. F. James Davis writes that this process of racial classification is unique to African Americans: "No other ethnic population in the nation, including those with visibly non-caucasoid features, is defined and counted according to a one-drop rule." (Davis 2002, 12) Indeed, the one-drop rule "emerged to protect slavery and . . . was consolidated in order to bolster Jim Crow segregation." (Davis 2002, 139) Because of the legal and social acceptance of the one-drop rule, people who are classified as "Black" possess an incredibly wide range of physical features and thus "are not a race group in the scientific sense." (Davis 2002, 15) But "because that category has a definite status position in the society it has become a self-conscious social group with an ethnic identity." (Davis 2002, 15) Although the one-drop rule originated in attempts to oppress people of African descent in the United States, many Black Americans have embraced hypodescent, largely in order to create a strong political contingent. Similarly, people from a wide variety of Indigenous nations within the United States founded the American Indian Movement in the late 1960s in order to achieve political and social change (Crenshaw 2018, 476).[10]

Yet the history of the construction of Native identity is quite different from the history of the construction of Black identity. While it takes only "one drop" of Black blood to make a person Black, it takes several drops of Indian blood to make a person Indian. Although the required blood quantum for Native status varies widely depending on who is quantifying and for what purpose, historically "proof" of Native blood has been a determining factor in "authenticating" Native identity. This is highly problematic for many reasons, not the least of which is that American Indian identity (and any ethnic identity, for that matter) also depends upon socialization, language, tribal enrollment, and cultural traditions. Yet even the power to determine who is a tribal member has been supplanted by the U.S. government. M. Annette Jaimes Guerrero explains that before the 1970s, "the tribes themselves determined who were members and thus would receive educational services as federal benefits. But during the 1970s, legislation was introduced that resulted in the infamous 506 forms, which were used to certify proof of tribal membership. This process was regulated by the BIA and required considerable paperwork for Indian parents and the tribes." (Guerrero 1996, 54–55) Because the Bush, Sr. administration claimed the power in 1992 to "declare any Indian tribe in the nation extinct, even if the tribe has been recognized by a congressionally ratified treaty," (quoted in Guerrero 1996, 55) many American Indians have little control over how they are officially counted (or whether they are counted at all). As a result, many people who should be eligible for government monies are denied opportunities for economic and personal advancement. Such attempts to disempower Indigenous peoples in this country underscore the ruthless greed that has characterized the dominant culture's interactions with Native Americans for the past 500 years. This process of classifying Indianness is, like the rationale for the one-drop rule for Blackness, economically driven. The fewer Indians there are, the fewer dollars need to be doled out to assuage European-American guilt over the dislocation and genocide of Native Americans. Thus while the process of classifying people as Black is inclusive, the process of identifying people as American Indian is exclusive. This may explain why there are so many more visual expressions of Native American identity in these portraits of Black Indians. Their "Blackness" is often read through their features, but some of these subjects must openly assert their Native American identity in order to make visible that part of their heritage which, historically, has been more difficult to prove.

Tucked between the Acknowledgments and the Table of Contents in *The Red-Black Connection* is quotation from a lecture given at the Southwest Museum in Los Angeles, California in 1998 by Professor Jack Forbes. A leading scholar in Black-Indian studies, Forbes has written many influential texts. He writes that: "You can't tell who people are by merely looking at them." (Dismukes 2007, v) Here Forbes repeats one of the foundational truths of race and identity: visual cues are misleading, especially when it comes to assessing racial or ethnic identity. Indeed, when we consider many of the images in Dismukes's collection, it is sometimes difficult to "tell" which of her subjects have Indian or European blood along with African blood. We think we know what a "white" person or a "Black" person or an "Indian" person looks like; but in fact, those categories are in flux and "realness" is an illusion. Visual clues can be deceptive. This lesson seems to be an impetus for Dismukes's project. But at the same time, her project suggests that the visual can tell us something. There is an underlying faith in the possibility that truth can be rendered through visual representation, in this case photographic representation. Ultimately, Dismukes and her subjects inhabit this contradiction: their visual and verbal self-inscriptions represent the possibility of redressing stereotypes and assumptions about people of Black, Native, and Black-Native ancestry, but they also gesture toward the incompleteness of the image as a mode for communicating the complexity of racial identity for those who straddle African and American Indian communities. In chapter 5, I analyze the life and work of Radmilla Cody, who uses performance and music to assert a blended identity through her reign as Miss Navajo in 1997–1998 and her work as a performer who is well known in contemporary Native music circles.

NOTES

1. Susan Searls Giroux puts it this way: "If the mid-century social welfare state was concerned, at least in theory, with citizens' social well-being in its performance of certain caretaking functions, for example the funding of education, healthcare and public housing – a set of commitments the civil rights struggle of the 1960s was meant to expand to all citizens—the neo liberal state that succeeded it grew more intrusive and more repressive, as resources drained from social safety nets were reallocated towards the police, military, prisons, border patrol, intelligence gathering, and an expanding homeland security apparatus" (Giroux 2008, 429).

2. One recent example of this attempt to "wave away" "historical legacies" "by declaring victory" is the U.S. Supreme Court's June 25, 2013 decision on Shelby

County v. Holder. In a 5-4 vote, the court rendered unconstitutional a section of the 1965 Voting Rights Act that "determine[s] which states must receive clearance from the Justice Department or a federal court in Washington before they made minor changes to voting procedures, like moving a polling place, or major ones, like redrawing electoral districts" (Liptak 2013). Writing on behalf of the majority, Chief Justice John Roberts asserted that "African-American voter turnout exceeded white voter turnout in five of the six states originally covered by Section 5" (Liptak 2013). Moreover, according to Chief Justice Roberts, the remedy provided by the 1965 act was no longer necessary because we have a Black president. Justice Ruth Bader Ginsburg dissented, saying that the legacy of Dr. Martin Luther King, Jr. and the "nation's commitment to justice had been 'disserved by today's decision'" (Liptak 2013). In her dissent, Justice Ginsburg also cited numerous recent examples of "race-based voter discrimination" and gave the following analogy: "Just as buildings in California have a greater need to be earthquake proofed, places where there is greater racial polarization in voting have a greater need for prophylactic measures to prevent purposeful race discrimination" (Sheppard 2013).

   3. One of the critiques that Michelle Elam offers is the way in which the mixed-race movement often portrays racial identity as a choice that is open to everyone equally. She cites Maria P.P. Root's 1993 manifesto "A Bill of Rights for Racially Mixed People" as an example of the ways in which "casting mixed race or as a state of mind or a question of privacy reinforces the idea that political agency is a matter of picking up a No. 2. pencil and shading in a bubble or two" (Elam 2011, 11–12). Also problematic are the ways in which visibility can become the end goal for mixed-race people, for "a simple move from invisibility to hypervisibility does not necessarily work as a political aesthetic strategy in the postcolonial and post-civil-rights-era" (Elam 2011, 158). As Ralina L. Joseph points out, racial ambiguity (which is related to but not always synonymous with racial mixture) can be deployed and coopted for different ends, including commodification (Joseph 2013, 145). Yet another problem among some members of the multiracial movement is the assumption that a multiracial identity is mutually exclusive from a Black identity. Rainier Spencer asserts: "Many multiracial advocates, but most especially some white mothers of so-called multiracial children, have gone to great lengths to prevent black/white multiracials from being categorized, labeled, or otherwise associated in any way with Afro-Americans (interesting, no such energy is expended to disclaim the whiteness of the same individuals)" (88). Spencer gives the example of Susan Graham, "Executive director of the multiracial advocacy organization Project RACE (reclassify All Children Equally)" who stated, "'My daughter is not black; my daughter is multiracial'" (Spencer 2006, 88).

   4. Clyde Taylor "use[s] the term *Arthistory* to indicate the institutionalization and control of knowledge about the world's cultural work, maintained through an inbred or very limited academic conversation. Arthistory's judgments must remain suspect because of the narrow range of its sympathies and allegiances" (Taylor 2001, 25).

   5. F. James Davis notes that four centuries of miscegenation in North America have created a group of people who are racially mixed, though they are defined as

Black because of the one-drop rule: "Estimates of the number of African Americans who have some white ancestry range from three-fourths to above 90 percent, and as many as one-fourth have Native American ancestry" (Davis 2002, 16).

6. Theda Perdue writes that nineteenth-century Indians in the Southeast "had no category for 'mixed bloods' and almost never used the term. On the rare occasions when they did, the term *half-breed* described or personified departure from traditional ways of doing things rather than identifying particular individuals by race" (Perdue 2004, 713).

7. Robert Miller, Sr. (Cherokee) writes: "I have a collection of weapons of war and pipes of peace, which I consider very important" (Dismukes 2007, 44). Another Cherokee woman, Synthia Saint James, asserts: "My living space abounds with Native American and African symbols: a framed feather from a powwow on Long Island; a couple of dream catchers; an arrow; a small bronze of an African woman by Tina Allen and a sand painting by an African artist. I also have drums and flutes and wear my moccasins almost every day" (Dismukes 2007, 52). Angela Y. Walton-Raji, Choctaw, has numerous family artifacts: "I have family documents I treasure, including artifacts that pertain to Sally's Land in the Choctaw nation. I also have the family Bible with birth and death dates of ancestors from Indian Territory" (Dismukes 2007, 63). There are numerous other examples in the collection. This emphasis on material manifestations of their heritage is evident in both the verbal narratives and many of the visual images in Dismukes's collection. That these objects are so treasured by many of these individuals may gesture towards the difficulty of uncovering (and, in some cases, "proving") their Native American heritage.

8. Ariela Gross begins her discussion of the ways in which race has been understood "at the intersection of law and local culture" (Gross 2008, 12) in the United States with the story of Alexina Morrison, an enslaved woman with "blue eyes and flaxen hair" who ran away from her master in Louisiana in 1857 and then sued her master for her freedom, arguing that she was a white woman who had been "kidnapped into slavery in Arkansas" (Gross 2008, 1). Over the course of three trials, various pieces of evidence were presented in order to "prove" her 'true' racial identity. "Expert" medical witnesses as well as lay community members relied on biological understandings of race to prove her whiteness (and, by extension, her unfitness for slavery): "Alexina brought more white witnesses who swore their certainty that she was white, arguing that a true Louisiana native could 'always detect in a person whether that person is of African origin,' just as 'the alligator . . . knows three days in advance that a storm is brewing.' Several doctors testified on her behalf that the shape of her hair follicles and the arches of her feet prove her whiteness" (Gross 2008, 2). The first trial ended in a hung jury, the second trial "found in Alexina Morrison's favor," and the final trial also ended in a hung jury (Gross 2008, 2). It is not clear what happened to Morrison (who likely did have some African ancestry, and thus would have been considered Black according to the "one-drop rule"), but "one way or another, found her freedom in 1862 or 1863" (Gross 2008, 2, 3). Gross uses this case to demonstrate how blood (and the ways in which it makes itself known, whether through physical features, behavior, or both) does not always "tell," despite a strong desire to believe that it does.

9. At least two of the contemporary book reviews I found address this issue. In her generally positive review, historian Clara Sue Kidwell writes that the book "leaves the impression, not dispelled by the photos and quotes from contemporary Indian people, that Indians were wiped out of history after that date [1890]" (Kidwell 1995, 518). In his searing critique, anthropologist William Wallard asserts that the "book should be properly entitled An Illustrated History of the Conquest of North American Indians. The Conquest is its central theme. It is another one-sided history of the defeat of 500 nations, not the history of those nations" (Wallard 1995, 78).

10. Christopher B. Crenshaw notes that Indigenous peoples have developed intertribal allegiances since the Europeans arrived in North America in the sixteenth century (473). But it is only in the past seventy years or so that American Indians have established Pan-Indian political organizations to protect their interests, such as the National Congress of American Indians in 1944 and the National Indian Youth Council in 1961(Crenshaw 2018, 476).

Chapter 5

Performing Race, Nation, and Self

The Life and Work of Radmilla Cody

In February 2014, operatic soprano Renée Fleming made history by becoming the first classical singer to perform "The Star-Spangled Banner" at the Super Bowl (Woolfe). In the days leading up to Fleming's live performance, my Facebook feed was filled with speculation about the significance of the choice of a singer best known for her career in opera (a genre that some "still believe is something with the potential to alienate more than inspire") to perform a song that is, by definition, of the masses (Woolfe 2014). Immediately after her performance, the singers in my Facebook network shared their take on Fleming's rendition of the national anthem, and their responses were wide-ranging and impassioned. Indeed, even Americans who do not consider themselves patriotic have a relationship to the anthem. It evokes a visceral response, as the reactions to Jimi Hendrix's psychedelic version of the piece that I discuss in chapter 3 demonstrate. Radmilla Cody's version of "The Star-Spangled Banner" also shows how the song functions as an expression of (sometimes competing) individual and collective identities. Cody, a GRAMMY-nominated singer of African-American and Navajo ancestry, included the Navajo-language version of the U.S. anthem on her 2000 debut album *Within the Four Directions*. Cody's version has become one of her signature pieces and a source of pride in Indian Country. One of Cody's earliest performances of the "Navajo National Anthem" occurred at the Kennedy Space Center in Florida in 2002 at a ceremony honoring Chickasaw astronaut John Herrington, the first enrolled American Indian to go to space (Chien 2002). The "honoring ceremony" was pan-Indian in nature, featuring a song by Cree musician and activist Buffy Sainte-Marie, a performance by the Chickasaw Dance Troupe, and a presentation of the "flags of the United States, Florida, and the Seminole Nations" by three Seminole veterans (Chien 2002). The ceremony itself and Cody's contribution to it reflect the ways in

133

which many contemporary American Indians are committed both to preserving their Indigenous practices, languages, and traditions, and to serving the United States, especially through civil or military service.[1]

Yet Cody is not just a Navajo woman singing "The Star-Spangled Banner" in Navajo; she is a Black Navajo woman doing so. As Kristina Jacobsen-Bia discusses in her 2014 article entitled "Radmilla's Cody's Voice: Music Genre, Blood Quantum, and Belonging on the Navajo Nation," both her musical influences and her voice itself mark her as a Black mixed-blood woman. While Cody sings traditional Navajo songs in Navajo, her singing style is marked by a "generous amount of vibrato (the signature sound of many opera singers and also used in slower soul, R & B, and pop ballads) and [she] also glides between notes, as did her childhood musical idols, Whitney Houston and Diana Ross." (Jacobsen-Bia 2014, 397) Her own recording label, Canyon Records, notes her hybrid and unique sound, "describ[ing] her voice as 'soaring vocals that deliver both traditional and contemporary sounds with a hint of gospel and soul.'" (quoted in Jacobsen-Bia 2014, 397) Moreover, Cody's nickname of the "Navajo Whitney Houston" serves as shorthand for the different ways in which her body and voice may be read, depending on audience and context (Jacobsen-Bia 2014, 385). Throughout her life in the public eye, Cody has resisted attempts to be defined solely by her racial and ethnic identities, a challenging feat in a time (the turn of the twenty-first century) and place (the United States) where authenticity remains the object of worship, often functioning as the metric for determining who belongs and who does not.

My study of Black-Native self-inscriptions ends with an examination of Radmilla Cody's public performances, both during her reign as Miss Navajo Nation 1997–1998 and more recently during her second act as a recording artist and activist deeply rooted in the Navajo Nation. Although all of the subjects in this book are aware of the ways in which certain narratives of racial, national, and tribal authenticity are mapped onto their bodies, Cody is explicitly reflecting on how her body becomes a text that can be mobilized for various purposes. Many of the challenges of belonging and authenticity that Long Lance, contributors to the WPA Slave Narratives, Jimi Hendrix, and participants in Dismukes's project faced are present for Cody as well. I argue that she practiced Radical Indigenism in order to assert her sense of belonging and to counter essentialist notions of membership in the Navajo Nation that ultimately serve to deaden rather than strengthen communities. As Garroutte asserts in her definition of Radical Indigenism, "[in] our [Native] communities we *already possess* the resources to meet the challenges of identity that confront us, and to do so without damaging those communities. We can only access those resources, however, when we come together to think through what our Original Instructions tell us—when community members of diverse talents bring their gifts to the process of working with the teachings, the stories, the histories." (Garroutte 2003, 143) Though Cody does not explicitly claim Radical Indigenism as a strategy for healing, her recourse to Diné ways of knowing and being and her engagement with the diverse members of the Navajo community resonates with the practice as Garroutte defines it. Cody finds a number of arenas in which to inscribe her identity and to reject entrenched definitions of Navajo (and Black) identity.

Born in 1975 to a Navajo mother and a Black father, Radmilla Cody was raised on the Navajo reservation in Arizona (Banks 2011). Cody's mother, who was eighteen when she gave birth to Radmilla, struggled with alcohol abuse and left her to be raised by her grandmother Dorothy (Banks 2011). From a young age, Radmilla sang in church and learned skills such as "rug-weaving and sheepherding." (Banks 2011) However, she often felt ostracized because she was biracial. In a 2011 article by Leo W. Banks, Cody recalls being scorned not just by her classmates but also by her own family: "It came out when they were drunk. . . . I remember sitting at the table and Uncle Elmer hitting me on the head with a spoon and calling me a black pig." (Banks 2011) At the age of twenty-two, Cody entered and won the Miss Navajo Nation competition. After serving as Miss Navajo Nation, Cody's singing career took off and she released her first album, entitled *Within the Four Directions,* in 2000 (Banks 2011). She has recorded three additional solo albums: *Seeds of Life* (2002), *Spirit of a Woman* (2006), *Precious Friends* (2008), and *Shi Keyah: Songs for the People* (2012). Cody has won multiple Native American Music Awards, and she was a 2013 GRAMMY nominee in the category of Best Regional Roots ("Biography," Radmilla Cody n.d.). She has also "become an activist, giving speeches on domestic violence to assemblies in Navajo schools—part of the Strong Spirit campaign – and in rallies at the state Capitol and elsewhere." (Banks 2011) According to her website, Cody has a Bachelor of Science degree in Public Relations with a minor in Sociology [from Northern Arizona University] and is currently pursuing a Masters in Sociology." ("Biography," Radmilla Cody n.d.)

But the event that threatened to overshadow all of these accomplishments was her 2001 federal indictment on drug charges (Banks 2011). At the age of nineteen, Cody became romantically involved with Darrell Bellamy, a drug runner based in the Phoenix area (Banks 2011). Physically and emotionally abusive, Bellamy forced Cody to "package marijuana" and "strap cocaine to her body . . . in a Phoenix airport." (Banks 2011) In 2001, Cody "pled guilty to misprision of a felony—failure to report a serious crime—and served 18 months in maximum security prison in Phoenix." (Banks 2011) Many members of her community were disturbed by the apparent hypocrisy of a Miss Navajo Nation participating in drug trafficking. Kelsey Begaye, a friend of Cody and a former Tribal President, said that: "A lot of the people who backed her after she won Miss Navajo thought, 'Well, now she's gone and gotten herself into this mess.' People were . . . wondering what kind of role model we had." (Banks 2011) Certainly there were people in her community who were disappointed in Cody for not representing the Navajo Nation appropriately; but many did support her through this time. In late 2002, as Cody was fulfilling her commitment to perform in various venues (even though some of her shows had been cancelled because of her conviction) while preparing to surrender herself to serve a sentence in federal prison, president-elect of the Navajo Nation Joe Shirley, Jr. said that, "yes, she's come up short of what is expected of her as an individual person, as a young lady, but we should be there for her, giving her support as a nation and as a family." (Abasta 2002) And it seems that Cody has emerged from her numerous struggles resilient and determined to share her story in the hope that it will help others. She states that: "I want people to hear about domestic violence from a survivor. . . . For me, a lot of this has been about taking back power." (Banks 2011) As a public figure, it is no wonder that Cody's remaking of herself has been public as well. An award-wining documentary entitled *Hearing Radmilla* by Angela Webb premiered in 2010 and has been screened all over the world (Banks 2011). Cody hopes that by sharing her own life, she can communicate the "message that anyone can make serious mistakes and recover from them, and that it's OK to be different." (Banks 2011) Cody's grappling with her mixed ancestry illuminates the ways in which the beauty pageant might function as a space of self-inscription. In this arena, public and private converge, and the stakes of proving one's belonging to a racial or ethnic group can be quite high.

In 1997, Radmilla Cody became the 46th Miss Navajo Nation, beating out six other finalists who competed in several categories such as Contemporary Skills and Talent, Traditional Skills and Talent, Traditional Techniques, Public Speaking, and Evening Gown ("About *Miss Navajo*" n.d.). Like many beauty pageants in Native communities, Miss Navajo Nation is concerned with performing a particular version of Indian-ness. Although the organization's official website declares that Miss Navajo Nation's goal is to "be a role model for young people everywhere," her primary focus is to serve as an ambassador of the Navajo Nation. The winner must demonstrate a thorough understanding of Navajo culture and language, and ever since the pageant's inception in 1952, Miss Navajo Nation has worked on behalf of members of the Navajo community and developed strong relations with other Nations ("History of Miss Navajo Nation" n.d.).

The competition itself, which filmmaker Billy Luther highlights in his 2007 film *Miss Navajo*, is physically and emotionally demanding. The competition is four days long, during which time contestants may not use cell phones or have any contact with their families. Luther filmed footage from the 2005 event, in which six young women from the Navajo Nation vie for the crown. (Only five made it through the entire competition, however. One contestant, Janene Yazzie, was hospitalized for "exhaustion" during the sheep butchering portion and did not return.) Before the competition begins, the contestants meet with a "beauty consultant" who gives them advice on how to take care of their hair, skin, and nails. She reminds them that Miss Navajo must be well-rested (or at least appear to be well-rested) while maintaining a grueling schedule of appearances. On the first day, the contestants are quizzed on aspects of Navajo government and history. On the second day, the contestants show their sheep butchering skills. They must wrangle the sheep, kill the sheep, cook the meat, and make the frybread that accompanies the meat—all while responding to judges' questions in Navajo about different aspects of the butchering. The image of these young women dressed in their finery (though they wear aprons and cover their moccasins with garbage bags to catch the blood splatter) is striking, and this event alone sets the Miss Navajo Nation Pageant apart from any other beauty pageant in the world. Later that day, contestants take a Navajo language test administered by former Miss Navajos. Although all of the contestants speak Navajo, few are fluent, and most struggle with this section. Day 3 marks the traditional skills portion of the competition. In the film, contestants showcase their talents in drumming, singing, storytelling, and traditional food preparation. At the end of Day 4, Miss Navajo is crowned, and the runners-up are announced. While the protagonist of the film, Crystal Frazier, does not win, she is first runner-up, and she says that participating in the contest made her "more organized" and a "better planner." (Luther 2007) Crystal also realizes the importance of self-confidence, especially when one is isolated from one's family during the four days of competition, and asserts that respecting oneself and others is essential. Luther's film provides insight into the courage, determination, and inner strength needed just to compete in this competition. In the words of Sunny Dooley (Miss Navajo 1982–1983), who appears throughout the film, the pageant "taps into the whole woman." (Luther 2007) Luther, whose mother, Sarah Johnson Luther, wore the 1966–1967 Miss Navajo crown, explains the motivation behind the film:

> MISS NAVAJO is dedicated to the Navajo woman, which is what the film is all about. Navajo women wear the trousers in Navajo society. They work the land, they raise the kids, and they preserve the culture and traditions. And they butcher the sheep! So you can see they are so much more than just a pretty face. My film isn't just about them, it's for them. (Independent Lens n.d.)

The competition requires young women to demonstrate mastery of skills that women are expected to have in Navajo culture, which is both matrilineal and matriarchal.

Because one of the duties of a Miss Navajo Nation is to serve as an "ambassador" for the Diné people, she must have a CDIB card, be bilingual, and demonstrate knowledge of "Navajo culture, history, and tradition." The rules of the Miss Navajo Nation competition stipulate that "Miss Navajo Nation must understand the position is not about glamour, but understand the role of Miss Navajo Nation is a highly respected position; therefore [she] must serve her ambassadorship with honor and respect by promoting and educating on the Navajo Culture, Language and Tradition." ("About the Pageant" n.d.) Here the pageant officials define Navajo-ness through a combination of blood, enrollment status, language facility, and traditional knowledge. However, as the scenes from Billy Luther's documentary film *Miss Navajo* indicate, familiarity with Navajo language and tradition varies widely among the participants. In one painful scene in the documentary, the contestants are interviewed in Navajo and expected to answer in Navajo. Most of the women struggle mightily; some answer in English, and one woman says nothing. Only one woman manages to answer the judges' question in Navajo (and she is ultimately crowned Miss Navajo Nation at the end of the competition) (Luther 2007).

There are also material benefits to being crowned Miss Navajo Nation. She "travels internationally and locally on behalf of the Navajo people and holds a salaried position for one year with the Navajo Nation." ("About the Pageant" n.d.) And at the end of her reign, each Miss Navajo Nation receives "an educational scholarship of $7,500 (for undergraduate students) or $15,000 (for graduate students)." ("About the Pageant" n.d.) This educational award is an important aspect of many beauty pageants on and off the reservation, including The Miss America Program, which "currently enjoys the status of being the largest scholarship program for women in the United States." (Banet-Weiser 1999, 45) Indeed, despite the focus on appearance in the Miss America Pageant, the organization expects that the goal of each contestant is to be an "educated woman." (Banet-Weiser 1999, 45) Miss Navajo Nation Pageant's focus on supporting young women's formal educational goals sits alongside its investment in promoting and retaining traditional knowledge of Navajo culture, for Miss Navajo Nation must be able to navigate both Native and non-Native worlds. She represents the possibility of retaining one's culture while also finding success in the world at large. Former Miss Navajo Nations have also discussed how winning the pageant gave them opportunities that they had never before imagined. For example, in the documentary film *Miss Navajo,* one former queen recalls with delight meeting Liberace. Another had the chance to hear Senator Robert Kennedy testify on American Indian education in Congress. She proudly recalls that when Kennedy came to the Navajo reservation a few years later, he immediately greeted her, saying, "It's so nice to see you again." (Luther 2007)

Because the women who wear the Miss Navajo Nation tiara are expected to literally embody authentic Navajo identity, the stakes of this competition are high. The collective investment in finding a suitable representative of the tribe was underscored when Radmilla Cody, the first Black Miss Navajo Nation, was crowned in 1997. Cody was prepared for the fact that her "reign [was not going] to be ordinary." ("Biracial Miss Navajo Nation" 1998) Born of mixed parentage, Cody entered the contest for cultural and political reasons. She told the *Daily Times,* a Farmington, New Mexico paper: "I really wanted to run for Miss Navajo to make a statement. And that statement is that biracial people such as I really want to be taken seriously." ("Biracial Miss Navajo Nation" 1998) Indeed, her year-long performance as a Miss Navajo Nation entailed a rejection of entrenched definitions of Navajo and Black identity and an assertion of pride in her multiracial heritage.

Some of the "Original Instructions" of the Navajo Nation that are central to the values of the tribe and of the Miss Navajo Pageant are rooted in the myth of Changing Woman. Navajos believe that Changing Woman, who was "discovered on top of Gobernador Knob" and "grew in twelve days to womanhood," created the original Navajo clans (Iverson 2002, 11). "She rubbed the skin from her breast, her back, and from under her arms to create" the four original clans (Iverson 2002, 11). There are now sixty Navajo clans, and a person inherits his or her clan matrilineally (Iverson 2002, 11). Changing Woman gave birth to twin boys, Born for Water and Monster (or Enemy) Slayer, who "embark on a long and dangerous journey, filled with the challenges that call upon them to employ all the good qualities emphasized in Navajo life." (Iverson 2002, 11) In some accounts of the myth, the twins return from their journey with "livestock as well as special prayer and medicine songs to be used for proper care of . . . animals." (Iverson 2002, 11) Navajo scholar Harry Walters summarizes the importance of Changing Woman and her sons in Navajo culture:

> Changing Woman's gift of mother's instinct and affection are the basis for the matrilineal clan system. The exploits of Monster Slayer and Born for Water are the basis for Navajo healing and protection ceremonies. The accomplishments of all three, mothers and sons, defined new terms and set standards of behavior on how the people should live and what to expect of life. (quoted in Iverson 2002, 12)

The myth of Changing Woman does not include any reference to skin color or ancestry. Rather, the story highlights the bond across generations, especially between mother and sons, that contributes to the survival of the Diné people. As Jennifer Denetdale writes, Changing Woman "is lauded for her powers of reproduction, for she alone has the power to produce the coming generations of Navajos." (Denetdale 2001, 18) The mother is the source of life, healing, and continuity. Miss Navajo "must have characteristics that reflect those of our female deities, particularly Changing Woman, who epitomizes the Navajo woman." (Denetdale 2001, 18) The fertility associated with Changing Woman must, however, be metaphorical in the case of the actual Miss Navajo Nation, who must not have children and "never have been pregnant." (Denetdale 2001, 18) Miss Navajo must keep the Navajo cultural traditions alive, but her labor should be productive, not reproductive, at least at this stage in her life.

Central to the controversy surrounding Cody's reign and the crowning of beauty queens at large is the question of representation: the winner of the beauty pageant purportedly represents the community or the nation. But who belongs to that community, and who defines membership in that community? An examination of Navajo social and political structures provides an answer to these two related questions.

Across time and space, women have been central to nation-building because of their role in reproducing citizens. Yet the other ways that women have contributed to the creation of the modern nation-state have been rendered invisible. As Anne McClintock puts it:

Excluded from direct action as national citizens, women are subsumed symbolically into the national body politic as its boundary and metaphoric limit. . . . Women are typically constructed as the symbolic bearers of the nation, but are denied any direct relation to national agency. (McClintock 1997, 261)

Thus even when women appear as symbolic figures of the nation (see, for example, the U.S. Statue of Liberty), they may not actually participate in the shaping of its values, policies, and institutions. Moreover, the gendering of citizenship in modern Europe, which was the focus of most theories of nationalism up until about thirty years ago, meant that "[a] woman's *political* relation to the nation was thus submerged as a *social* relation to a man through marriage. For women, citizenship in the nation was mediated by the marriage relation with the family." (McClintock 1997, 262–263) This is yet another way in which women's participation in nation-building has been suppressed.

For Diné people, the politics of gender and nation-building are inflected by their history of colonization by Americans, Spanish, and Mexicans. While most written accounts of Navajo history before European American contact do not include references to women's involvement in public life, Navajo oral tradition and other accounts note that "it was not unheard of for women to serve as headmen or chiefs." (Denetdale 2006, 11) When the Navajo Nation signed a treaty with the federal government in 1868 allowing them to return to part of their homeland, Navajo men were the primary negotiators, but as historian Ruth Roessel points out, women's "thoughts and feelings were evident in the treaty." (cited in Denetdale 2006, 12) Although Navajo maintained their traditional lifeways through the early twentieth century, federal Indian policies in the 1930s imposed "Western democratic principles" that "undermined Navajo women's traditional rights including land-use rights, property and livestock rights, and primary care and control of children." (Dentedale 2006, 13) The education of Navajo children at boarding schools further led to the inculcation of Western values around gender roles in which "Navajo women were expected to relegate themselves to the domestic realm which is associated with little political or economic power." (Denetdale 2006, 13) This trend has continued into the twenty-first century, as "no Navajo woman has been elected as president of the Navajo Nation," though one woman, LeNora Fulton, ran for president in 1998 and met resistance from some Navajo men who told her that "the presidency is men's work." (Denetdale 2006, 15) Jennifer Denetdale writes that Navajo women are involved in government as "council delegates in various offices at the chapter levels." (Denetdale 2006, 15) But the most visible and prominent woman in the Navajo public community is not a politician but a beauty queen: Miss Navajo Nation. Denetdale argues that this contest serves as "further evidence of the bifurcation of men's and women's roles wherein men participate fully in the public sphere while women are related to specific and limited participation in the same sphere." (Denetdale 2006, 17) Denetdale's assessment of the ways in which the body of Miss Navajo Nation Pageant, even as it celebrates "ideal Navajo Womanhood," reinforces oppressive "Victorian ideals of purity, chastity, and domesticity," provides a counterpoint to the empowering rhetoric of the pageant that is highlighted in the film *Miss Navajo* (Denetdale 2006, 17). Without painting Navajo women as victims, Denetdale highlights how nation-building in the Diné community reflects both how Anglo values have influenced how people think about gender roles and how "tradition" is often invoked as a reason to keep Navajo women out of public office.[2]

Navajo is the most widely spoken Indigenous language in the United States, but whether or not the Navajo Nation is the largest tribe in the country is debatable. If we consider full-blooded members, the Navajo Nation is the most populous with 286,000 members, and the Cherokee Nation is the second most populous, with 284,00 members, according to the 2010 U.S. Census (Yurth 2012). However, if we include mixed-blood members in the count, Cherokee far outnumber Navajo, with 819,000 and 332,000, respectively (Yurth 2012). Complicating this further is the fact that different tribes determine membership differently. For instance, while there is no minimum blood quantum requirement for membership in the Cherokee Nation, an applicant must show proof of a "lineal ancestor listed on the Dawes Rolls, also known as the Final Rolls of Citizens and Freedmen of the Five Civilized Tribes, taken between 1899 and 1906 in Indian Territory, now Oklahoma." (Hunter

142   *Chapter 5*

2019) This means that some members of the Cherokee Nation (including some but not all descendants of Cherokee freedmen) are not Cherokee by blood, though some members of the tribal government are keen to change the requirements. The Navajo Nation, on the other hand, "defines their citizenry through blood quantum and lineal descent." (Lee 2006, 89) Navajo scholar Lloyd Lee outlines the three ways in which someone may be enrolled in the Navajo tribe:

(1) Person's name appears on the official roll of the Navajo tribe maintained by the Bureau of Indian Affairs; (2) Person with at least one-fourth degree Navajo blood, but who has not previously enrolled as members of the tribe, is eligible for tribal membership and enrollment; (3) children born to any enrolled member of the Navajo tribe shall automatically become members of the Navajo tribe and shall be enrolled, provided they are at least one-fourth degree Navajo blood. (Lee 2006, 90)

While some members find other factors, which Lee calls "historical Navajo cultural identity markers" and include "worldview, language, kinship, and land," to be problematic, blood and descent remain the official markers of Navajo identity (Lee 2006, 89, 90). According to the Navajo Nation's own guidelines, Radmilla Cody would definitely be a member of the Nation, as her mother is an enrolled member and Cody herself possesses a one-half blood quantum. Yet as the responses to her crowning suggest, Cody's phenotype and the fact that she is not a full-blooded Navajo woman rendered her an inadequate representative of the Nation. Rather than appeal to blood definitions of Navajo-ness, however, Cody performed[3] her identity as a Navajo woman according to a more holistic, and, some would say, traditional, understanding of Navajo identity. Yet she did this without denying her Black ancestry, a challenging feat given her upbringing.

Growing up in a Navajo family on the Navajo reservation, Cody identified as Navajo, even though she was singled out for being different not only by her peers but also by her own family. As a child, she was cruelly called "zhini," a Navajo word that means "black." She did not have a relationship with her father and did not grow up around African-American people; as a result, her understanding of Black culture and history was quite limited (Linthicum 1998). In a newspaper article published in March 1998 during her reign, Cody recalls a moment in high school in which her ignorance of African-American history became painfully clear. She remembers seeing a Black student donning a t-shirt featuring a large "X." She said to him,

"You have an X on your T-shirt. I guess I'll go and get me an R for Radmilla." His facial expression was like "What planet are you from?" I had not the slightest idea who Malcolm X was. The only person I was aware of as a black leader was Martin Luther King and that was just briefly. (Linthicum 1998)

Over the course of her reign as Miss Navajo, however, Cody "made it a point to learn about black history." (Linthicum 1998) In the years follow-ing her tenure as Miss Navajo, Cody has continued to educate herself about African-American history and culture, and in 2012 she was awarded the Black History Makers Crystal Microphone Award by "'Initiative Radio with Angela McKenzie,' a weekly program based in New York City." (Davis 2012) In her acceptance speech, Cody said that "being the treasure and icon for culture unity . . . is so important in a sense that I'm at a place where I created a balance of both my beautiful cultures." (Davis 2012) Cody has also incorporated into her vocabulary a new term for African Americans in Navajo, one that replaces the cries of "zhini" that followed her on the school playground as a child. On her personal website she describes the origins of this word:

> The term Naahiłii is a new term that was passed down to Radmilla from a Diné practitioner when she inquired about a more positive, respectful, and empower-ing term to identify those whom she is born for, the African Americans. The following is the Diné description of the term Naahiłii/Nahiłii: "Na(a)"—Those who have come across. "hił (slash in the l)"—dark, calm, have overcome, persevered and we have come to like. "ii"—oneness. ("Biography," Radmilla Cody n.d.)

Cody's claiming of this word to describe her paternal ancestry not only heals her wounds but also offers a new way for Navajo people, both mixed-blood and not, to conceive of people of African ancestry within their communities.

During her year-long reign as Miss Navajo Nation, Cody fulfilled the duties that all Miss Navajo Nations before her have executed. She spoke at "schools and meetings on the reservation" and "represent[ed] the Navajo Nation at intertribal functions." (Linthicum 1998) Cody kept a "punishing schedule of two, three or four appearances a day" while serving as an ambas-sador to the tribe (Linthicum 1998). She also frequently sang one of her sig-nature pieces, a version of "The Star-Spangled Banner" in Diné and spoke out against domestic violence, an issue that was painfully close to her (Linthicum 1998). Though she hid it from the public, Cody was being physically abused by her boyfriend Darrell Dwight Bellamy. She recalls in a 2002 newspaper article, "There were times I went up there (on stage) with a black eye and lied to the people, 'I was in a car accident.'" (Marley 2002) As the first Black Miss Navajo Nation, she also became an advocate for mixed-blood Navajos and became a bridge between African-American and Navajo communities.

However, after Cody's victory, some members of the Native community spoke out against her appointment and argued that she was an unfit representative for the tribe. Cody's body was not deemed racially pure and thus not authentically Indian (Brooks 2002, 16). Orlando Tom of Blue Gap, Arizona wrote in a letter to *Navajo Times*: "Miss Cody's appearance and physical characteristics are clearly Black, and are thus representative of another race of people. . . . It is the very essence of the genetic code which is passed down to us from generation to generation that makes us who we are. Miss Cody should focus on her African American heritage and stay out of Navajo affairs." (Tom 1997) For Tom, Cody was an inadequate spokesperson for the Navajo Nation, despite the fact that she was intimately familiar with and active in Diné culture. Many people responded to Tom's letter by defending Cody, including some Navajo people who identified as biracial. Rick Abasta asserted that, "it's unfortunate that Navajos like Mr. Tom are willing to discredit the accomplishments of another tribal member due to their biracial background. Such a blighted view of people is an unadulterated example of racism, and to have a minority express contempt upon another minority (let alone an Indian upon another Indian), is absolutely ludicrous." (Abasta 1997) As Celia Naylor points out in her examination of the debate, after the initial flurry of responses to Tom's opinion subsided, in March 1998 another person from the Navajo Nation rekindled the controversy with a letter to the editor of *Navajo Times* (Naylor 2006, 152). Leona R. Begay stated that "the whole concept of having a Miss Navajo is just that, in the title itself, Navajo. Anyone can learn to speak Navajo, learn to butcher a sheep/goat, learn another's culture. But it takes a full-blooded Navajo to be a hundred percent Navajo. This Navajo would then have every right to call herself Miss Navajo." (Begay 1998) Begay's comments led community members like Ivis Daniel Peaches to highlight the troubling racial politics that inform such a viewpoint. Peaches wrote that:

> [W]hen a person like Miss Cody is discredited in representing the Navajo Nation just because she is not "100 percent Navajo," they might as well discredit our forefathers (i.e., Manuelito, Barboncito) and the great Native American athletes (i.e., Billy Mills, Jim Thorpe). If you have not noticed, the majority of our forefathers have Spanish names, what makes you so sure that they are not bi-racial? . . . Not all Navajos, such as myself, feel that Miss Cody is a threat to the future of the Navajo people, but is a blessing. (Peaches 1998)

Peaches not only points out the ethnic and racial diversity that exists (and has existed for a long time) among Navajo people, but she also notes that many people who are considered heroes in Diné communities were mixed-blood. "Born into the Bit'ahnii clan near Bear Ears, Utah around 1818," Manuelito was a central leader of the Navajo resistance to American expansion in the nineteenth century (Denetdale 2007, 57). Though he is "[k]known to the Diné by several names, including 'Askii Diyinii (Holy Boy), Naabaahi Jóta' (Warrior Grabbed Enemy), Naabáána badaaní (son-in-law of late Texan), and Hastin Ch'il Hajin (Man of Black Weeds), he is best known to non-Navajos and younger Navajos as Manuelito, a name given to him by the Mexicans and adopted by the Americans." (Denetdale 2007, 57) Manuelito, who died in 1894 "from a combination of alcoholism and pneumonia" (Denetdale 2007, 83), is revered among Navajos today "as a warrior who resisted foreign domination, voiced convictions about resistance as an appropriate response, and always fought for Diné sovereignty." (Denetdale 2007, 53) Barboncito "was born into the Coyote Pass Clan around 1820" and was known as Hastiin Hastiin Daagi ("Full-bearded Man"), Bislahalani ("the Orator"), and ("Beautyway Chanter") (Carey, 2009). He fought alongside Manuelito during the Navajo Wars and was a central negotiator of the Treaty of 1868 (Iverson 2002, 63). This treaty ended the conflict between the U.S. government and the Navajo Nation and "allowed the Navajo to return to only a small portion of their original homeland in Arizona and New Mexico." ("Peoples of the Mesa Verde Region: The Long Walk" 2014) Though I have found no evidence to suggest that these two leading figures were not full-blooded Navajo, Peaches may have assumed that Manuelito and Barboncito had Mexican blood because of the Spanish names they were given. Nevertheless, her point about the self-defeating tyranny of blood quantum, both within Navajo communities and outside them, is valid.[4]

Another community member who supported Cody's crowning was Sean Walker, a leader in the chapter of the local NAACP chapter in Gallup, New Mexico. Walker squarely confronted the hypocrisy of accepting mixed-blood Navajos when the mixture comes from European or Mexican ancestry but not when it comes from African ancestry: "In the past, hasn't there been mixed-blood Miss Navajos? It wasn't a problem then, so why is it a problem now? Could it be because Ms. Cody is part African American?" (Walker 1998) Although I have been unable to locate the blood quantum records or clan affiliations of previous Miss Navajo Nations, Jennifer Denetdale points out that "Navajos claim an ancestry that includes the adoption and intermarriage of neighboring Pueblos and Mexicans." (Denetdale 2006, 19) Indeed, it is quite likely that mixed-blood Miss Navajo Nations have been crowned in the past without incident, as long as their family trees did not include African heritage. Jennifer Denetdale cites Circe Sturm's research on anti-Black discrimination within the Cherokee tribe and suggests that the replication of hegemonic values is not limited to the Cherokee: "Just as Cherokees have responded to U.S. racism in ways that are unique to their own history and nation building, so too have Navajos reproduced, reinterpreted, and

redeployed dominant race-thinking." (Denetdale 2006, 19–20) It is not unrea-
sonable to suspect that anti-Blackness played a role in the backlash against
the first Black Miss Navajo.

Moreover, one cannot underestimate the role of colorism in the debate surrounding Cody's crowning. Just a few years after Cody's win, Lillian Sparks
was crowned Miss Indian World at the Gathering of Nations Pow Wow in
Albuquerque in 2000 (Westerly 2000). A member of the Rosebud Sioux
tribe, Sparks also has African ancestry. But to my knowledge, there was no
controversy about her biracial status, either when she was crowned Miss
Rosebud Sioux or when she won Miss Indian World. This lack of outcry can
be interpreted in a number of ways. Cody's reign a couple of years earlier
might have opened minds within American Indian communities about how
equating Indian authenticity with 100 percent blood quantum can be divisive
and deeply problematic. The politics of tribal membership and inclusion in
the Navajo Nation are also very different from those in the Rosebud Sioux
Nation. (In order to enroll in the Rosebud Sioux Nation, "applicants must
provide three generations of lineal descent born after April 1, 1935" and
"must have one or both parents enrolled with our tribe." ["Enrollment" n.d.]
There is no blood quantum requirement.) Or phenotype could explain the two
different scenarios. Though Sparks has what might be considered "Black"
facial features, she is considerably lighter-skinned than Radmilla Cody. The
picture of her on the U.S. Department of Health and Human Services website, where she currently works as Commissioner of the Administration of
Native Americans, shows a light-skinned woman with straight hair who does
not "read" as Black in the same way that Radmilla Cody does. To be sure,
such assessments are highly subjective, but they do operate both consciously
and unconsciously. That Sparks could represent not only the Rosebud and
Oglala Sioux tribe but also all American Indians suggests that the female
body that stands in for the (non-Black) nation must not bear the visible signs
of Blackness.[5]

Although the majority of people in the Navajo community did not oppose
Cody's appointment, the opinions of Tom and Begay indicated a lingering desire for authenticity in defining a Native identity, even among some
Natives themselves. Indeed, Radmilla Cody was accused of "playing Indian,"
despite the fact that she was (and still is) deeply rooted in Diné culture. While
some were disturbed by Cody's title, other people in the Navajo community
openly supported Cody. For instance, Daphne Thomas asserted that: "Ethnic
blood cleansing has no place in Navajo society, because the Navajo way
teaches that beauty is everywhere." (Thomas 1997) This response indicates
an understanding that blood quantum is only one part of Native identity, and
that being Navajo also means speaking Navajo, practicing Navajo traditions,
being recognized by the community, being aware of Navajo history, and, in

Cody's case, growing up on the Navajo reservation in Arizona. It is important to note that nobody from the Black community spoke out against Cody for being a representative of the Navajo Nation. In fact, Cody was featured in an article in *Jet*, a magazine with a predominantly African-American subscription base. The 305-word article also included a picture of Radmilla Cody in traditional Navajo dress ("Biracial Miss Navajo Nation" 1998). This lack of outcry among African Americans is consistent with the history of the racialization of African Americans, who have welcomed people with Black heritage, no matter how small that "drop" of blood. This is not to say, however, that there are not deep divisions among African-Americans, especially along the lines of skin color. But it does highlight the distinct ways that Blackness and Indian-ness have been defined in the United States.

Although Cody used the arena of the beauty pageant as a site of self-making, she was crowned to represent the Navajo Nation. Her self-expression during her year-long reign was subsumed by her performance as the female epitome of Navajo-ness. In the years following her reign, Cody has continued to navigate between allegiances to self and to nation(s), exploring her multiracial and multicultural identity through performance. The videos on her personal website, radmillacody.net, demonstrate how Cody is informed but not limited by her racial, ethnic, national, or tribal affiliations.

The first video listed on Cody's website, "Tears," is a powerful act of self-inscription. Like many of Jimi Hendrix's lyrics, Cody's narrative in this song appears autobiographical. The combination of sounds and images in this video highlights Cody's struggle with adversity as well as the strength that she has cultivated to overcome trials. The video begins with an image of Cody sitting in a dark room writing in a journal at a desk that has three mirrors. She is wearing a t-shirt and jeans, beaded, dangly earrings, and a large turquoise ring. There are three reflections of Cody in the mirrors, perhaps symbolizing the fragmented sense of self that is portrayed in the lyrics. This image of adult Cody alternates with various images that fade in and out during the four-minute video and reflect the story that she narrates. We see images of a little biracial girl alone, Cody as an adult sitting in a Southwestern landscape, a silhouette of a man and woman physically fighting while a young biracial girl frowns and watches furtively from the next room, images of news articles about Cody with headlines that read "Proud of Her Heritage," "Fall From Grace," and the "Long Road Home," and shots of Radmilla and her maternal grandmother, Dorothy Cody, both dressed in traditional Navajo garb in her native Arizona. Interspersed with these shots are images of the two musicians who accompany Cody's singing, a flautist dressed in Navajo regalia, and a guitarist wearing jeans and a black loose-fitting shirt. The final scene of the video features Cody sitting with her grandmother, Dorothy, lovingly standing beside her (Cody 2006).

The images in "Tears" complement the lyrics, which reflect a desire to reconcile with a difficult past. Cody begins by describing the scene in third person: "She sits on a hill behind her childhood home, and stares out to the land afraid, alone." (Cody 2006) She goes on to say that she is "trying to understand much of its [life's] predicaments." (Cody 2006) She expresses both sadness as well as her frustration that "[h]er cry remains an unheard call" to the Creator (Cody 2006). Despite the pain of her distant and recent past, Cody finds strength in her Navajo belief system and cultural practices. In the song's chorus, Cody describes how the tears that flow represent "joy and love and pain." (Cody 2006) She sings that one day this woman (presumably Cody, though she does not speak in first person) will "remember that the tears of a woman/ is her inner divine, at its best." (Cody 2006) The final image in the video of Cody with her grandmother symbolizes the continuity of tradition across generations and the matrilineal nature of Diné culture. Cody was raised by her maternal grandmother, Dorothy Cody, and she asserted in a 2012 speech: "My grandmother is the cornstalk of my life. . . . She has nurtured and supported me throughout my life. She planted me with the Navajo language." (Largo 2012) Dorothy Cody also shaped her musically, as Radmilla began singing in the choir at the Pentecostal church she attended with her grandmother as a child (Jacobsen 2017, 90). "Tears" illustrates both Cody's willingness to confront some of the painful aspects of her past and her reliance on cultural practices to sustain her moving forward.

The second video on this page, "A Beautiful Dawn," reveals a different side of Cody. An a cappella song written by her uncle Herman Cody and performed in Diné, this piece is at the opposite end of the spectrum from "Tears," which is sung entirely in English and is accompanied by guitar and flute. "A Beautiful Dawn" is a much simpler video, featuring Cody and a young Navajo girl in Navajo country. The natural world is an important element, and the relationship between Cody and this young girl is at the heart of the video's narrative. Cody approaches the young girl, who is wearing traditional Navajo clothing and jewelry and weaving reeds on the side of a hill. As Cody sings, she wraps a blanket gently around the little girl (Cody 2005). Here Cody is framed as a maternal figure who is passing wisdom and tradition on to the next generation. Just as Cody's grandmother served as a supportive presence for Cody, especially during difficult times, Cody nurtures this young Navajo girl. In her 2012 TED Talk, Cody explains the significance of the dawn in Navajo culture before singing this piece: "As Navajos we believe that we come into this world from the east. It is that direction that we give our offerings to the holy people." (Cody 2012) She says that they ask for blessings from these holy people "so that we can walk in beauty through our thoughts, our plans, our life with hope that all goes well in a beautiful way." (Cody 2012) The song's emphasis on the connection between land and spirit, between past and present is echoed in the video. And although "A Beautiful Dawn" may seem to reflect more strongly Cody's connection to her Navajo heritage, Kristina Jacobsen-Bia articulates her movement away from traditional performance practice and toward the creation of a hybrid sound that reflects her multiple cultural and musical influences. Instead of "accentuating register shifts or 'breaks' between head and chest voice" as is common in country music, "here Radmilla seamlessly integrates her 'head' and 'chest' voice so that we don't hear the voice breaks at all." (Iwashita 2014) Jacobsen-Bia also notes that the "nasality" heard is Navajo traditional singing is almost absent in Cody's performance, stating that "breath here becomes an expressive resource utilized to communicate emotional involvement and investment on the singer's part in the vocal performance." (Iwashita 2014)

This blending of cultures and influences is also on display on the next video on the page, a thirty-second video of a television broadcast at the 55th Annual GRAMMY Awards Ceremony. Cody, who is dressed in traditional Navajo clothing and jewelry, begins by introducing herself in Navajo, stating her clan affiliations, and then translating into English. Cody says that this is how she introduces herself and how she identifies as a woman (Cody 2013). Her identity as a bilingual and biracial woman is foregrounded, and the two "sides" of herself seem to blend seamlessly in her brief welcome.

Radmilla Cody also emphasizes the marriage of multiple ancestries in the final video on this page, a three-minute video in which she accepts the Black History Maker Award in 2012. The video begins with the sound of Cody singing an a cappella song in Diné and then cuts to Cody standing in the studio with the microphone-shaped award in front of her. Her hair is tied back, she wears beaded earrings, and she dons a turquoise bracelet and rings. Cody begins by introducing herself in Navajo and then in English. Then she states poignantly: "I treasure my varied background, but my parents' ethnicity does not define who I am. I am always Navajo. I am always African American. And a child of the American culture. I blend all of these things. But ultimately, I am Radmilla." (Cody 2012) Here Cody walks a fine line between embracing her multiple cultures (African American, Navajo, American) and refusing to be pigeonholed by them. Her final statement, that she is, above all, Radmilla, reflects a fierce sense of individualism, a trait that is often coded as uniquely American. This is different from the message that she (by virtue of the title itself) sent while serving as Miss Navajo Nation. The tension between being an individual and being a representative of a group (or many groups) is still present here, as Cody is accepting an award that honors African-Americans. But she has more leeway without the crown. Cody goes on to say that this award "belongs to many people" and acknowledges the family and friends from both "sides" of her ancestry who have supported her (Cody 2012). Interestingly, she acknowledges "her late father, Troy Davis" and her brothers, aunt, and uncle (Cody 2012). She says that these "family connections are relatively new but are very important to [her]." (Cody 2012) Cody also thanks two African-American women who have supported her: Angela Webb, the creator of the 2010 documentary *Hearing Radmilla*, and Adina Howard, an R & B singer who is probably best known for her 1995 hit "Freak Like Me" ("Biography," Adina Howard n.d.). Cody ends by saying "Thank You" in Navajo and English, and as the credits roll, Cody is heard singing in Navajo the same song that preceded the video.

Although Cody has popularized the Navajo version of "The Star-Spangled Banner," she was not the first person to sing it. That honor goes to Katherine Duncum, a Diné woman who was born in a "traditional Hogan in the Black Mesa area." (Donovan 2005) After teaching "Navajo culture and language courses" for many years, Duncum translated and recorded songs in Navajo and recorded a tape entitled "American and Patriotic Songs in Navajo and English" in 1988 (Donovan 2005). In a 2005 *Gallup Independent* article written by Bill Donovan, Duncum recalls receiving positive feedback from other Navajo "who praised her for doing something no one else had ever done before." (Donovan 2005) Duncum describes the trend that she witnessed during her career: "When I first started, the dominant language among the students was Navajo. . . . Now the dominant language is English." (Donovan 2005) The 2005 reissue of the tape in CD format provided one weapon in the fight against the decline in the number of Navajo speakers. Paraphrasing Duncum, the interviewer notes that "learning a song in Navajo . . . is one of the best ways to preserve the Navajo language." (Donovan 2005)

A perusal of YouTube videos uploaded in the past decade reveals the extent to which Radmilla Cody's rendition has inspired others. Most of the roughly forty videos are amateur recordings of Navajo people singing the "Star-Spangled Banner" in schools and at Indian events such as pow-wows, though there are a few videos that were recorded in the privacy of people's bedrooms. The vast majority performing the anthem are young people under the age twenty-five, and most of the time they are singing it a cappella, though there is one young man who sings it while beating a drum (Tabaaha92 2012). There are two recordings of Shaylin Shabi, Miss Native American USA 2012–2013, singing it (Shaylin 2014). As a non-Navajo speaker, I cannot evaluate the pronunciation of these performances, though the musicianship varies widely (which is not surprising, given that it is a challenging song for a non-trained singer to perform, especially unaccompanied). But the pride with which these people sing the piece and the enthusiastic reactions of the audiences (in the case of public or recorded performances) indicate the determination to keep the Navajo language alive, especially for the next generation. As language teachers everywhere know, it is much easier to learn a language if those words are set to a tune—especially a tune that is already familiar. Though it is impossible to know how many of the singers of the Navajo version of the U.S. anthem speak Navajo fluently, the increased visibility of the Navajo version of the anthem has sparked an interest among young Navajo people to learn more about their Indigenous language, thus furthering the goals of language preservation and revitalization that are central to Natives around the world.

By far Radmilla Cody's recording of the anthem is the most viewed video of the Navajo National Anthem on YouTube. As of February 2, 2020, the video, which was first posted in 2009, had 211, 366 views with 1,200 likes and 52 dislikes. Posted by someone whose screen name is Daybreak Warrior, the video features the U.S. flag onto which is superimposed a word-by-word bilingual presentation of the anthem. The piece ends with a man (presumably Daybreak Warrior) saying Happy Fourth of July in Diné and English (Cody 2009). This version reflects a kind of hyphenated identity that many American Indians navigate. The independence of the United States is celebrated by Natives, despite the ugly history of the federal government's treatment of Indigenous people. Sung in Navajo by mostly young people, "The Star-Spangled Banner" represents the ways in which the blending of cultures need not be a process of assimilation in which, as Gloria Anzaldúa puts it, a person of color goes through the "mill with its razor white teeth" and emerges "smelling like white bread but dead." (Anzaldúa 1987, 217) While some might balk at the idea of "The Star- Spangled Banner" being sung in any language other than English, any country whose motto is "e pluribus unum" must make room for different interpretations of its national anthem, interpretations that reflect the reality of its citizens.[6]

Cody's a cappella version of "The Star-Spangled Banner" reflects the multiple intersecting identities that Cody inhabits. Cody has a distinctive voice—so distinctive, in fact, that she was named by NPR as one of the fifty great voices in their special series that highlights the "stories of awe-inspiring voices from around the world and across time" ("50 Great Voices" n.d.). Her voice has a lovely timbre and though she sings the anthem (which has a notoriously wide pitch range) accurately, she does not stick to the notes on the page. Cody embellishes the melody a bit and "uses techniques like bending the notes: common among blues, jazz and pop singers." (Contreras 2010) But what is perhaps most distinctive about her performance is that the tune Americans all know from sporting and civic events is sung not in English but in Diné,a tonal language that is unfamiliar to the vast majority of Americans. In her NPR interview with Felix Contreras, Cody says of her singing: "I think the soul comes in from the black side," Radmilla says, laughing, "and with the Navajo [side], just the beauty and the language in itself." (Contreras 2010) Her statement seems to capitulate to essentialist notions of what it means to be Black and Navajo, respectively. That is, Black people are soulful and Navajo people are beautifully dignified, rooted in tradition. But the laughter that breaks up her sentence suggests an awareness of how those notions are both true and false. Perhaps her laughter also stems from the language of "sides" that is so common in discourse about mixed-race identity. Compartmentalizing the self along racial and ethnic lines might work in the abstract, but people's lived experiences rarely reflect the maintenance of strict, nonporous boundaries. As a bilingual woman of African and Navajo heritage who is a citizen of the United States and of the Navajo Nation, Cody creates a self that revises boundaries of race, nation, gender, and language. Like the other subjects in this book, Cody grapples with discourses of racial and ethnic authenticity that are often imposed by others. The question of how to define Black-Native identity remains as complicated (and perhaps in some ways more complicated) for Cody as it was for Long Lance 100 years ago. Cody's self-inscription in the pageant arena and in her musical performances reflects an ongoing navigation of the rules of belonging to various communities. The initial on Radmilla's metaphorical baseball cap is ever-shifting. Whether she claims A for American, X for Black, N for Navajo, or R for Radmilla, Cody's sense of self is circumscribed by often competing discourses of authenticity in a time and place where authenticity is politicized and commodified as never before.

NOTES

1. One of the apparent ironies within Indian Country is the pride that many natives take in serving the United States, a nation that was founded on the genocide of Indigenous peoples and the forced labor of Africans.

2. In her 1980 autobiography, Irene Stewart, who was involved in Navajo politics in the mid-20th century, tells the Navajo legend of Asfdzáá Naat/áani (woman Chief). She was a "Queen of the underworld" who was morally "lax," which led to women "becom[ing] loose in their morals." Men became frustrated with the women's behavior and established a "new home far across a big sea." Life was difficult for everyone, but "the queen and her daughter remained stubborn and would do nothing to bring the sexes back together." Eventually "an old wise owl" warned the women that the extinction of the Diné people was imminent if they "continued with their foolishness. This made them admit that they were wrong, and ever since the men have taken over as rulers." Stewart concludes: "My people have this story in mind when they criticize a woman leader. They say there will be confusion within the tribe whenever a Navajo woman takes office" (Stewart and Dawdy1980, 61).

3. Cody was not performing Indian-ness in the way that Sylvester Long Lance, who drew from multiple Indigenous cultures and literally created various Indian identities for himself that did not reflect the reality of his ancestry or his upbringing. Cody was born and raised in the Navajo community, and so the ways in which her Navajo identity manifested (and still manifest) are grounded in her own lived experience. Yet

the nature of pageantry and the position of Miss Navajo Nation both require a kind of performance of self and nation that may or may not always reflect one's "authentic" self.

4. Peaches also mentions two legendary Native American athletes who are sources of pride for Native communities but are not full-blooded Indians. Billy Mills (b. 1938) is a mixed-blood Oglala Sioux "who is the only runner from the United States to win the 10,000-meter race at the Olympics," which he accomplished at the 1964 Summer Games in Tokyo (Longman 2003). Now in his seventies, Mills maintains a busy schedule a "motivational speak[er]" and has worked to "gain representation for Native Americans in Congress and on the Supreme Court so as to give more urgency to matters like tribal sovereignty, gaming, treaty rights and water and land issues" (Longman 2003). Football player Jim Thorpe (1887-1953) was deemed one of the greatest athletes of the twentieth century. He "won the pentathlon and decathlon at the first worldwide Olympic Games in Stockholm" ("The Life of Jim Thorpe" 2013). He was born in Oklahoma to two mixedblood parents: his father was Irish and Sac and Fox, and his mother was French and Potawatomi ("The Life of Jim Thorpe" 2013).

5. The opposite sentiment can operate in a country that perceives of itself as a "Black" nation. Natasha B. Barnes recounts the outcry (which included the hurling of cups, bottles, and oranges at the pageant ceremony) in 1986 at the crowning of Lisa Mahfood as Miss Jamaica (Barnes 1994, 471). Mahfood was "the daughter of a Lebanese Jamaican entrepreneurial family" who was 'European' by the standards of Jamaican racial identity and hence had no business representing what to many of the Miss Jamaica onlookers was a black country" (Barnes 1994, 472).

6. In April 2006, several "Latin pop stars" recorded a version of "The Star-Spangled Banner" in Spanglish. Entitled "Nuestro Himno," the translation is "relatively faithful to the spirit of the original," though the "more obscure second stanza is almost a rewrite, with phrases such as 'we are equal, we are brothers'" (Montgomery 2006). Meant to "be an anthem of solidarity of what has drawn hundreds of thousands of people to march peacefully for immigrant rights in Washington and cities across the country," the song drew criticism from both a group of Republican senators who sponsored a bill "ruling that the anthem never be recited or sung in a foreign language" and "pro-immigration groups such as the National Council of La Raza" (Goldstein 2006). However, as *Washington Post* journalist David Goldstein points out, the "US government gave its blessing" to a Spanish version of the anthem that has existed in the Library of Congress since 1919 "without so much as a sniff of disapproval (Goldstein 2006). There are also "vintage translations in Polish, French, Italian, Portuguese, and Armenian, among others (Goldstein 2006).

Coda

"Too Many Masters to Serve"

In the spring of 2014, Oklahoma State House Speaker T. W. Shannon attracted considerable local and national press when he announced his decision to run for U.S. Senate. Shannon is an enrolled member of the Chickasaw Nation (Martin 2014). His father is Chickasaw and his mother is African American (Martin 2014). And he is a Republican (Martin 2014). All of these details, including the fact that if he won he would represent Oklahoma, a state in which 9.2 percent of the population identified as "American Indian" or "Alaska Native" in 2012 (compared to 1.2 percent of the U.S. population) ("QuickFacts: Oklahoma") and Indians "collectively constitute the state's largest nongovernment employer outside of Walmart," (Martin 2014), were notable. The construction of T. W. Shannon by others reveals a wide range of political agendas and demonstrates the ways in which, as Ralina L. Joseph points out, multiracial people and their bodies have been coopted to suit a variety of ideological purposes.[1]

For instance, one-time Republican vice presidential hopeful Sarah Palin exclaimed at a rally of Shannon supporters in Tulsa in April 2014: "His name alone! . . . The Democrats accuse us of not embracing diversity? Oh, my goodness, he is—he's it. He is the whole package." (Martin 2014) Palin uses T. W. Shannon's name to stand in for the "diversity" that Republicans allegedly shun. His full name is Tahrohon Wayne Shannon, and one can imagine how Palin sees different ethnic strands in each part of his name: Tahrohon, "a family name with Amerindian roots,"[2] symbolizes his "Indian" side, Wayne represents his "Black" heritage, and Shannon nods to his Irish roots (Greene 2013). His name itself screams "difference" and represents the ethnic and racial diversity that people at both ends of the political spectrum often hail as the essence of America. Perhaps a more subtle expression of that sentiment comes from Oklahoma State Senator David

Holt: "You've got to project a face from your party that reflects America, and America is changing." (Martin 2014) Despite the fact that America has always been multiracial (while the "browning" of America is seen as relatively recent trend, America was, in fact, brown (and red and black) before it was white), Holt's point seems to be that Republicans must cultivate a racially and ethnically heterogeneous constituency if they are to survive. Other Republicans, like Texas Senator Ted Cruz, shy away from "identity politics and smear campaigns, which is the specialty, sadly, of the Modern Democratic party" and instead "discuss how to turn this country around." (Martin 2014) Cruz aims to shift the emphasis away from Shannon's racial and ethnic ancestry (and perhaps even de-race him in an attempt to practice colorblind politics) and toward the policies that need to be enacted to promote change.

But the message and rhetoric of an April 2014 open letter signed by "Oklahoma Tea Parties and Grassroots Conservatives" who do not support Shannon are particularly striking:

> Your endorsement will not make T. W. Shannon become conservative, he has too many masters to serve, the Indian tribes, Tom Cole, big business and the Chamber of Commerce—once in office, he will dance with the one that brought him to the dance and it won't be Ted Cruz, Mike Lee or Sarah Palin. Shannon is being very well handled—he is whatever you want him to be at the time. (Faught 2014)

The letter writers express fear that Shannon is not his own man because he has "too many masters to serve." This is a particularly charged turn of (biblical[3]) phrase, given the history of enslavement of people of African descent by both Europeans and American Indians, including the Chickasaw Nation.[4] Yet the conservatives who oppose Shannon do not include African Americans on the list of groups to which Shannon will express allegiance. Perhaps this is because African Americans make up a smaller percentage of the Oklahoma state population,[5] and, perhaps more importantly, they lack the political and economic clout of "Indian tribes." Or the writers of the open letter may be attempting *not* to sound anti-Black by not even mentioning his African ancestry or the fact that he might want to serve the interests of his Black constituents. Yet the very use of the word "master" has an undeniable racial connotation: they are, in essence, calling Shannon a slave, and despite the history of enslavement in the Americas, which began with the forced labor of Indigenous peoples, "slave" is often synonymous with "Black." Whether intentional or not, the turn of phrase highlights Shannon's Blackness in a disturbing and derogatory manner. But how does T. W. Shannon understand his own racial, ethnic, and/or national identity?

In an interview for a May 6, 2014 *New York Times* article, Shannon stated that while he was "'very proud' of his heritage," he was "an American first, and that's the most important thing." (Martin 2014) Emphasizing his identity as American seems to be a way to assure voters that his primary allegiance is to the United States and not to the Chickasaw Nation. But such a statement also downplays his racial identity, an identity that he does not share with the majority of Oklahomans. In a piece published a year earlier in *Tulsa World* on April 28, 2013, journalist Wayne Greene focuses on Shannon's political accomplishments but does mention his dual heritage, stating: "If you say that T. W. Shannon is a black man, you're only half right. Shannon clearly honors his Chickasaw heritage equally with his black heritage." (Greene 2013) Greene includes these words of praise from Chickasaw Governor Bill Anoatubby: "T. W. exhibits the best qualities of what it means to be Chickasaw. He has the indomitable spirit, courage, humility and compassion needed to be a true servant leader." (Greene 2013) But the words from Shannon himself in this section of the article about his heritage relate to his unusual name that many find hard to pronounce: "I've never met another one," he said. "I told my wife when our son was born, I had to suffer with it, so does he." (Greene 2013) According to the article, he changed his name to T. W. in college "in an effort to sound more sophisticated," though childhood friends still call him Tahrohon (Greene 2013). People change their names for a variety of reasons, and it can be dangerous to make assumptions about such personal decisions. But Shannon's sense that T. W. would seem "more sophisticated" may speak to a desire to de-race himself, to not be othered by an Indian name that most people cannot pronounce. Indeed, names mark gender, socioeconomic class, language, nation, race, and ethnicity in ways that shape how we see ourselves and how others see us. "T. W. Shannon" reads very differently than "Tahrohon Wayne Shannon."

Shannon's self-representation on his official campaign website supports his selective discussion of his racial background. The "Meet T. W." section of his website features two family photos: one in which he poses on a grassy hillside with his phenotypically Black wife and their two children and another in which he stands with his daughter, Audrey, outside of what looks like a government building. The verbal narrative begins with a statement about his faith: "T. W. Shannon learned the values of faith, family, in the pews of Bethlehem Baptist Church in Lawton, Okla. He still serves there today as a Sunday School teacher." ("Meet T.W." 2014) The rest of the biography focuses on his political achievements, which include "author[ing] welfare reform," "shrink[ing] the size of state government," and "le[a]d[ing] the ways to lower income tax rates." ("Meet T.W." 2014) The biography highlights his pro-life stance and notes that he "has been married to his college sweetheart Devon, for twelve years" and that "they have two children, Audrey Grace and T. W. II." ("Meet T.W." 2014) The third paragraph matter-of-factly highlight's Shannon's racial identity: "Chosen by his Republican House colleagues, T. W. became Oklahoma's youngest and first African American House speaker. He is also an enrolled member of the Chickasaw Nation." ("Meet T. W." 2014) The biography also mentions that Shannon worked for the Chickasaw Nation, but the emphasis is not on Shannon's personal connection to the tribe: "At a young age fresh out of college, T. W. served as the chief administrative officer for the Chickasaw Nation, one of the most prosperous Native American tribes in the country." ("Meet T. W." 2014) This detail is framed as a precocious achievement that led to economic victory.

The "Media" section of Shannon's website, which includes several videos and full-color photos, similarly emphasizes his conservative values and only certain aspects of his identity: namely, his nationality (American) and his religion (Christian). His "I'm In" video features Shannon sitting in church and talking about its centrality in his family's lives for several generations (Shannon January 29, 2014). The video of his wife, "Devon's Story," begins with her saying that they met at Cameron University as undergraduates and that T. W. led her to know Jesus Christ as her Lord and Savior (Shannon April 14, 2014). Most of the photos feature Shannon in smiling conversation with various Oklahomans, most of whom appear to be European American, in the streets, in factories, and on farms. There are several photos of Shannon with his young, photogenic family and a scanned photograph of his maternal grandparents. He presents himself as rooted in the church, devoted to family and tradition, eager to meet the needs of everyday Oklahomans, and, as indicated by a formal photo with Mike Lee, Ted Cruz, and Sarah Palin, vetted by conservative leaders with national reputations.

Like the scrapbooks of Long Lance, the oral testimonies of Black Indian former slaves, the songs of Jimi Hendrix, the photographs of Valena Dismukes, and the reign of Radmilla Cody, Shannon's performance of self serves as an example of the complex negotiation of multiple discourses about racial belonging and authenticity that people who straddle Black and Native cultures often engage in. He seems to situate himself as a post-racial candidate whose interests and allegiances will not be dictated by his blood and cultural ties. Even in his videos featured on the Chickasaw TV website, many of which highlight his connection to the Chickasaw Nation, Shannon emphasizes that "Chickasaw values are Oklahoma values," perhaps to anticipate criticism that his allegiances will be to the Chickasaw Nation and not to the state of Oklahoma but also to remind viewers that the past, present, and future is intimately connected to the numerous American Indian tribes that live there ("Chickasaw Values" 2021). Ultimately, T. W. Shannon lost his bid for Senate, though he continues to be active civically. He was "appointed by the Speaker of the House to the Transportation Commission in March 2019, representing District 3, an 11-county area of east-central Oklahoma." ("T.W. Shannon" n.d.) His page on the Oklahoma Department of Transportation website, which highlights his election "as Oklahoma's youngest and first African American Speaker of the Oklahoma House of Representatives in 2013" and his work as "Chief Administrative Officer for the Chickasaw Nation" is yet another self-inscription of his Black-Native identity ("T.W. Shannon" n.d.).

The autobiographical acts of the figures I have examined in this project reflect the range of modes of self-inscription that fall under the umbrella of life writing. These multiracial Americans challenge narrow definitions of autobiography as a purely written form about a single individual by expressing themselves through sound, image, and performance and by situating themselves in relationship to a larger community. Sylvester Long Lance, formerly enslaved Black Indians, Jimi Hendrix, the subjects of Valena Dismukes's portraits, and Radmilla Cody navigate their Black-Native ancestries in a variety of genres and have different ways of understanding what it means to belong to a community. For some of these subjects, blood is a vitally important metric of identity; for others, political allegiances and cultural practices determine belonging. But no matter how they measure ethnoracial belonging and no matter how they choose to name themselves, they all understand themselves within the context of a larger group. Defining a self, especially a racialized self, is a dialogic project that cannot happen in isolation.

A recent memoir by a woman of mixed Black, Indigenous, and European ancestry reflects an understanding of how the individual and the community are deeply intertwined. Published in 2018, Darnella Davis's *Untangling a Red, White, and Black Heritage: A Personal History of the Allotment Era* delves into her family's history and in the process encourages readers to reckon with the voices of "mixed-race peoples" whose "voices have been muted or stilled in the telling of the American myth." (Davis 2018, 4) She places her story as a "skinny little colored girl" growing up in Detroit in the mid-twentieth century to a mother who was Muscogee Creek and a father who was descended from Cherokee freedmen within the context of a larger movement to understand the complex, contingent, and "shifting racial identities" in the United States (Davis 2018, 8, 9). This reckoning with peoples and histories that have often been obscured in official narratives of American history necessitates an explosion of the autobiographical form, as Davis relies on and interweaves "archival documents, oral histories, and family records" to tell the story of a multiracial family that is also a microcosm of the story of America (Davis 2018, 8). She writes in her conclusion that:

> This work places a clearer picture of the value of my ancestors' lives in the hands of their descendants. For others, it offers a different, an alternative view

of an American family and the American promise of democracy, a glimpse of the future of our mixed-race and multiethnic society in a crisper image of the past. (Davis 2018, 137)

Davis's text represents an important contribution to explorations of Black-Indigenous identity and history, and she situates her narrative in relation to the work of many of the scholars that I have cited in this project, including Theda Perdue, Celia Naylor, Tiya Miles, Claudio Saunt, Barbara Krauthamer, and Circe Sturm (Davis 2018, 115–118). She affirms the value of multiple forms of engagement with this particular aspect of U.S. history, asserting that "there should be no shame in stressing experience over theory." (Davis 2018, 118) On the contrary, there is tremendous value in "the nexus of historical writing and personal voice." (Davis 2018, 118) Like Davis, I have attempted to merge individual voices with collective stories, to connect family lore with official histories, and to link theoretical frameworks with lived experiences. The complexity of our racialized past, present, and future calls for new forms of scholarship and personal narrative that bend generic expectations.

Despite the chronological nature of this book, I do not propose a progress narrative that suggests that people of Black and Indian ancestry have become less bound by the rhetoric of authenticity since the early twentieth century. It is true that the social and historical realities that influenced Long Lance's rejection of his Black ancestry and adoption of a variety of American Indian identities are quite different today, nearly 130 years after his birth. Perhaps he would have been able to embrace his mixed-blood identity today in a way that was impossible in the early twentieth century. But as the more recent expressions of Black-Native identity by Radmilla Cody and the subjects of Valena Dismukes's portrait series illustrate, mixed-blood people still navigate the minefield of authenticity. Because of the history of non-Indian people falsely claiming Indian heritage for personal gain and narrow conceptions of what a "Real Indian" looks like, some have accused "individuals of mixed Native American and African American heritage [of being] 'wannabe Indians.'" (Collins 2009, 183) Micah Fitz-Patrick, an artist of African, European, and Blackfeet ancestry, writes that:

I don't want to come off as a wannabe, trying to cash in on the culture or tribal funds, especially since I don't fit the stereotypical view of what an Indian is supposed to look like. It's the tired, old game of divide and conquer theory and always having to prove yourself to others, even worse, to each other. (Dismukes 18)

And the struggles for citizenship faced by freedmen descendants demonstrate on a larger scale the challenges of measuring ethnoracial authenticity as well as the stakes for both the freedmen descendants *and* the tribes that want to determine their own citizenship criteria. The creative ways that people who straddle Black and Native identities have negotiated questions of belonging, authenticity, and representation in the past 120 years testify to the empowering possibilities of expanding definitions of autobiography. Through scrapbooks, oral history, music, photography, and performance, Black Indians have engaged in anti-hegemonic modes of self-inscription that challenge both racial and generic boundaries. They model resistance to staid, narrow narratives about who is allowed to claim an identity, narratives that are rooted in the colonial mindset upon which the United States was founded. They offer inspiration in the fight against the white supremacy that is built into our nation's structures and emerges in the rhetoric of both everyday citizens and holders of public office. Their acts of self-inscription demonstrate the heterogeneous ways in which racial identities can be challenged, claimed, and reconciled.

NOTES

1. In *Transcending Blackness: From the New Millennium Mulatta to the Exceptional Multiracial,* Joseph reads Barack Obama as "the paradigmatic multiracial African American subject" who is "represented as a flexible racialized body, a floating signifier, or an empty vessel who can conveniently be filled with any desired racialized image from hyperraced or starkly racist (calling up controlling images of black masculinity) to de-raced or e-raced (evoking stereotypes of race transcendence, mixed-race, and post-race)" (Joseph 2013, 165).

2. Shannon doesn't think Tahrohon is Chickasaw and speculates that "[i]t may come from the Iowa tribe" (Greene 2013). Tahrohon is the name of an Ioway warrior who fought against the Osage and the Sioux ("Tahoron, Ioway Warrior" n.d.).

3. "No man can serve two masters: for either he will hate the one, and love the other; or else he will hold to the one, and despise the other. Ye cannot serve God and mammon" (Matthew 6:24 King James Bible).

4. I am still trying to discern how and if slavery fits in to Shannon's family history. Wayne Greene writes that Shannon's "Chickasaw ancestors came to Oklahoma six generations ago, part of the Indian removal policy of Andrew Jackson" and that his family "still holds allotment land just north of Ardmore" (Greene 2013). It is unclear whether his Chickasaw ancestors were enslavers and whether his maternal ancestors were enslaved.

5. According to 2010 U.S. Census data, "Black[s] or African American[s] alone" constituted 7.6 percent of Oklahoma's population ("QuickFacts: Oklahoma").

Bibliography

"50 Great Voices." *NPR*. Accessed December 23, 2020. https://www.npr.org/series /122287224/50-great-voices.

Abasta, Rick. "Award-winning Singer Plans to Keep Public Schedule." *Navajo Times* (Window Rock, AZ), December 12, 2002. http://jpllnet.sfsu.edu/login?url=https:// www-proquest-com.jpllnet.sfsu.edu/newspapers/award-winning-singer-plans-keep -public-schedule/docview/225310412/se-2?accountid=13802.

Abasta, Rick. "Disturbed by Racial Attack." *Navajo Times*, December 30, 1997.

"About the Pageant." Independent Lens. Accessed December 23, 2020. https://www .pbs.org/independentlens/missnavajo/aboutpageant.html.

"About this Collection." Born in Slavery: Slave Narratives from the Federal Writers' Project, 1936 to 1938. Accessed December 17, 2020. https://www.loc.gov/colle ctions/slave-narratives-from-the-federal-writers-project-1936-to-1938/about-this -collection/.

Agent, Dan. "The Cherokee Nation Under Siege." In *IndiVisible: African-Native American Lives in the Americas*, edited by Gabrielle Tayac, 122–126. Washington, DC: Smithsonian Institute, 2009.

Alexander, Amy. "Truth and Consequences." *The Nation*, March 6, 2008. https://ww w.thenation.com/article/archive/truth-and-consequences/.

Alexie, Sherman. "Because My Father Always Said He Was the Only Indian Who Saw Jimi Hendrix Play 'The Star-Spangled Banner' at Woodstock." In *The Lone Ranger and Tonto Fistfight in Heaven*, edited by Sherman Alexie, 24–36. 1993. Reprint, New York: Grove Press, 2005.

Alexie, Sherman. "Harmful Jazz." In *Summer of Black Widows*, 77. Brooklyn, NY: Hanging Loose Press, 1997.

Andrews, William L. "An Introduction to the Slave Narrative." *Documenting the American South*. Accessed December 23, 2020. https://docsouth.unc.edu/neh/intro .html.

Anzaldúa, Gloria. *Borderlands/La Frontera: The New Mestiza.* 1st ed. San Francisco: Spinsters/Aunt Lute Books, 1987.

Aptheker, Herbert. "Maroons Within the Present Limits of the United States." In *Maroon Societies: Rebel Slave Communities in the Americas*, edited by Richard Price, 151–167. Baltimore: Johns Hopkins University Press, 1996.

"At Southwest Museum—Red-Black Connection: The Cultural Heritage of Black Native Americans." *Los Angeles Sentinel*, February 1, 2001: http://jpllnet.sfsu.edu/login?url=https://www-proquest-com.jpllnet.sfsu.edu/newspapers/at-southwest-museum-red-black-connection-cultural/docview/369355061/se-2?accountid=13802.

Baker, Brian Alan. Review of *In Whose Honor?* By Jay Rosenstein. *Teaching Sociology* 26, no. 2 (April 1998): 153–156. https://doi-org.jpllnet.sfsu.edu/10.2307/1319291.

Baker, T. Lindsay and Julie P. Baker, eds. *The WPA Oklahoma Slave Narratives*. Norman and London: University of Oklahoma Press, 1996.

Banet-Weiser, Sarah. *The Most Beautiful Girl in the World: Beauty Pageants and National Identity*. Berkeley and Los Angeles: University of California Press, 1999.

Banks, Leo W. "Radmilla Cody: An Unusual Miss Navajo." *High Country News* (Paoniam CO), March 7, 2011. https://www.hcn.org/issues/43.4/an-unusual-miss-navajo.

Banks, Sandy. "Why Would Author Label Fiction as Fact?" *LA Times*, March 8, 2008. https://www.latimes.com/archives/la-xpm-2008-mar-08-me-banks8-story.html.

Barnes, Natasha B. "Face of the Nation: Race, Nationalisms and Identities in Jamaican Beauty Pageants." *The Massachusetts Review* 35, no. 3/4 (Autumn 1994): 471–492. Accessed December 29, 2020. http://search.ebscohost.com.jpllnet.sfsu.edu/login.aspx?direct=true&AuthType=ip,cookie,url,uid&db=a9h&AN=9412051622&site=ehost-live.

Bates, Karen Grigsby. "Color Complexity: How Much Black Makes One Black?: Does Personally Acknowledging Many Ethnic Roots Mean Self-Pride Or Self-Loathing?" *Emerge*, June 1993. http://jpllnet.sfsu.edu/login?url=https://www-proquest-com.jpllnet.sfsu.edu/magazines/color-complexity-how-much-black-makes-one-does/docview/230821451/se-2?accountid=13802.

Bay, Mia. "The Historical Origins of Afrocentrism." *Amerikastudien/American Studies* 45, no. 4 (2000): 501–512. Accessed December 29, 2020. https://www.jstor.org/stable/41157604.

Bederman, Gail. *Manliness and Civilization: A Cultural History of Gender and Race in the United States, 1880-1917*. Chicago and London: University of Chicago Press, 1995.

Begay, Leona R. "Times Are Changing." *Navajo Times*, March 26, 1998.

Berry, S.L. "Picture this: A Red-Black Connection." *Indianapolis Star*, Jul 11, 2004. http://jpllnet.sfsu.edu/login?url=https://www-proquest-com.jpllnet.sfsu.edu/newspapers/picture-this-red-black-connection/docview/240703006/se-2?accountid=13802.

Bey, Yasiin. "Rock N Roll." Genius. Accessed January 21, 2021. https://genius.com/Yasiin-bey-rock-n-roll-lyrics.

Bhabha, Homi K. *The Location of Culture*. London: Routledge, 1994.

Bhabha, Homi K. "Of Mimicry and Man." In *The Performance Studies Reader*, edited by Henry Bial, 279–286. New York: Routledge, 2004.

Bibb, Henry. *Narrative of the Life and Adventures of Henry Bibb, An American Slave, Written by Himself.* 1850. In *Slave Narratives*, edited by William L. Andrews and Henry Louis Gates, Jr., 425–566. Reprint, New York: Library of America, 2000.

"Biography." *Adina Howard.* Accessed December 17, 2020. https://www.adinahoward.com/bio.

"Biography." *Radmilla Cody.* Accessed December 22, 2020. http://radmillacody.net /biography.html.

"Biracial Miss Navajo Nation Surprises Some on Indian Reservation in Arizona." *Jet.* July 6, 1998. http://search.ebscohost.com.jpllnet.sfsu.edu/login.aspx?direct=true &AuthType=ip,cookie,url,uid&db=ulh&AN=834659&site=ehost-live.

Blu, Karen I. *The Lumbee Problem: The Making of an American Indian People.* Cambridge: Cambridge University Press, 1980.

"Boe Glasschild." *Amazon.* Accessed December 23, 2020. https://www.amazon.com /Boe-Glasschild/e/B00EDQERTW.

Boyle, Kevin. "The Fire Last Time; 40 Years Later, the Urban Crisis Still Smolders" [Final Edition] *The Washington Post,* July 29, 2007. Accessed December 29, 2020. http://jpllnet.sfsu.edu/login?url=https://www-proquest-com.jpllnet.sfsu.edu/news papers/fire-last-time-40-years-later-urban-crisis-still/docview/410091655/se-2?a ccountid=13802.

Brennan, Jonathan. Introduction to *When Brer Rabbit Meets Coyote: African-Native American Literature*, 1–97. Edited by Jonathan Brennan. Urbana and Chicago: University of Illinois Press, 2003.

Brooks, James F. Introduction to *Confounding the Color Line*, 1–18. Edited by James F. Brooks. Lincoln and London: University of Nebraska Press, 2002.

Browder, Laura. *Slippery Characters: Ethnic Impersonators and American Identities.* Chapel Hill: University of North Carolina Press, 2000.

Brumble, H. David, III. *American Indian Autobiography.* Lincoln and London: University of Nebraska Press, 1988.

Bruss, Elizabeth. *Autobiographical Acts: The Changing Situation of a Literary Genre.* Baltimore: Johns Hopkins University Press, 1976.

"Bureau of Indian Affairs." Accessed December 17, 2020. https://www.bia.gov/bia.

Butler, Judith. "Performative Acts and Gender Constitution: An Essay in Phenomenology and Feminist Theory." In *The Performance Studies Reader*, edited by Henry Bial, 154–165. New York: Routledge, 2004.

Calt, Stephen, and Gayle Wardlow. *King of the Delta Blues: The Life and Music of Charlie Patton.* Newton, NJ: Rock Chapel Press, 1988.

Carey, Harold, Jr. "Barboncito, Navajo Political and Spiritual Leader." November 16, 2009. Accessed December 23, 2020. https://navajopeople.org/blog/barboncito -navajo-political-and-spiritual-leader/.

Carlson, Nicholas. "At Last - The Full Story of How Facebook Was Founded." *Business Insider*, March 5, 2010. https://www.businessinsider.com.au/how-facebo ok-was-founded-2010-3#we-can-talk-about-that-after-i-get-all-the-basic-functiona lity-up-tomorrow-night-1.

Carter, Ray. "Freedmen ask Choctaw for Their Rights." *Tulsa Beacon*, August 27, 2020. http://tulsabeacon.com/freedmen-ask-choctaws-for-their-rights/.

Chien, Philip. "STS-113 Delayed: NASA Scrambles to Fix Leak on Astronaut John Herrington's Shuttle Flight Put on Hold for Eight Days." *Indian Country Today* (Oneida, NY). November 20, 2002. http://jpllnet.sfsu.edu/login?url=https://www -proquest-com.jpllnet.sfsu.edu/newspapers/sts-113-delayed-nasa-scrambles-fix-lea k-on/docview/362718036/se-2?accountid=13802.

Chickasaw Nation. "Chickasaw Values: Embracing Diversity." Chickasaw TV. Video, 2:00. Accessed January 21, 2021. https://www.chickasaw.tv/videos/chi ckasaw-values-embracing-diversity.

"Choctaw Language Learning Resources." *Mississippi Band of Choctaw Indians.* Accessed December 23, 2020. http://www.choctaw.org/culture/cllr.html.

Chow, Kat. "Judge Rules That Cherokee Freedmen Have Right to Citizenship." August 31, 2017. *NPR.* https://www.npr.org/sections/thetwo-way/2017/08/31/5477 05829/judge-rules-that-cherokee-freedmen-have-right-to-tribal-citizenship.

Cody, Radmilla. "A Beautiful Dawn Music Video." 2005. YouTube. April 13, 2013. Video, 4:16. https://www.youtube.com/watch?v=xny8znDmPUY.

Cody, Radmilla. "A Message to the Navajo People." *Navajo Times.* December 5, 2002.

Cody, Radmilla. "Radmilla Cody Presenting at the 55th Annual GRAMMYs." 2013. YouTube. February 10, 2013. Video, 0:33. https://www.youtube.com/watch?v =UJVOiRlHPow.

Cody, Radmilla. "Radmilla Cody at TEDx Women 2012," Filmed December 2012 in Washington, DC. TEDxWomen. 8:57. https://www.youtube.com/watch?v=Yii EkkDW620.

Cody, Radmilla. "The Star-Spangled Banner (Navajo Lyrics) (National Anthem)." YouTube. July 4, 2009. Video, 1:58. https://www.youtube.com/watch?v=6NU j_w38FNM.

Cody, Radmilla. "Tears Music Video." 2006. YouTube. April 13, 2013. Video, 4:03. https://www.youtube.com/watch?v=PafWhcXPb0s.

Collins, Robert Keith. "What is a Black Indian?: Misplaced Expectations and Lived Realities." In *IndiVisible: African-Native American Lives in the Americas*, edited by Gabrielle Tayac, 183–195. Washington, DC: Smithsonian Institute, 2009.

Considine, JD. "Replays -- Blues by Jimi Hendrix / Smokey Robinson and the Miracles: The 35th Anniversary Collection by Smokey Robinson and the Miracles / One More Mile by Muddy Waters / and others." *Rolling Stone* 682. May 19, 1994. http://jpllnet.sfsu.edu/login?url=https://www-proquest-com.jpllnet.sfsu.edu/maga zines/true-believers-hard-road/docview/220147652/se-2?accountid=13802.

Contreras, Felix. "Radmilla Cody: Two Cultures, One Voice." *NPR.* May 10, 2010. http://www.npr.org/templates/story/story.php?storyId=126638085.

Cook-Lynn, Elizabeth. *Why I Can't Read Wallace Stegner and Other Essays.* Madison: University of Wisconsin Press, 1998.

Cornatzer, Mary, and Rob Christensen. "Lumbee Recognition Gets Bipartisan Support." *The News & Observer* (Raleigh, NC), August 1, 2011.

Crenshaw, Christopher B. "Pan-Indianism." In E*ncyclopedia of the Atlantic World, 1400-1900: Europe, Africa, and the Americas in an Age of Exploration, Trade, and*

Empire, edited by David Head, 473–477. Santa Barbara: ABC-CLIO, LLC, 2018. Accessed January 7, 2021. ProQuest Ebook Central.

Daley, Mark. "Land of the Free. Jimi Hendrix: Woodstock Festival, August 18, 1969." In *Performance and Popular Music: History, Place and Time,* edited by Ian Inglis, 52–57. Burlington, VT: Ashgate, 2006.

Davis, Darnella. *Untangling a Red, White, and Black Heritage: A Personal History of the Allotment Era.* Albuquerque: University of New Mexico Press, 2018.

Davis, F. James. "Defining Race: Comparative Perspectives." In *Mixed Messages: Multiracial Identities in the "Color-Blind" Era,* edited by David L. Brunsma, 15–31. Boulder, CO: Lynne Rienner Publishers, Inc., 2006.

Davis, F. James. *Who Is Black?: One Nation's Definition.* University Park: Pennsylvania State University Press, 2002.

Davis, Glenda Rae. "Radmilla Cody receives Black History Maker Award." *Navajo Times,* February 23, 2012. http://jpllnet.sfsu.edu/login?url=https://www.proquest.com/newspapers/radmilla- cody-receives-black-history-maker-award/docview/92 8450117/se- 2?accountid=13802.

Deloria, Philip J. *Indians in Unexpected Places.* Lawrence, Kansas: University Press of Kansas, 2004.

Deloria, Phillip J. *Playing Indian.* New Haven: Yale University Press, 1998.

Deloria, Vine, Jr. *Custer Died for Your Sins: An Indian Manifesto.* New York: Avon Books, 1969.

Denetdale, Jennifer Nez. "Chairmen, Presidents, and Princesses: The Navajo Nation, Gender, and the Politics of Tradition." *Wicazo Review* 21, no. 1 (Spring 2006): 9–28. Accessed December 29, 2020. http://www.jstor.org/stable/4140296.

Denetdale, Jennifer Nez. *Reclaiming Diné History: The Legacies of Navajo Chief Manuelito and Juanita.* Tucson: University of Arizona Press, 2007.

Dichek, Bernie, dir. *Long Lance.* 1986; Edmonton National Film Board of Canada, Northwest Centre, DVD.

Dismukes, Valena Broussard. *The Red-Black Connection: Contemporary Urban African-Native Americans and Their Stories of Dual Identity.* Los Angeles: Grace Enterprises. 2007.

Donovan, Bill. "'Oh Say, Can You See' in Navajo." *Gallup Independent* (Gallup, NM), March 25, 2005. http://www.gallupindependent.com/2005/mar/032505navajo.html.

Dow, Timothy. *Light Writing and Life Writing: Photography in Autobiography.* Chapel Hill: University of North Carolina Press, 2000.

Durkin, Pat. Introduction to *Heart of the Circle: Photographs by Edward S. Curtis of Native American Women,* 4–23. Edited by Sara Day. San Francisco: Pomegranate Artbooks, 1997.

Dyson, Eric Michael. Foreword to *Who's Afraid of Post-Blackness?,* xi–xviii. By Touré. New York: Free Press, 2011.

Earle, Jonathan. *The Routledge Atlas of African American History.* New York and London: Routledge, 2000.

Elam, Michele. *The Souls of Mixed Folk: Race, Politics, and Aesthetics in the New Millennium.* Stanford: Stanford University Press, 2011.

"Enrollment." *Rosebud Sioux Tribe.* Accessed December 17, 2020. https://www.ros ebudsiouxtribe-nsn.gov/enrollment.

Evans, D. "Charley Patton: The Conscience of the Delta." In *The Voice of the Delta: Charley Patton and the Mississippi Blues Traditions,* edited by R. Sacre, 111–214. Liège: Presses Universitaires Liège, 1987.

Fabi, M. Giulia. "'The Unguarded Expressions of the Feelings of the Negroes': Gender, Slave Resistance, and William Wells Brown's Revisions of *Clotel.*" *African American Review* 27, no. 4 (Winter 1993): 639–654. Accessed December 29, 2020. https://link.gale.com/apps/doc/A15342586/LitRC?u=sfsu_main&sid=Li tRC&xid=86d1b8f7.

Fairchild, John. "Sources: Print, Audio, Video and Jimi's Own Hand – The Obsessive Task." *Starting at Zero.* Accessed March 4, 2014. http://starting-at-zero.com/book /sources/.

Faught, Jamison. "OK Tea Party Leaders Announce opposition to T.W. Shannon." April 24, 2014. MuskogeePolitico.com. Accessed December 23, 2020. https://ww w.muskogeepolitico.com/2014/04/ok-tea-party-leaders-announce.html?m=1.

Fiege, Gale. "Tulalip Woman on Journey to Photograph Nation's Tribes." *The Herald* (Everett, WA), November 24, 2012. https://www.heraldnet.com/news/tulalip-w oman-on-journey-to-photograph-nations-tribes/.

Forbes, Jack D. *Africans and Native Americans: The Language of Race and the Evolution of Red-Black Peoples.* Urbana and Chicago: University of Illinois Press, 1993.

Ford, Richard Thompson. *Racial Culture: A Critique.* Princeton: Princeton University Press, 2005.

Frady, Marshall. "Children of Malcolm." In *A Malcolm X Reader,* edited by David Gillen, 273–310. New York: Carroll & Graf Publishers, Inc., 1994.

Gamble-Williams, Penny. "Red Power/Black Power: The People, the Land, and the Movement." In *Indivisible: African-Native American Lives in the Americas,* edited by Gabrielle Tayac, 217–223. Washington, DC: Smithsonian Institution, 2009.

Garroutte, Eva. *Real Indians: Identity and Survival in North America.* Berkeley: University of California Press, 2003.

Gates, Henry Louis, Jr. "'Authenticity,' or the Lesson of Little Tree." *The New York Times,* November 24, 1991. https://www.nytimes.com/1991/11/24/books/authentic ity-or-the-lesson-of-little-tree.html.

Gates, Henry Louis, Jr. "The 'Blackness of Blackness': A Critique of the Sign and the Signifying Monkey." *Critical Inquiry* 9, no. 4 (June 1983): 685–723. Accessed December 29, 2020. http://ejournals.ebsco.com.jpllnet.sfsu.edu/direct.asp?Artic leID=4C77B29FFB6C6FE4A2A1.

Gidley, Mick. "Reflecting Cultural Identity in Modern American Indian Photography." In *Mirror Writing: (Re)-Constructions of Native American Identity,* edited by Thomas Claviez and Maria Moss, 257–282. Berlin: Galda + Wilch Verlag.

Gilmore, Paul. "The Indian in the Museum: Henry David Thoreau, Okah Tubbee, and Authentic Manhood." *Arizona Quarterly* 54, no. 2 (Summer 1998): 25–63. Accessed December 29, 2020. DOI: 10.1353/arq.1998.0019.

Giroux, Susan Searls. "Notes on the Afterlife of Dreams: On the Persistence of Racism in Post-Civil Rights America." *JAC* 28, no. 3/4 (2008): 423–442. Accessed December 29, 2020. https://www.jstor.org/stable/20866851.

Goellnicht, Daniel C. "Passing as Autobiography: James Weldon Johnson's *The Autobiography of an Ex-Colored Man.*" *African American Review* 30, no. 1 (Spring 1996): 17–33. Accessed December 29, 2020. https://link.gale.com/apps/doc/A183 72101/LitRC?u=sfsu_main&sid=LitRC&xid=24ef2822.

Goldstein, David. "National Anthem in Other Languages? Heard This Before." *The Seattle Times,* May 6, 2006. Accessed December 29, 2020. https://infoweb-news bank-com.jpllnet.sfsu.edu/apps/news/document-view?p=AMNEWS&docref=new s/1117BA210BEC704D.

Gonzales, Angela. "Racial Legibility: The Federal Census and the (Trans) Formation of 'Black' and 'Indian' Identity, 1790-1920." In *IndiVisible: African-Native American Lives in the Americas,* edited by Gabrielle Tayac, 57–67. Washington, DC: Smithsonian Institute, 2009.

Gonzales, Angela. "The (Re)Articulation of American Indian Identity: Maintaining Boundaries and Regulating Access to Ethnically-Tied Resources." *American Indian Cultural and Research Journal* 22, no. 4 (1998): 199–225. Accessed December 29, 2020. http://search.ebscohost.com.jpllnet.sfsu.edu/login.aspx?dire ct=true&AuthType=ip,cookie,url,uid&db=hft&AN=509693127&site=ehost-live.

Good, Katie Day. "From Scrapbook to Facebook: A History of Personal Media Assemblage and Archives." *New Media & Society* 15, no. 4 (September 30, 2012): 557–573. Accessed December 29, 2020. https://doi.org/10.1177/14614448124 58432.

Green, Rayna. "The Tribe Called Wannabee: Playing Indian in America and Europe." *Folklore* 99, no. 1 (1988): 30–55. Accessed December 29, 2020. https://www.jstor .org/stable/1259567.

Greene, Wayne. "Oklahoma House Speaker T.W. Shannon Making Name for Himself." *Tulsa World,* April 28, 2013.https://cole.house.gov/tulsa-world-oklah oma-house-speaker-tw-shannon-making-name-himself.

Gross, Ariela. *What Blood Won't Tell: A History of Race on Trial in America.* Cambridge, MA: Harvard University Press, 2008.

Guerrero, M. Annette Jaimes. "Academic Apartheid: American Indian Studies and 'Multiculturalism.'" In *Mapping Multiculturalism,* edited by Avery F. Gordon and Christopher Newfield, 49–63. Minneapolis: University of Minnesota Press, 1996.

Hafen, P. Jane. "Rock and Roll, Redskins, and Blues in Sherman Alexie's Work." *Studies in American Indian Literature* 9, no. 4 (Winter 1997): 71–78. Accessed December 29, 2020. https://www.jstor.org/stable/20739426.

Halliburton, R. Jr. *Red Over Black: Black Slavery Among the Cherokee Indians.* Westport, CT: Greenwood Press, 1977.

Hall, Jacquelyn Dowd. "The Long Civil Rights Movement and the Political Uses of History." *The Journal of American History* 91, no. 4 (March 2005): 1233-163. Accessed December 29, 2020. https://www.jstor.org/stable/3660172.

Helfand, Jessica. *Scrapbooks: An American History*. New Haven: Yale University Press, 2008.

Henderson, David. "Jimi Hendrix Deep Within the Blues and Alive Onstage at Woodstock – 25 Years after Death." *African American Review* 29, no. 2 (Summer 1995): 213–216.

Henderson, David. *'Scuse Me While I Kiss the Sky: The Life of Jimi Hendrix*. New York: Bantam, 1983.

Hendrix, Jimi. "Black Gold." Metro Lyrics. Accessed January 21, 2021. https://www.metrolyrics.com/black-gold-lyrics-jimi-hendrix.html.

Hendrix, Jimi. "Castles Made of Sand." Recorded October 29, 1967. Track 9 on *Axis: Bold as Love*. 1967. Track, Spotify.

Hendrix, Jim. "Cherokee Mist." Recorded May 2, 1968. Track 13 on *Both Sides of the Sky*. 2018. Legacy, Spotify.

Hendrix, Jimi. "Cherokee Mist." Recorded June 14, 1970. Track 9 on *The Jimi Hendrix Experience*. 2000. MCA, Spotify.

Hendrix, Jimi. "Hear My Train A Comin." Recorded December 19, 1967. Track 1 on *Blues*. 1994. MCA, Spotify.

Hendrix, Jimi. "House Burning Down." Genius. Accessed January 21, 2021. https://genius.com/The-jimi-hendrix-experience-house-burning-down-lyrics.

Hendrix, Jimi. "I Don't Live Today." Track 6 on *Are You Experienced*. 1967. Track, Spotify.

Hendrix, Jimi. "Jimi Hendrix (1973) - Hear My Train A Comin' (Acoustic)." YouTube. March 6, 2017. Video, 3.13. https://www.youtube.com/watch?v=Vrs0XgnXsxk.

Hendrix, Jimi. "National Anthem U.S.A. (Woodstock 1969)." YouTube. August 16, 2019. Video, 3.44. https://www.youtube.com/watch?v=ezI1uya213I.

Hendrix, Jimi. *Starting at Zero: His Own Story*. 1st U.S. ed. New York: Bloomsbury, 2013.

Hill, Lynda M. "Ex-Slave Narratives: The WPA Federal Writers' Project Reappraised." *Oral History* 26, no. 1 (Spring 1998): 64–72.

Hirsch, Mark. "Race, Citizenship, and Sovereignty in the Cherokee Nation." In *IndiVisible: African-Native American Lives in the Americas*, edited by Gabrielle Tayac, 117–121. Washington, DC: Smithsonian Institute, 2009.

"History." *Narragansett Indian Tribe*. Accessed December 17, 2020. http://narragansettindiannation.org/history/perseverance/.

"History and Culture." *Lumbee Tribe of North Carolina*. Accessed December 22, 2020. https://www.lumbeetribe.com/history-and-culture.

"History of Miss Navajo Nation." Office of Miss Navajo Nation. Accessed December 30, 2020. https://www.omnn.navajo-nsn.gov/History.

Hughes, Langston. "The Negro Artist and the Racial Mountain." In *The Portable Harlem Renaissance Reader*, edited by David Levering Lewis, 91–95. 1926. Reprint, New York: Penguin Books, 1994.

Huhndorf, Shari. *Going Native: Indians in the American Cultural Imagination*. Ithaca: Cornell University Press, 2001.

Hunter, Chad. "Cherokee Nation Registration Officials Give Advice to Applicants." October 1, 2019. *Cherokee Phoenix*. https://www.cherokeephoenix.org/Article/index/103590.

Independent Lens. "Filmmaker Statement: *Miss Navajo*." Accessed December 23, 2020. https://www.pbs.org/independentlens/missnavajo/statement.html.

"IndiVisible: African-Native American Lives in the Americas, NY." February 9, 2012–October 1, 2012. Accessed December 17, 2020. https://americanindian.si.edu/explore/exhibitions/item?id=907.

"Interview with Fountain Hughes." North Carolina Digital History. Accessed December 17, 2020. https://www.ncpedia.org/anchor/interview-fountain-hughes.

Iverson, Peter. *Diné: A History of the Navajos*. Albuquerque: University of New Mexico Press. 2002.

Iwashita, Ann. 2014. "Radmilla's Voice: Music Genre, Blood Quantum, and Belonging on the Navajo Nation: Supplemental Material." *Society for Cultural Anthropology*. May 1, 2014. https://culanth.org/fieldsights/radmillas-voice-music-genre-blood-quantum-and-belonging-on-the-navajo-nation-supplemental-material.

Jacobsen, Kristina. *The Sound of Navajo Country: Music, Language, and Diné Belonging*. Chapel Hill: University of North Carolina Press, 2017.

Jacobsen-Bia, Kristina. "Radmilla's Cody's Voice: Music Genre, Blood Quantum, and Belonging on the Navajo Nation." *Cultural Anthropology* 29, no. 2 (May 2014): 385–410. Accessed December 29, 2020. https://journal.culanth.org/index.php/ca/article/view/ca29.2.11/305.

Japtok, Martin and Jerry Rafiki Jenkins. "What Does It Mean to Be 'Really' Black? A Selective History of Authentic Blackness." In *Authentic Blackness/"Real" Blackness: Essays on the Meaning of Blackness in Literature and Culture,* edited by Martin Japtok and Jerry Rafiki Jenkins, 7–51. New York: Peter Lang, 2011.

Johnson, E. Patrick. *Appropriating Blackness: Performance and the Politics of Authenticity*. Durham and London: Duke University Press, 2003.

Joseph, Peniel E. *The Black Power Movement: Rethinking the Civil Rights-Black Power Era*. New York and London: Routledge, 2006.

Joseph, Ralina L. *Transcending Blackness: From The New Millennium Mulatta to the Exceptional Multiracial*. Durham, NC: Duke University Press, 2013.

Josephy, Alvin M. Jr. *500 Nations: An Illustrated History of North American Indians*. New York: Random House, Inc., 1994.

Justice, Daniel Heath. "A Lingering Miseducation: The Legacy of Little Tree." *Studies in American Indian Literature* 12, no. 1 (Spring 2000): 20–36. Accessed December 29, 2020. https://www.jstor.org/stable/20736948.

Katz, William Loren. *Black Indians: A Hidden Heritage*. New York: Aladdin Paperbacks, 1997.

Keenan, Jerry. *Encyclopedia of American Indian Wars, 1492-1890*. Santa Barbara, CA: ABC-CLIO, Inc., 1997. http://search.ebscohost.com.jpllnet.sfsu.edu/login.aspx?direct=true&AuthType=ip,cookie,url,uid&db=nlebk&AN=56838&site=ehost-live.

Kelley, Robin D.G. "People in Me: 'So, What Are You?'". *ColorLines* 1, no. 3 (Winter 1999): 5–7. http://jpllnet.sfsu.edu/login?url=https://www-proquest-com.j

pllnet.sfsu.edu/magazines/people-me-so-what-are-you/docview/215531591/se-2? accountid=13802.

Kidwell, Clara Sue. Review of *500 Nations: An Illustrated History of North American Indians. The Western Historical Quarterly* 26, no. 4 (Winter 1995): 517–518. Accessed December 30, 2020. https://doi-org.jpllnet.sfsu.edu/10.2307 /970852.

King, C. Richard. "Apologies and Apologists: The Disavowal of Racism and the Abjuration of Anti-racism in the Contemporary United States." *Studies in Media & Information Literacy Education* 4, no. 4 (November 2004). *Academic Search Premier Publications*: n.p. DOI:10.3138/sim.4.4.002.

Klopotek, Brian. "Of Shadows and Doubts: Race, Indigeneity, and White Supremacy." In *IndiVisible: African-Native American Lives in the Americas*, edited by Gabrielle Tayac, 85–89. Washington, DC: Smithsonian Institute, 2009.

Krauthamer, Barbara. *Black Slaves, Indian Masters: Slavery, Emancipation, and Citizenship in the Native American South*. Durham: University of North Carolina Press, 2013.

Kroskrity, Paul V. "Sustaining Stories: Narrative as Cultural Resources in Native American Projects of Cultural Sovereignty, Identity Maintenance, and Language Revitalization." In *Telling Stories in the Face of Danger: Language Renewal in Native American Communities,* edited by Paul V. Kroskrity, 3–20. Norman, OK: University of Oklahoma Press, 2012.

Lance, Chief Buffalo Child Long. *Long Lance*. New York: Cosmopolitan Book Corporation, 1928.

Largo, Jim. "Offerings to the Holy People." *Navajo Times* (Window Rock, AZ), March 22, 2012. http://jpllnet.sfsu.edu/login?url=https://www-proquest-com.jpllne t.sfsu.edu/newspapers/offerings-holy-people/docview/1009680321/se-2?accountid =13802.

Lawrence, Sharon. *Jimi Hendrix: The Man, the Magic, the Truth*. 1st ed. New York: Harper Entertainment, 2005.

Lee, Lloyd. "Navajo Cultural Identity: What Can the Navajo Nation Bring to the American Indian Identity Discussion Table?" *Wicazo Sa Review* 2, no. 2 (Autumn 2006): 79–103. Accessed December 29, 2020. https://www.jstor.org/ stable/4140269.

Lejeune, Phillippe. "The Autobiographical Pact." In *The Routledge Auto/Biography Studies Reader,* edited by Ricia Anne Chansky and Emily Hipchen, 34–48. 1975. Reprint, London and New York: Routledge, 2016.

"The Life of Jim Thorpe." *Standard-Speaker* (Hazleton, PA), May 15, 2013. Updated April 17, 2020. https://www.standardspeaker.com/news/the-life-of-jim-thorpe/ article_4398f3cf-47e0-557b-9afd-3d080705ff62.html.

Linthicum, Leslie. "Queen of Two Cultures." *Albuquerque Journal,* March 1, 1998. http://jpllnet.sfsu.edu/login?url=https://www-proquest-com.jpllnet.sfsu.edu/news papers/queen-two-cultures/docview/323884234/se-2?accountid=13802.

Lionnet, Françoise. *Autobiographical Voices: Race, Gender, and Self-Portraiture*. Ithaca and London: Cornell University Press, 1989.

Lippard, Lucy. Introduction to *Partial Recall*, 13–45. New York: The New Press, 1992.

Liptak, Adam. "Supreme Court Invalidates Key Part of Voting Rights Act." *New York Times.* June 25, 2013. Retrieved April 3, 2014.

"Local Woman's Life Looks Bearable in Scrapbook." *The Onion.* December 8, 2004. https://local.theonion.com/local-womans-life-looks-bearable-in-scrapbook-1819567636.

Long Lance, Chief Buffalo Child Collection. University of Calgary Archives and Special Collections, Calgary, Alberta, Canada. https://glenbow.ucalgary.ca/finding-aid/chief-buffalo-child-long-lance-fonds/.

Longman, Jere. "Drawing Inspiration from Struggle." *The New York Times.* October 26, 2003, Late Edition (East Coast). http://jpllnet.sfsu.edu/login?url=https://www-proquest-com.jpllnet.sfsu.edu/newspapers/drawing-inspiration-struggle/docview/432529517/se-2?accountid=13802.

Lowery, Malinda Maynor. *Lumbee Indians in the Jim Crow South: Race, Identity, & the Making of a Nation.* Chapel Hill: The University of North Carolina Press, 2010.

Luther, Billy, dir. *Miss Navajo.* 2007; New York, NY: Cinema Guild. Academic Video Online: Premium.

Lyman, Christopher M. *The Vanishing Race and Other Illusions: Photographs of Indians by Edward S. Curtis.* Washington, DC: Smithsonian Institution Press, 1982.

McClintock, Anne, Aamir Mufti, and Ella Shohat, eds. *Dangerous Liaisons: Gender, Nation, and Postcolonial Perspectives.* Minneapolis: University of Minnesota Press, 1997.

McCorkle, Robert. "Texas Buffalo Soldier to be honored posthumously." September 13, 2013. Accessed December 17, 2020. https://tpwd.texas.gov/newsmedia/releases/?req=20130930b.

McCulloch, Anne Merline and David E. Wilkins. "'Constructing' Nations Within States: The Quest for Federal Recognition by the Catawba and Lumbee Tribes." *American Indian Quarterly* 19, no. 3 (Summer 1995): 361–388. Accessed January 7, 2021. http://jpllnet.sfsu.edu/login?url=https://www-proquest-com.jpllnet.sfsu.edu/scholarly-journals/constructing-nations-within-states-quest-federal/docview/61450217/se-2?accountid=13802.

McGrath, Gareth. "Despite Support from Trump and Biden, Lumbees Will Have to Wait for Federal Recognition." *The Fayetteville Observer*, December 21, 2020. https://www.fayobserver.com/story/news/2020/12/21/lumbee-tribe-north-carolina-wont-see-federal-recognition-2020/3997808001/.

McKay, Nellie. "The Narrative Self: Race, Politics, and Culture in Black American Women's Autobiography." In *Women, Autobiography, Theory*, edited by Sidonie Smith and Julia Watson, 96–107. Madison: University of Wisconsin Press, 1998.

Mahtani, Minelle and April Moreno. "Same Difference: Towards A More Unified Discourse in 'Mixed Race' Theory." In *Rethinking 'Mixed Race,'* edited by David Parker and Miri Song, 65–75. London: Pluto Press, 2001.

Mailhot, Terese. "Native American Lives Are Tragic, But Probably Not in the Way You Think." *Mother Jones,* November/December 2018. https://www.motherjones .com/media/2018/11/native-american-story-tragic-terese-mailhot-tommy-orange-p overty-porn/.

Mangione, Jerre. *The Dream and the Deal: The Federal Writers' Project, 1935-1943.* Boston and Toronto: Little, Brown, 1972.

Margolis, Eric and Jeremy Rowe. "Images of Assimilation: Photographs of Indian Schools in Arizona." *History of Education* 33, no. 2 (March 2004): 199–230. Accessed December 29, 2020. DOI: 10.1080/0046760032000151456.

Marley, Shebala. "Fall from Grace: Ex-Miss Navajo Radmilla Cody Recounts Story that Led to Drug-related Charges and Prison." *Navajo Times* (Window Rock, AZ), December 12, 2002. http://jpllnet.sfsu.edu/login?url=https://www-proquest-com .jpllnet.sfsu.edu/newspapers/fall-grace-ex-miss-navajo-radmilla-cody-recounts/ docview/225310054/se-2?accountid=13802.

Martin, Jonathan. "GOP Hopeful Finds Tribal Tie Cuts Both Ways." *The New York Times.* May 3, 2014. Accessed December 17, 2020. https://www.nytimes.com/2 014/05/04/us/politics/gop-hopeful-finds-tribal-tie-cuts-both-ways.html.

Masouri, John. "The Story of the Book: The Autobiography That Was Banished into Exile." *Starting at Zero.* Accessed January 7, 2021. http://starting-at-zero.com/ book/story/.

Maxwell, Tom. "Shelved: Jimi Hendrix's Black Gold Suite." *Longreads*, March 2019. https://longreads.com/2019/07/16/shelved-jimi-hendrixs-black-gold-suite/.

Mecklenburg-Faenger, Amy. "Trifles, Abominations, and Literary Gossip: Gendered Rhetoric and Nineteenth-Century Scrapbooks." *Genders,* no. 55 (Spring 2102): 1–46. Accessed December 29, 2020. https://web.archive.org/web/201305122315 32/http://www.genders.org/g55/g55_mecklenburg-faenger.html.

MediaAssassin. "Margaret B. Jones/Seltzer's Lie-All Gangsta Video – Exposed!" April 29, 2008. YouTube. Video, 1:29. https://www.youtube.com/watch?v=RVx s5t2wyzs.

"Meet T.W." *T.W. Shannon.* Accessed May 15, 2014. www.twshannon.com.

Miles, Tiya. "Taking Leave, Making Lives: Creative Quests for Freedom in Early Black and Native America." In *IndiVisible: African-Native American Lives in the Americas*, edited by Gabrielle Tayac, 139–149. Washington, DC: Smithsonian Institute, 2009.

Miles, Tiya. "Uncle Tom Was an Indian: Tracing the Red in Black Slavery." In *Confounding the Color Line: The Indian-Black Experience in North America*, edited by James F. Brooks, 137–160. Lincoln and London: University of Nebraska, 2002.

Minges, Patrick N. *Black Indian Slave Narratives.* Winston-Salem, NC: John F. Blair, Publisher, 2004.

Montgomery, David. "An Anthem's Discordant Notes; Spanish Version of 'Star-Spangled Banner' Draws Strong Reactions: [FINAL Edition]." *The Washington Post,* Apr 28, 2006. Accessed December 29, 2020. http://jpllnet.sfsu.edu/login?url =https://www-proquest-com.jpllnet.sfsu.edu/newspapers/anthems-discordant-note s-spanish-version-star/docview/409995579/se-2?accountid=13802.

Moskowitz, David. *The Words and Music of Jimi Hendrix*. Santa Barbara, CA: Praeger, 2010.

Murray, Charles, Shaar. *Crosstown Traffic: Jimi Hendrix and the Rock 'n' Roll Revolution*. New York: St. Martin's, 1989.

Mwalim (Morgan James Peters). "We Heard it in the Fields: The Native American Roots of the Blues." In *Indivisible: African-Native American Lives in the Americas*, edited by Gabrielle Tayac, 211–215. Washington, DC: Smithsonian Institution, 2009.

Natambu, Kofi. *Critical Lives: The Life and Work of Malcolm X*. Indianapolis: Alpha Books, 2002.

National Congress of Black Indians (@ncbai). "Radmilla Cody accepts the Initiative Radio 2012 Black History Makers Award as 'National Treasure & Icon of Cultural Unity.'" Facebook, September 5. 2014. https://www.facebook.com/watch/?v=2 97619247090745.

Naylor, Celia. "'Playing Indian?' The Selection of Radmilla Cody as Miss Navajo Nation, 1997-1998." In *Crossing Waters, Crossing Worlds: The African Diaspora in Indian Country*, edited by Tiya Miles and Sharon P. Holland, 145–163. Durham and London: Duke University Press, 2006.

Naylor-Ojurongbe, Celia. "'Born and Raised among These People, I Don't Want to Know Any Other': Slaves' Acculturation in Nineteenth-Century Indian Territory." In *Confounding the Color Line: The Indian-Black Experience in North America*, edited by James F. Brooks, 161–119. Lincoln and London: University of Nebraska, 2002.

Neal, Larry. "The Black Arts Movement." *The Drama Review* 12, no. 4 (Summer 1968): 28–39. Accessed December 29, 2020. https://doi-org.jpllnet.sfsu.edu/10.2307/1144377.

Neeley, Bill. *The Last Comanche Chief: The Life and Times of Quanah Parker*. New York: John Wiley & Sons, Inc., 1995.

Nitopi, Bill, ed. *Cherokee Mist: The Lost Writings of Jimi Hendrix*. New York: HarperCollins Publishers, Inc., 1993.

Oakley, Giles. *The Devil's Music: A History of the Blues*. 2nd ed. New York: Da Capo Press, 1997.

Ogbar, Jeffrey Obgonna Green. *The Black Power Movement: Rethinking the Civil Rights-Black Power Era*. New York and London: Routledge, 2006.

Olney, James. "'I Was Born': Slave Narratives, Their Status as Autobiography and as Literature." *Callaloo* no. 20 (Winter 1984): 46–73. Accessed December 29, 2020. https://doi-org.jpllnet.sfsu.edu/10.2307/2930678.

Osborne-McKnight, Juilene. Review of *500 Nations: An Illustrated History of North American Indians*. *Antioch Review* 53, no. 4 (Fall 1995): 495–496.

Ott, Katherine, Susan Tucker, and Patricia Buckler. Introduction to *The Scrapbook in American Life*, 1–28. Philadelphia: Temple University Press, 2006.

Owens, Louis. *Mixedblood Messages: Literature, Film, Family, Place*. Norman: University of Oklahoma Press, 1992.

Packard, Jerrold. *American Nightmare: The History of Jim Crow*. New York: St. Martin's Press, 2002.

Parker, David and Miri Song. Introduction to *Rethinking 'Mixed Race,'* 1–22. Edited by David Parker and Miri Song. London: Pluto Press, 2001.

Pasquaretta, Paul. "African-Native American Subjectivity and the Blues Voice in the Writings of Toni Morrison and Sherman Alexie." In *When Brer Rabbit Meets Coyote: African-Native American Literature,* edited by Jonathan Brennan, 278–291. Urbana: University of Illinois Press, 2003.

Patnaik, Deba P. "Diasporic Double Vision." In *Committed to the Image: Contemporary Black Photographers,* edited by Barbara Head Millstein, 29–39. London: Merrell Publishers, Limited, 2001.

Patterson, Orlando. *Slavery and Social Death: A Comparative Study.* Cambridge, MA and London: Harvard University Press, 1982.

Peaches, Ivis Daniel. "Different Hogan." *Navajo Times,* April 16, 1998.

Penn, William S. Introduction to *As We Are Now: Mixblood Essays on Race and Identity,* 1–11. Edited by William S. Penn. Berkeley and Los Angeles: UC Press, 1998.

"The Peoples of the Mesa Verde Region: The Long Walk." Crow Canyon Archaeological Center. 2014. Accessed December 23, 2020. https://www.cro wcanyon.org/EducationProducts/peoples_mesa_verde/historic_long_walk.asp.

Perdue, Theda. "Native Americans, African Americans, and Jim Crow." In *IndiVisible: African-Native American Lives in the Americas,* edited by Gabrielle Tayac, 21–33. Washington, DC: Smithsonian Institute, 2009.

Perdue, Theda. "Race and Culture: Writing the Ethnohistory of the Early South." *Ethnohistory* 51, no. 4 (Fall 2004): 701–723. Accessed December 29, 2020. http://ejo urnals.ebsco.com.jpllnet.sfsu.edu/direct.asp?ArticleID=44F5A83A8B57A3DE672E.

Perdue, Theda. *Slavery and the Evolution of Cherokee Society, 1540-1866.* Knoxville: University of Tennessee Press, 1987.

Peretti, Burton W. *The Creation of Jazz: Music, Race, and Culture in Urban America.* Urbana: University of Illinois Press, 1994.

Piper, Adrian. "Passing for White, Passing for Black." *Transition: An International Review* no. 58 (1992): 4–32. Accessed December 29, 2020. https://doi-org.jpllnet .sfsu.edu/10.2307/2934966.

Ponder, Justin. "'A Patchwork Heritage': Multiracial Citation in Barack Obama's *Dreams from My Father.*" In *Obama and the Biracial Factor: The Battle for a New American Majority,* edited by Andrew J. Jolivette, 61–80. Bristol and Chicago: The Policy Press, 2012.

"QuickFacts: Oklahoma." *U.S. Census Bureau.* Accessed December 22, 2020. https:// www.census.gov/quickfacts/OK.

Rawick, George P. *The American Slave: A Composite Autobiography.* Vol. 1, *From Sundown to Sunup: The Making of the Black Community.* Westport, CT: Greenwood Publishing Company, 1972.

Rich, Motoko. "Gang Memoir, Turning Page, Is Pure Fiction." *New York Times,* March 4, 2008. Late Edition (East Coast). http://jpllnet.sfsu.edu/login?url=https: //www-proquest-com.jpllnet.sfsu.edu/newspapers/gang-memoir-turning-page-is-pure-fiction/docview/433815101/se-2?accountid=13802.

Roby, Steven. *Black Gold: The Lost Archives of Jimi Hendrix.* New York: Billboard Books, 2002.

Roby, Steven and Brad Schreiber. *Becoming Jimi Hendrix: From Southern Crossroads to Psychedelic London, the Untold story of a Musical Genius.* Cambridge, MA: Da Capo Press, 2010.

Rosier, Paul C. *Serving their Country: American Indian Politics and Patriotism in the Twentieth Century.* Cambridge: Harvard University Press, 2009.

Rugg, Linda Haverty. *Picturing Ourselves: Photography and Autobiography.* Chicago: University of Illinois Press, 1997.

Ryan, Andrew. "Mashpee Tribe Wins Federal Recognition." *Boston Globe*, February 16, 2007. Accessed December 17, 2020. http://archive.boston.com/news/local/art icles/2007/02/16/mashpee_tribe_wins_federal_recognition/.

Saunt, Claudio. *Black, White, and Indian: Race and the Unmaking of an American Family.* Oxford University Press, 2006.

Saunt, Claudio, Barbara Krauthamer, Tiya Miles, Celia E. Naylor, Circe Sturm. "Rethinking Race and Culture in the Early South." *Ethnohistory* 53, no. 2 (Spring 2006): 399–405. DOI: 10.1215/00141801-53-2-399.

Shabi, Shaylin. "Star Spangled Banner in Navajo." February 20, 2014. YouTube. Video, 1:29. https://www.youtube.com/watch?v=WYjW3WktfNs.

Shabi, Shaylin. "Star Spangled Banner in Navajo 2." February 20, 2014. YouTube. Video, 1:42. https://www.youtube.com/watch?v=lNAdvPrKm04.

Shannon, T.W. "Devon's Story." April 14, 2014. YouTube. Video, 2:41. https://www .youtube.com/watch?v=phGxltebZAI&lc=Ughycktzpnt4s3gCoAEC.

Shannon, T.W. "I'm In." January 29, 2014. YouTube. Video, 1:25. https://www.you tube.com/watch?v=PchqSJUMu8Q.

Shapiro, Harry and Caesar Glebbeek. *Jimi Hendrix: Electric Gypsy.* New York: St. Martin's Press, 1990.

Shaw, Stephanie J. "Using the WPA Ex-Slave Narratives to Study the Impact of the Great Depression." *The Journal of Southern History* 69, no. 3 (August 2003): 623–658. Accessed December 29, 2020. https://doi-org.jpllnet.sfsu.edu/10.2307 /30040012.

Sheppard, Kate. "The Best Lines from Ginsburg's Dissent on the Voting Rights Act Decision." *Mother Jones.* June 25, 2013. Accessed December 29, 2020. https:// www.motherjones.com/crime-justice/2013/06/best-lines-ginsburg-dissent-voting-rights-act-decision/.

Sider, Gerald. *Living Indian Histories: Lumbee and Tuscarora People in North Carolina.* Chapel Hill and London: The University of North Carolina Press, 2003.

Silko, Leslie Marmon. "The Indian With a Camera." In *Yellow Woman and a Beauty of the Spirit: Essays on Native American Life Today*, 175–179. New York: Simon & Schuster, 1996.

Smith, Chris. "Going to the Nation: The Idea of Oklahoma in Early Blues Recordings." *Popular Music* 26, no. 1 (January 2007): 83–96. Accessed December 29, 2020. http://ejournals.ebsco.com.jpllnet.sfsu.edu/direct.asp?ArticleID=46159 723FD0CA1433A59.

Smith, Donald B. *Chief Buffalo Child Long Lance: The Glorious Impostor.* Red Deer, Alberta, Canada: Red Deer Press, 1999.

Smith, Sidonie and Julia Watson. *Reading Autobiography: A Guide for Interpreting Life Narratives.* Minneapolis: University of Minnesota Press, 2010.

Sontag, Susan. *On Photography.* Harmondsworth, England: Penguin, 1979.

Spencer, Rainier. "New Racial Identities, Old Arguments: Continuing Biological Reification." In *Mixed Messages: Multiracial Identities in the "Color-Blind" Era,* edited by David L. Brunsma, 83–102. Boulder, CO: Lynne Rienner Publishers, Inc. 2006.

Spindel, Donna. "Assessing Memory: Twentieth-Century Slave Narratives Reconsidered." *The Journal of Interdisciplinary History* 27, no. 2 (Autumn 1996): 247–261. Accessed December 29, 2020. https://doi-org.jpllnet.sfsu.edu/10.2307/205156.

Spingarn, Adena. *Uncle Tom: From Martyr to Traitor.* Stanford, CA: Stanford University Press. 2018.

Stempel, Jonathan. "Brothers' row with Facebook nears finish." *The Independent.* June 24, 2011. Accessed December 29, 2020. https://www.independent.co.uk/life-style/gadgets-and-tech/news/brothers-row-with-facebook-nears-finish-2302043.html.

Stepto, Robert B. *From Behind the Veil: A Study of Afro-American Narrative.* Urbana: University of Illinois Press, 1979.

Stewart, Irene, and Doris Ostrander, Dawdy. *A Voice in Her Tribe: A Navajo Woman's Own Story.* Socorro, NM: Ballena Press, 1980.

Strong, Pauline Turner and Barrik Van Winkle. "'Indian Blood': Reflections on the Reckoning and Refiguring of Native North American Identity." *Cultural Anthropology* 11, no. 4 (November 1996): 547–576. Accessed December 29, 2020. https://www.jstor.org/stable/656667.

Sutherland, Steve. "Acid Rain: Woodstock/Woodstock II." *Melody Maker* May 6, 1989: 34.

"T.W. Shannon." *Oklahoma Department of Transportation.* Accessed December 22, 2020. https://oklahoma.gov/odot/about/transportation-commission/t-w-shannon.html.

Tabaaha92. "National Anthem in Navajo." September 6, 2012. YouTube Video, 1:38. https://www.youtube.com/watch?v=u2R1Nw9WFeg.

"Tahoron, Ioway Warrior." *Access Genealogy.* Accessed December 22, 2020. https://accessgenealogy.com/native/tahrohon-ioway-warrior.htm.

Tallbear, Kim. "DNA, Blood and Racializing the Tribe." *Wicazo Sa Review* 18, no. 1 (Spring 2003): 81–107. Accessed December 29, 2020. https://www.jstor.org/stable/1409433.

Taylor, Clyde. "Empowering the Eye." In *Committed to the Image: Contemporary Black Photographers,* edited by Barbara Head Millstein, 15–25. London: Merrell Publishers, Limited, 2001.

Teves, Stephanie Nohelani. "Blood." In *Native Studies Keywords,* edited by Stephanie Nohelani Teves, Andrea Smith, and Michelle H. Raheja, 199–208. Tucson: University of Arizona Press, 2015.

Thomas, Daphne. "Interracial Marriages Have Deep Ties." *Navajo Times*, December 30, 1997.

Tom, Orlando. "Sense of Identity." *Navajo Times*, December 23, 1997.

Touré. *Who's Afraid of Post-Blackness?: What It Means To Be Black Now*. New York: Free Press, 2011.

"Tribal History." *The Mashantucket (Western) Pequot Tribal Nation*. Accessed December 17, 2020. https://www.mptn-nsn.gov/tribalhistory.aspx.

Tubbee, Okah and Laah Ceil. *The Life of Okah Tubbee*. 1852. Reprint, Lincoln: University of Nebraska Press, 1988.

"Up Where We Belong: Native Musicians in Popular Culture." *Smithsonian National Museum of the American Indian*, July 1, 2010–January 2, 2011. Accessed December 17, 2020. https://www.si.edu/exhibitions/where-we-belong-native-m usicians-popular-culture%3Aevent-exhib-907.

Viola, Herman. "The Buffalo Soldiers." In *IndiVisible: African-Native American Lives in the Americas*, edited by Gabrielle Tayac, 53–54. Washington, DC: Smithsonian Institute, 2009.

Ventre, Michael. "Hendrix Created Banner Moment at Woodstock." *Today.com*. August 10, 2009. https://www.today.com/popculture/hendrix-created-banner -moment-woodstock-2D80555766.

Waksman, Steve. "Black Sound, Black Body: Jimi Hendrix, the Electric Guitar, and the Meanings of Blackness." *Popular Music and Society* 23, no. 1 (1999): 75–113. DOI: 10.1080/03007769908591726.

Walker, Richard. "Photographer Matika Wilbur's Three-Year, 562-Tribe Adventure." *Indian Country Today* (Oneida, NY), January 15, 2013. https://indiancountrytoda y.com/archive/photographer-matika-wilbur-s-three-year-562-tribe-adventure-1 Plm98CuNEaTwM6XC36XBw.

Walker, Sean. "Sovereign Racism." *Navajo Times*, January 22, 1998.

Wallard, William. Review of *500 Nations: An Illustrated History of North American Indians,* by Alvin M. Josephy. *Wicazo Sa Review* 11, no. 2 (Autumn 1995): 78.

Welburn, Ron. "Native Americans in Jazz, Blues, and Popular Music." In *Indivisible: African-Native American Lives in the Americas*, edited by Gabrielle Tayac, 201–209. Washington, DC: Smithsonian Institution, 2009.

Wells, Liz and Derrick Price. "Thinking about Photography: Debates, Historically and Now." In *Photography: A Critical Introduction*, edited by Liz Wells, 11–54. London: Routledge, 1997.

Westerly, Suzanne. "Miss Indian World Pageant." *News from Indian Country (Hayward, WI)*. May 31, 2000. http://jpllnet.sfsu.edu/login?url=https://www-proq uest-com.jpllnet.sfsu.edu/newspapers/miss-indian-world-pageant/docview/3674 84028/se-2?accountid=13802.

Wilkinson, Charles. *Blood Struggle: The Rise of Modern Indian Nations*. New York and London: W.W. Norton & Company, 2005.

Womack, Craig. "Howling at the Moon: The Queer but True Story of My Life as a Hank Williams Song." In *As We Are Now: Mixblood Essays on Race and Identity,* edited by William S. Penn, 32–49. Berkeley and Los Angeles: University of California Press, 1997.

Wong, Hertha Dawn. *Sending My Heart Back Across the Years: Tradition and Innovation in Native American Autobiography.* Cary: Oxford University Press, 1992.

Woolfe, Zachary. "With Renée Fleming, Super Bowl XLVIII Gets an Operatic Opening." *The New York Times*, February 2, 2014. https://artsbeat.blogs.nytimes .com/2014/02/02/with-renee-fleming-super-bowl-xlviii-gets-an-operatic-openi ng/?mtrref=www.google.com&gwh=6B9CBEB4360544475C3C5153E8F0F1B6 &gwt=pay&assetType.

Works Progress Administration. *Slave Narratives: A Folk History of Slavery in the United States from Interviews with Former Slaves: Indiana Narratives.* Washington: Library of Congress, 1941. http://www.gutenberg.org/files/13579 /13579-h/13579-h.htm.

Wortham, Jenna. "A Site That Aims to Unleash the Scrapbook Maker in All of Us." *The New York Times*, March 12, 2012. https://www.nytimes.com/2012/03/12/techn ology/start-ups/pinterest-aims-at-the-scrapbook-maker-in-all-of-us.html.

"The WPA and the Slave Narrative Collection." *Born in Slavery: Slave Narratives from the Federal Writers' Project, 1936 to 1938.* Accessed December 17, 2020. https://www.loc.gov/collections/slave-narratives-from-the-federal-writers-project -1936-to-1938/articles-and-essays/introduction-to-the-wpa-slave-narratives/wpa- and-the-slave-narrative-collection/.

Yurth, Cindy. "Census: Native Count Jumps by 27 Percent." *Navajo Times* (Window Rock, AZ), January 26, 2012. http://jpllnet.sfsu.edu/login?url=https://www-proq uest-com.jpllnet.sfsu.edu/newspapers/census-native-count-jumps-27-percent/d ocview/922208242/se-2?accountid=13802.

Index

Index

NIYC. *See* National Indian Youth Council (NIYC)

Obama, Barack, 3, 8–9, 161n1
Olney, James, 69nn9–10
one-drop rule. *See* hypodescent

Parker, Quanah, 126
Patton, Charlie, 74–75
photography: as autobiography, 106–7; as mode of liberation, 109–11; as propaganda, 38; as tool of oppression, 109
"playing Indian," 16, 23, 25, 27–28, 36, 88, 96, 103nn22–24, 146
post-Blackness, 14, 17
post-race, 14, 161n1
Project 562. *See* Wilbur, Matika

Radical Indigenism, 14–18, 122, 134, 135
Reconstruction, 71n15
The Red-Black Connection, origins of, 112, 116
The Red-Black Connection, subjects in: Davenport, Don "Little Cloud," 122–24; Fitz-Patrick, Micah, 160; Glasschild, Boe Bvshpo Lawa (Many Knives), 117–19, *118*; Midget, Melanie, 119–21; Miller, Robert Sr., 131n7; Parker, Samuel L. Sr., 125–27; Procello, Richard, 121–22; St. James, Synthia, 131n7; Walton-Raji, Angela Y., 131n7; Webb-Mitchell, Elnora Tena, 124–25
Red Power Movement. *See* American Indian Movement
removal, Indian, 10, 15, 52, 65–67, 70n14, 161n4

scrapbooks, 30–32
Seltzer, Peggy. *See* Jones, Margaret
Seminole, 10–11, 53, 59, 114, 123, 133
Shannon, T.W., 155–59

signifyin(g), 81, 96, 111
The Silent Enemy, 26, 31–32
Silko, Leslie Marmon, 7, 9, 110
slave narrative genre, 2–3, 7, 50, 60, 67, 69nn9–10
slavery: of American Indians, 52; in Cherokee Nation, 10–11, 52–53; in Chickasaw Nation, 10–11, 53–54, 156; in Choctaw Nation, 10–11, 53–54, 60, 63–64; in Creek Nation, 10–11, 54; in Seminole Nation, 10–11
Smith, Sidonie, 3, 51–52, 68n2, 70n12
social death, 92
Sontag, Susan, 109, 113
Sparks, Lillian, 146
"The Star-Spangled Banner": performed by Jimi Hendrix, 73–74, 81–82, *98*, 100–101n7, 101n10; performed by Katherine Duncum, 150; performed by Radmilla Cody, 133, 144, 151; performed by Reneé Fleming, 133
stereotypes, American Indian: Cherokee Princess, 78–79; Noble Savage, 20n1, 26, 27, 34, 39, 88; Vanishing Indian, 20n1, 33, 34, 43, 108, 109

Thorpe, Jim, 40–41, 144, 153n4
Touré, 14, 21–22n6
Trail of Broken Treaties, 76–77
Tubbee, Okah, 9, 21n3, 27

Vizenor, Gerald, 4, 20n1

wannabe Indians, 16, 79, 160
Watson, Julia, 3, 51–52, 68n2, 70n12
Wilbur, Matika, 112–13
WPA Slave Narrative Project, 50, 54–59
Wounded Knee Massacre, 65, 70n13, 125

X, Malcolm, 117–19, 143

zhini, 142

About the Author

Sarita Cannon is professor of English at San Francisco State University where she teaches courses on twentieth- and twenty-first-century U.S. Literature. A global citizen committed to cross-cultural exchange, she travels frequently and has presented her work at conferences in Spain, France, Portugal, Japan, South Africa, Tunisia, Morocco, Ghana, and Australia. Her scholarship has appeared in *Interdisciplinary Humanities, Asian American Literature: Discourses and Pedagogies, the quint, Ethnic Studies Review, CEA Critic, MELUS,* and *Biography.*